Sink or Swim

Sink or Swim

*Capitalist Selfhood
and Nineteenth-Century
American Literature*

Andrew Kopec

The University of North Carolina Press CHAPEL HILL

© 2025 Andrew Kopec
All rights reserved
Set in Merope Basic by Westchester Publishing Services
Manufactured in the United States of America

Library of Congress Cataloging-in-Publication Data
Names: Kopec, Andrew, author
Title: Sink or swim : capitalist selfhood and nineteenth-century American
   literature / Andrew Kopec.
Description: Chapel Hill : The University of North Carolina Press, 2025. |
   Includes bibliographical references and index.
Identifiers: LCCN 2025013746 | ISBN 9781469690162 cloth |
   ISBN 9781469690179 paperback | ISBN 9781469679587 epub |
   ISBN 9781469690186 pdf
Subjects: LCSH: American literature—19th century—History and criticism |
   Economics in literature | Capitalism in literature | Self in literature |
   BISAC: LITERARY CRITICISM / Modern / 19th Century | POLITICAL
   SCIENCE / Political Ideologies / Capitalism | LCGFT: Literary criticism
Classification: LCC PS217.E35 K67 2025 | DDC 810.9/3553—dc23/eng/20250528
LC record available at https://lccn.loc.gov/2025013746

Cover art from the Wild West Press kit, Walden Font Company.

Portions of chapter 1 were adapted from the article, "Irving, Ruin, and Risk," originally published in *Early American Literature* 48, no. 3 (Winter 2013). Used by permission of the University of North Carolina Press. www.uncpress.org.

A small portion of chapter 3 was adapted from the article, "Emerson, Labor, and Ages of Turbulence," originally published in *ESQ: A Journal of Nineteenth-Century American Literature and Culture* 60, no. 2 (2014): 251–84. Copyright by the Board of Regents of Washington State University.

A small portion of the epilogue was adapted from the article, "1819–1857: Romantic Cycles from the Panic of 1819 to the Panic of 1857," originally published in *Timelines of American Literature*, edited by Cody Marrs and Christopher Hager. Used by permission of the Johns Hopkins University Press.

For product safety concerns under the European Union's General Product Safety Regulation (EU GPSR), please contact gpsr@mare-nostrum.co.uk or write to the University of North Carolina Press and Mare Nostrum Group B.V., Mauritskade 21D, 1091 GC Amsterdam, The Netherlands.

*For Lydia, Hannah, and Zoey,
three big swimmers*

Contents

List of Illustrations ix
Acknowledgments xi

INTRODUCTION
Contemplating Crisis 1
Antebellum Literature and the Romance of Trade

CHAPTER ONE
Irving, Risk, and Ruin 22

CHAPTER TWO
Sedgwick, Failure, and the Romance in Real Life 44

CHAPTER THREE
Emerson, the Scholar, and the Pace of Enterprise 63

CHAPTER FOUR
Hawthorne's Soft Ambition, Melville's Bright Future, and Fern's Repeated Failures 82

CHAPTER FIVE
Early African American Literature and the Freedom to Fail 105

EPILOGUE
War and Institutions 131
Striving in the Transbellum Office

Notes 139
Bibliography 165
Index 179

Illustrations

0.1 Edward Williams Clay, *The Times* (1837) 3

0.2 Detail from Edward Williams Clay, *The Times* (1837) 4

1.1 *King Andrew the First* (1833) 42

2.1 Nicolino Calyo, *View of the Ruins After the Great Fire in New York, 1835* (1837) 49

2.2 Edward Williams Clay, *New Edition of Macbeth. Bank-Oh's! Ghost* ["The Ghost of Commerce"] (1837) 58

4.1 Ruth Hall's Seton Bank stock (Fanny Fern, *Ruth Hall* [1855]) 104

E.1 John Cameron, *Running the "Machine"* (1864) 133

Acknowledgments

This book explores how notions of "success" or "failure" as individual identities were negotiated by American writers before the US Civil War. Some of the texts these writers produced are skeptical of the idea that one truly makes or breaks the self—that one sinks or swims alone. Although it is customary to assert that the pages that follow, faults and all, are "mine"—and that is true—it is equally true that I (like nearly all authors) have benefitted from the comradery, collegiality, love, and support of many during this book's long gestation. So, I am pleased to acknowledge many of those people here.

A now distant version of this project began as a dissertation at Ohio State University. I remain grateful to members of my committee, including Jared Gardner, Steve Fink, Beth Hewitt, whose scholarship in literature and economics always awes me, and Elizabeth Renker, from whose counsel on the discipline and the profession I continue to profit. These faculty members, along with people like Aman Garcha, Sandra Macpherson, and Jim Phelan, made my time in Columbus something to cherish. Classmates at OSU, including Kristina Garvin and Ali Salerno, and, especially Lindsay DiCuirci, who read portions of this manuscript in draft form, and Adam Stier, remain professional and personal inspirations to me today. As I completed my dissertation, I was also fortunate to spend time as a short-term fellow of the Library Company of Philadelphia's Program in Early American Economy and Society. I thank staff, especially Jim Green and Cathy Matson, and members of my fellowship cohort.

In a stroke of good fortune, Elizabeth Renker introduced me to the Civil War Caucus of the Midwest Modern Language Association, which is directed by Kathleen Diffley, as I completed my doctorate. Directly and indirectly, I owe much to this group's generosity and intelligence, and I am pleased to thank, in addition to Kathleen, Jane Schultz, Justine Murison, Jeff Insko, Tim Donohue, Mike Stancliff, and many others. For invitations to contribute to edited volumes and good counsel, I thank Chris Hager, Cody Marrs, and Chris Hanlon. And for his willingness to read good chunks of this manuscript in draft form, thanks to John Barnard, whose friendship and sage advice I also appreciate. In addition to those colleagues I routinely see in November,

I also thank Rachel Blumenthal, James Finley, and Greg Laski, who each offered impressionable feedback on an early draft. And thank you to Gordon Hutner for his advice on an early version of this project, Bob Levine, and especially Howard Horwitz, who has graciously debated economics and literature with me since meeting on a train from Baltimore to DC long ago.

I also thank the editors and presses with whom I published much earlier versions of this work as a doctoral candidate and a junior faculty member at Purdue University Fort Wayne. Portions of chapter 1 were adapted from the article, "Irving, Ruin, and Risk," originally published in *Early American Literature* 48, no. 3 (Winter 2013). The article is used by permission of the University of North Carolina Press (www.uncpress.org). A much different version of chapter 3 appeared as "Emerson, Labor, and Ages of Turbulence" in *ESQ: A Journal of Nineteenth-Century American Literature and Culture* 60, no. 2 (2014): 251–84. Copyright by, and used with the permission of, the Board of Regents of Washington State University. And finally, a small portion of chapter 4 was adapted from Cody Marrs and Christopher Hager, eds. *Timelines of American Literature*, pp. 123–33 (2019). Copyright by, and reprinted with the permission of, Johns Hopkins University Press. I gratefully acknowledge these publishers for their permission to reprint and the journals' editorial staffs that facilitated these pieces' original publications.

I have been fortunate at Purdue University Fort Wayne to benefit from the collegiality of many across campus. In English, I thank the literature faculty, including longtime chair and friend Hardin Aasand, Rachel Hile, Lidan Lin, Lewis Roberts, M. L. Stapleton, and Lachlan Whalen. Colleagues in writing, including our new chair, Suzy Rumsey, the current Poet Laureate of Indiana, Curtis Crisler, Karol Dehr, Deb Huffman, Sarah Sandman, and Kate White, have offered steadfast support. Troy Bassett, Damian Fleming, and Shannon Bischoff have especially encouraged me to complete a book-length study, and I am grateful for their professional wisdom and friendship. I also thank Shanté Howard and Carrie Adams in the department office for their support and good cheer. Colleagues from across the campus, including Deborah Bauer, Noor Borbieva, and Steve Buttes, kindly read a portion of the manuscript. My work has benefited from support from the College of Liberal Arts and the Office of Academic Affairs, and I thank Dean Janet Badia and Provost Carl Drummond. And I also acknowledge the generosity of the Purdue Research Foundation, that funded a summer grant to support this project.

I will always feel lucky to have found Lucas Church's email inbox at the University of North Carolina (UNC) Press. I thank him, Thomas Bedenbaugh, and the entire production team at the press. I am also grateful to Matt Seybold and the press' readers for their rigorous and good faith suggestions to improve this manuscript.

It is with great pleasure (and relief) that I thank my family and friends for their support and encouragement as I worked to complete this book. Longtime friends Nick Bridewell, Andy Goddard, Bryan Di Matteo, Matt McCartney, Jason Stanley, and Jeff Thompson offered good cheer and polite inquiries about my work—and Kevin Fitzgerald (supposedly) read a small portion of this book. In Columbus, I had the enviable experience to complete graduate school near my in-laws, Chris and George Mychkovsky, who offered love, support, and food during those lean years. Likewise, Les Krisa has become a cherished member of my family. I am equally grateful for the love and friendship of my brother-in-law, Alex Mychkovsky—longer-than-expected (and, at times, wanted) bike rides in Northern Michigan helped remind me that I can do hard things. I thank, too, my sister-in-law Martha Mychkovsky and our nephew Roman Mychkovsky for their love and support. In Fort Wayne, in addition to Deborah Bauer, Seth Weinglass, Ben Groeneweg, and Steve Knight. I thank Kevin and Sharon Knuth, whose love of historic neighborhoods, dog walks, boat rides, show choir, and good-natured teasing of Zoey has been a boon to our family.

To my parents, Mike and Chris Kopec, who have always cheered my writing and nourished my love of letters, thank you. I appreciate the self-belief, the resilience, and the kindness that I see modeled in you both, and I would not have the life I have without you. Thank you, too, to my brother Matt Kopec and his partner Joe Becherer, whose talents and love I so admire.

Finally, my deepest thanks go to Lydia Kopec and our daughters, Hannah and Zoey Kopec. Your love, support, and hard work make the dilemma of sinking or swimming feel less urgent, and I am grateful for the people you are and the life we, along with our pets Maisie, Felix, and Sasha, have made. I doubt this book will help you clarify to family, friends, coworkers, and classmates what it is, exactly, I do, but I hope you see it as a sign of your sustaining belief in me.

Sink or Swim

INTRODUCTION

Contemplating Crisis
Antebellum Literature and the Romance of Trade

What does Walt Whitman's "barbaric yawp" have to do with business fluctuations in the nineteenth-century United States?[1] Ideally, at least from the poet's perspective, not much. In the preface to *Leaves of Grass* (1855), Whitman argues that just as the United States is "essentially the greatest poem," so, too, is it a nation that "need never be bankrupt while corn grows from the ground or the orchards drop apples or the bays contain fish or men beget children upon women."[2] This optimism for lasting abundance makes sense in its historical moment: the mid-1850s, one economic historian writes, was a period of "unbroken" development.[3] A break would happen with the Panic of 1857, but in *Democratic Vistas* (1871), Whitman would worry about the "hollowness" of the coming Gilded Age.[4] By 1888, however, he avoided direct economic critique altogether. Indeed, that year's ode to failures, "To Those Who've Fail'd," notably omits business insolvents and dignifies instead "unnam'd soldiers," "devoted engineers," and other poor souls who found their "aspiration vast . . . quench'd by an early death": "Cut off before their time."[5] Preferring not to liken broken merchants to noble but doomed artists, the poem ultimately solves the problem of late nineteenth-century capitalism's grasp on identity by romanticizing it—that is, by idealizing the fact that such protocols of personality, the very stuff of "their time," are trials never to be faced.

These selections from Whitman respectively construe the realities of bankruptcy as unimaginable, lament the United States' acquisitive urge, and, finally, eschew business culture's psychological implications for everyday life. With this range of reactions to market society in mind, we can probably envision these texts reinforcing certain economic interpretations of nineteenth-century writing. Perhaps the 1855 preface is suffused with a financially tinged American exceptionalism. And to compensate for this early naivety, maybe the 1888 poem resists the commodification of identities that would occur across the nineteenth century by removing "failure" from the arena of the market and dropping it instead into the opposed one of art. And yet, as I argue throughout this study, "romantic optimism" and idealistic

1

escapism can only hint at how midcentury writers found their bearings in an era in which the "sky was always falling," with individuals, compelled to sink or swim, always on the verge of drowning.[6]

This book's premise is that business fluctuations, the struggle to establish an identity, and antebellum American literature were intimately entwined. Recurring financial spasms in the United States raised a host of questions as they threatened individuals with failure, but also allured them with success. What exactly do these categories, "failure" and "success," mean? How would one recognize, claim, or avoid them as identities? What speculative risks, financial and psychological, do such selves entail as one faces the challenge of sinking or swimming? According to the *Oxford English Dictionary*, this idiom, *sink or swim*, dates to late-fourteenth-century England and "indicat[es] the arrival of a personal turning point"; it would be codified in US literature with Horatio Alger's rags-to-riches tale of the same name (1870).[7] Closer to Alger than to Whitman—who imagines "a bold swimmer" in "Song of Myself" (1892) in the context of life-affirming leisure, not financial profit-seeking—James Fenimore Cooper, Washington Irving, Catharine Maria Sedgwick, Ralph Waldo Emerson, Nathaniel Hawthorne, Herman Melville, Fanny Fern, Frank J. Webb, Frederick Douglass, and the other figures examined here point to surprising answers to the questions raised above.[8] For their writing, the dilemma of securing the self proceeds most forcefully when it rejects an anxious retreat from the market's fluidity and engages deliberately with it. And grappling with systemic events like the Panics of 1819, 1837, 1857, and 1865, in addition to business vicissitudes more generally, their work invites us to reconsider how midcentury literature questioned the contingencies of capitalist identities that, now naturalized, seem mandatory today.

The mid-nineteenth-century United States was an era of financialization.[9] And the chapters that follow unfold historicist readings about literature amid profound reorientations for the understanding of the self along the axes of loss and gain. To consider the ruptures that such a shift entailed, we can begin with the fact that many Americans needed new words to ground themselves in the present—"derangements," "delusions," and "follies"; "manias," "revulsions," and "moral epidemics"; "pressures," "crises," and "panics." But the writers I study did not simply coin new terms. Rather, they reconfigured such commercial shocks, whatever they were called, as provocations for self-reflection. And this imaginative transformation of crisis into a drama of the self's accounting required strict observation from market participants.

FIGURE 0.1 Edward Williams Clay's 1837 lithograph, *The Times*, portraying the social chaos of the Panic of 1837. Courtesy of the Library of Congress.

A background figure in Edward Williams Clay's *The Times* (1837) suggests this counterintuitive phenomenon in which a society gone distracted might find self-understanding (see fig. 0.1). The "iconic image of the Panic of 1837," Clay's lithograph illustrates the pandemonium of a failed market, ushered in (from his perspective) by President Andrew Jackson's goldbug fiscal policies.[10] The image's gritty realism emphasizes displaced laborers, evicted widows, drunkards, suicides, and, in the language of the Library of Congress's description of the lithograph, a mob of "frantic customers" during a run on the Mechanics Bank.[11] In contrast, a well-dressed man in the background calmly smokes on the Custom House steps (see fig. 0.2). It is impossible to know what this man—probably a business clerk—imagines in viewing the violent consequences of a market gone bust. Is he contemplating the success or failure of his—or his firm's—financial investments? Taking pleasure "of a low sort" in the evaporation of other people's money?[12] Is he composing an anti-Whitmanian ode to the ruined lives, or apprehending the melee, perversely, as a "romance of trade," in Washington Irving's phrase from 1840?

Contemplating Crisis 3

FIGURE 0.2 Background detail from Edward Williams Clay's 1837 lithograph, *The Times*. Courtesy of the Library of Congress.

Does the man's relaxed demeanor suggest that he has insulated himself from market volatility—or that he, like many Americans, will want to do so to weather future storms? What does his seeming ease tell us about the others' lack thereof?

This figure raises the question in short: In contemplating a financial crisis, what lessons does one perceive about the self and how identity relates to the United States' economic institutions? It is this dilemma, I contend, that we find ourselves confronted with time and time again in mid-nineteenth-century US literature.

By reading their works in relation to this conundrum, my book shows how financial instability is significant for some of this era's major writers amid a developing relationship between literature and commercial culture. Individual texts, as we will see below, exposed the paradoxes of capitalist selfhood, in which the security of one's identity was anchored by financial unrest. In doing so, they negotiated—and thereby transformed—what it meant to conceive of the self as an entity that was coextensive with the market. To arrive at my thesis of nineteenth-century literature's textualization of identity thus entails specific approaches to uncertainty that counteract the escapism usually imputed to romantic-era writers. That market fluctuations are thematically, formally, and theoretically meaningful to this writing, indeed, can elude those who dwell on either the supposed absence of major works about the Panic of 1837 or the category of "anxiety" to the point where it threatens to flatten any sense of these writers' participation in business culture. I elaborate on these points below. For now, this is to say that the periodic movements from speculative exuberance to economic contraction do not necessarily result in complicity or distraction among the era's literary figures. In response to such swings, writers just as often got down to business, a word that meant both "matters demanding attention" and "commercial transactions."[13] Irving's biography illustrates just these psycho-financial resonances. In response to his brothers' bankruptcy in the late 1810s in Liverpool, England, he devised a "plan," *The Sketch-Book* (1819). At the mercy of the economy's swings, Irving moves from insecurity to text, worry to attention, inaction to trade. He thus suggests a way of living and writing within, in Marx and Engels's incisive phrase from the *Communist Manifesto* (1848), an epochal "everlasting uncertainty."[14]

The Genres of Panic

Although the economy in the early United States was a tumultuous one, with harmful retrenchments in 1792 and 1795–96, commercial disruptions during the republican era were confined mostly to "land speculators and seaport merchants."[15] In the antebellum era, by contrast, "unprecedented growth [and] unprecedented volatility" affected most Americans.[16] The result of "increasing the size of the market for American manufactured goods"—as commerce encompassed a growing share of midcentury Americans' productive activity—cultural evidence bears out a thesis of a qualitative shift in the lived experiences of the economy for the greater "number of workers who toiled for wages."[17] If the implications of the Industrial Revolution are evident in the mechanical analogies of Emerson's essays and in the fictionalized industrialists and inventors of Hawthorne's and Melville's short works, the psycho-financial ones for the era's strivers stand out in my study. For I especially focus on the implications of this qualitative shift among those Americans who sought to "strike out on their own" and secure their identities through market-based risks.[18] Uneven and contested throughout the century, such developments drew increasing commentary among those who sought to understand—and exploit—them. Indeed, the inchoate field of US political economy was just beginning to theorize the volatility of markets, but popular writing about "the times" boomed.[19] The era's indispensable business newspaper, *Niles' Weekly Register*, put the matter succinctly in 1821—economic unrest made "the whole people . . . political economists."[20]

That this democratization of debates over the significance of risk-taking occurred in the depression-era year of 1821 is no surprise. For Samuel Rezneck, one of the earliest cultural historians of US business swings, "the depression phase of the business cycle in particular inspired a voluminous literature."[21] The Panics of 1819, 1837, and 1857 yielded a wide discourse that ranged from sermons to editorials, essays to fiction, poems to treatises. Across these genres, writers struggled to apprehend a reality in which prosperity could morph without warning into widespread ruin. And like a Freudian compulsion to repeat, words like "sudden" and "hasty" permeated their analyses. In 1819, one American periodical contributor explained, "the business of five years has been done in one."[22] The culprit of this time compression—as noted by the English writer and acquaintance of Sedgwick and Emerson, Harriet Martineau, in her travelogue *Society in America* (1837)—was the United States' "hasty enterprise."[23] *Niles'* rued the "zeal 'to make haste to be rich.'"[24] In 1857, businessmen with memories of the Panic of 1837 looked backward to map the ripple effects of the present distress. Whichever way they glanced, dislocations seemed to have accelerated . . . and intensified. In one diarist's words from 1857: "This attack is far more sudden, acute, and prostrating than that of 1837. Will the banks stand it? I think *not*, and predict their downfall within ten days."[25]

Between financial shocks, more than institutions hung in the balance. So, too, did the identities of the individuals who patronized "the banks." Because crises of fiscal solvency foregrounded the self's vulnerability to what the cultural historian Jean-Christophe Agnew has called "the new systemic rules of capitalism as a market form of life," they raised questions about the ability to make or break on one's own.[26] This individual drama preoccupies the writers I study here. Perhaps unsurprisingly, the era's political economists touched on this relation between a sense of self and the unpredictable movement of the economy. Almost solely concerned with the macroeconomy, however, they did so to belittle the importance of any one person's bust. In one of the earliest economic textbooks by an American author, *Thoughts on Political Economy* (1820), the Baltimore politician Daniel Raymond dismisses the "common expression" that business failures "will be a serious injury to the country, and will retard [its] prosperity." "Nothing is more erroneous," he concludes. Such "occurrences, no doubt, cause much distress and calamity among individuals." That being said, "they produce no permanent injury to the country, nor do they diminish a nation's wealth."[27] From the perspective of early political economy, an individual failure simply confirmed a healthy, competitive commercial system.

The era's vernacular fictions countered the dispassionate view of the political economist in urban novels about wrecked business strivers. These sensationalist narratives expose the plight of a new class of "paper money men," David Anthony's resonant term for a group of "aspiring professionals who found themselves the victim of the new and unstable paper economy."[28] The New York bookseller Asa Greene's *The Perils of Pearl Street* (1834), for instance, laments how the "wheel of fortune is constantly moving. . . . The merchant knows little to-day of what he shall be on the morrow."[29] Another New Yorker, the prominent editor Charles Frederick Briggs, targets the merchant's susceptibility to flux during the depression of the 1840s in *The Adventures of Harry Franco: A Tale of the Great Panic* (1839) and *Bankrupt Stories* (1843). One victim, the eponymous hero of *Harry Franco*, a foolish cotton factor, keeps buying the commodity in 1837 until "suddenly a panic seized upon the minds of the whole people."[30] The event cut him to the quick. "The suddenness of the change which had taken place in my prospects," he states, "unsettled the fixed purpose of my soul."[31] For the political economist Raymond, Franco's break might "produce no permanent injury to the country."[32] But, from the microeconomic perspective of these sensationalist texts, unsettling existential questions about the individual remain: What of the self—the "soul"—whose loss is "too great for grief"?[33]

My study contends that major writers of the midcentury United States likewise sought to understand what it meant, in Horatio Alger's pithy phrase from his rags-to-riches novel, *Ragged Dick* (1868), to "feel like a capitalist" in the throes of economic crisis.[34] And yet I argue that literature—as a prime vehicle for revealing what Agnew calls "the cognitive and affective structures" that were adapted for a "disruptive" market culture—allows us to see how individual and structural scales connect in the experience of everyday life under emergent capitalism in the United States.[35] Political economy could snub questions about one person's relation to the broader economy, while topical writers like Greene and Briggs could linger on the psychological effects of economic convulsions for members of the grasping professional class.[36] Beyond the genres of "panic" or "economic" writing, the nineteenth-century figures I study, rather, worked at this intersection. Whether written by women or men, Black Americans or white people, so many of the era's historical romances, sentimental sketches and tales, transcendentalist essays, short stories, slave narratives, and novels obsessively heeded the shifting terms of the affective systems that authorized, upheld, or undid the self.

My book demonstrates, then, that these heterogenous coordinates of form and identity are each critical sites on which the economic self unfolds. From Irving's study of bankruptcy in *The Sketch-Book* to Webb's reflections on the hypocrisies of capitalist subjectivity in the urban North, antebellum writers probed the nature of, the justification for, and the parameters of selfhood central to the reproduction of exchange. They set about exploring market identity, approaching it as a set of contested practices far more complex than either political economists or topical writers tended to acknowledge.

Go-Aheadism in Antebellum America

In their attempts to "'bring the economy back' into American social and cultural history," scholars in what has come to be called a new history of capitalism conceive of the antebellum era as a vital site of "capitalism's transformation into an 'ism.'"[37] For this era witnessed the blossoming of a society where "exchange transcend[ed] the temporal and spatial boundaries to which it had long been confined . . . and c[a]me to characterize all spheres of life."[38] To chart this transcendence among the professional classes, cultural historians like Thomas Augst, Scott A. Sandage, and Brian P. Luskey address the installation of personal striving as an index of one's value. Indeed, as these historians demonstrate, the capitalist mode of production can be apprehended as a "form of selfhood."[39] For Sandage, the central psychocultural assemblage that emerged here was *go-aheadism*—a midcentury modality that prodded people into the belief that their (voluntary) individual exertions could "achieve" an identity.[40] John Russell Bartlett's *Dictionary of Americanisms* (1848) defined "go ahead" as "to proceed; to go forward. A seaman's phrase which has got into very common use."[41] "Perpetual striving," Sandage writes, "tipped the balance between identity and oblivion."[42] And this cultural transaction gave rise to the terms "success" and "failure" not merely as markers of business endeavors, but as genres of the self.

Competitive self-making, in which the rise and fall of a market encompasses the interior life of the self, attended "the imperceptible processes of commodification and financialization" in the antebellum United States.[43] Previously, writers imagined the self as secured from failure by God or by landed wealth. So, although John Winthrop's "A Model of Christian Charity" (1630) acknowledges the reality of economic turbulence, the sermon reassures its audience that one can rely on predetermined rules of behavior to ride it out. The "Gospel propounds," Winthrop writes, "a difference of seasons and occasions. There is a time when a Christian must sell and give to the poor. . . . There is also a time when a Christian . . . must give beyond their ability."[44] Nearly 150 years after Winthrop's speech aboard the *Arbella*, the "elite class of American Revolutionaries," as Jennifer J. Baker has written in *Securing the Commonwealth: Debt, Speculation, and Writing in the Making of Early America* (2005), wanted to "ground civic personality in property ownership [as] an idealized transcendence of market involvement."[45] By the antebellum era, alternatively, figurative conceptions of the self increasingly marked one's relation to intangible but market-based forms of wealth—think less God's covenant, landed estates, or gold bullion, and more paper money, stocks, bonds, and equity in business partnerships.[46]

How an individual navigated these displacements of traditional institutions by market culture has attracted the attention of American and British literary criticism. Whether explicitly working under the rubric from the late 1990s of the New Economic Criticism or not, scholars have shown, for example, how an array of new financial genres trained readers in market epistemology.[47] The literary form of the novel has emerged for critics of British literature, in particular, as a key technology for preparing people to understand fluid, and increasingly abstract, social relations.[48] From these valuable perspectives, literature could undertake the cultural work of facilitating market exchanges amid new conditions of uncertainty. But, as this scholarship equally asserts, it could also "diagnose a litany of economically induced" anxieties.[49] Indeed, as Americanist studies have noted, literature often deflects worries over unstable currencies, rampant speculation, insecure property, and the growth of insurance practices like underwriting.[50]

No doubt, *anxiety* has been a key term for economically oriented Americanist critics who want to understand how literary texts register shifts in people's understandings of, feelings about, and knowledge of market capitalism. The term has also been central for studies that track representations of and ideologies of identity—not just how people conceive of the market, but how people comprehend themselves within that structure. Anthony sees "capitalist selfhood" as an exemplar of a "kind of fiscal neurotic, given over to insecurity, anxiety, depression, and irrational fears" who struggles to make sense of the "drama and dynamism of capitalist exchange."[51] Anthony's criticism builds on David Leverenz's research that finds in the antebellum era an ideology of manhood that is "a compensatory response to fears of humiliation" posed by bankruptcy, which, despite Whitman's insouciance in 1855, became a new reality for more and more Americans.[52] Thus Briggs's *Bankrupt Stories* deplores that the "sudden breaking up and overturning the family of a merchant when overtaken by bankruptcy" results in one, now

Contemplating Crisis 9

unmanned, "feel[ing] that his respectability has oozed out of him."[53] For many of these literary and cultural studies of midcentury anxiety—because such oozing transpired within a social reality in which "business kept revising its own premises and practices in a ceaseless effort to negotiate a better deal"—literature offered insight into the "creative coping mechanisms" meant to hold the self fast within an endlessly changing, and suddenly shifting, world.[54] From these viewpoints—whether focused on working-class dime novels, as with Michael Denning, or the travails of the aspiring merchant class, as with Anthony—literature offers a "process of fantasy resolution" to calm the constantly nervous self.[55]

Literature's role in deflecting business fluctuations is an important topic for my book. In what follows, I would like to resist the idea, however, that financial uncertainty as a rule impelled individuals to distraction, escapism, fantasy, victimhood, or avoidance.[56] It just as readily led the mostly canonical writers I study here to participate purposefully in culture-wide debates over identity and its link to economy. For writers from Irving to Webb, the threat of ruin would become the basis for self-making: an affect that had to be reckoned with, rather than fantasized away. So, what Denning assesses in popular culture as working-class dreams of sudden wealth, which are (in his argument) payoffs for the "impossibility of imagining 'realistic' actions by powerful agents," would be for the writers I study here the stuff of nightmares. After all, such visions of easily attained (because unearned) riches would undermine the stringent faith among go-getters that one's work alone, undertaken amid uncertainty, will yield an identity.

In pursuing less anxious stances toward the market than other Americanist studies of economics and literature, then, my book participates in a project recently named the Economic Humanities. I aim to "focus on the broader historical imaginary" of capitalist culture in the midcentury United States "through an anatomy of the necessary fictions underpinning economics" and finance.[57] For what we encounter in the texts examined in the chapters that follow is often the belief that writers or characters *become* "powerful agents" by addressing "the very psychology of success and failure in modern America," rather than avoiding it.[58] As one contemporary put it, "the ambition to do a *great business* is here universal," and commercial crises could confirm such ambition.[59] Compulsory striving in times flush or fallow—a "necessary fiction" of antebellum capitalism indeed—demanded safety mechanisms, especially considering an unregulated market. And yet the writers I study saw in turbulence a chance to gain a foothold on slippery economic terrain. They considered what is now an old saw of neoliberal capitalist culture—that roiled financial markets are, for the shrewd prospectors, but precursors to profits. To understand midcentury literature's relation to market culture, then, means not just highlighting the anxieties that flux produced, but also engaging the psychological alternatives that financial innovation dramatically brought to the fore as new categories of the self.

The Romance and Finance: Hawthorne's *The House of the Seven Gables* and the Paradox of Capitalist Selfhood

Now, an example—Nathaniel Hawthorne's *The House of the Seven Gables* (1851), perhaps the midcentury text that most indelibly marks the ambitions of an economically oriented Americanist criticism.[60] The tale traces the financial ups and downs of the Pyncheon family in New England from the Salem Witch Trials to the 1840s. Seemingly cursed by a greedy forebear who expropriated land from a poor seventeenth-century settler, Matthew Maule, the Pyncheons in the novel's present are divided. Judge Pyncheon enjoys wealth and power, while his cousins, Hepzibah and the wrongfully imprisoned Clifford, suffer indigence. To provide for themselves, the patrician but destitute Hepzibah opens a cent shop. Ill-suited to this enterprise, she is saved by a distant relation, the young, bright country girl, Phoebe, whose domestic acumen integrates effectively into the urban core. Phoebe eventually falls in love with Hepzibah's lodger, the itinerant Holgrave. When the judge dies unexpectedly, leaving Hepzibah, Clifford, and Phoebe to inherit, the novel ends in a marriage that joins the Pyncheons (Phoebe) and Maules (Holgrave). The Pyncheons' "ill-gotten" wealth is cleansed in the process.[61]

Readings of this historical romance's relation to "the entropic energies of" nineteenth-century capitalism abound.[62] Whether focusing on Phoebe's transcendent commercial acuity like Gillian Brown or Clifford's idleness like David Anthony, addressing the novel's Lockean sensibility like Mark Rifkin or its hopeless immersion in market capitalism like Walter Benn Michaels, critics of different stripes have productively read this text as "a parable of the market revolution."[63] In addition to these impressive critical studies, the novel has also inspired scholarship about authorial reactions to shifts in the material basis of nineteenth-century literature's production. So, Michael T. Gilmore, in a foundational argument, tracks Hawthorne's ambivalence toward a structural transformation of the national literary marketplace, while Meredith McGill sees in *House*'s formal stutters Hawthorne's struggle to "disavow" (her word) his prior work, which had resonated in a formerly regional, decentralized literary sphere.[64]

More recent studies attend to the romance's critique of capitalist forms of identity.[65] Such arguments build on Michaels's classic formulation of *House* as an imaginary "escape from capitalism."[66] This escapist project spells trouble for the novel's archvillain, Judge Pyncheon, as the romance's search for stability entails gleefully killing off this most obvious representative of nineteenth-century go-aheadism.[67] In a formally distinct chapter told in the present tense, the narrator mocks the typically busy, grasping judge. This irony is manifested in the chapter title, "Governor Pyncheon," a position to which the Essex County justice aspires but has not just yet obtained. The narrator also mocks him, "a gentleman" so typically "burthened with engagements," through imagining what "was to have been such a busy day!" (*HSG*, 269) The thwarted itinerary seems ripped from a profile in today's *CEO Magazine*. Meetings with insurance executives, a "State-street broker," "note-shaver[s]," real estate auctioneers, and political kingmakers—all for naught (*HSG*, 271). "What!," the narrator sardonically muses over the judge's inanimate body, "Thou art not stirred . . . ? No; not a jot!" (*HSG*, 283) The narrator's proliferation of jeering exclamation points in this direct address to a corpse is matched only by the business opportunities that the judge's death indefinitely forestalls.[68]

With Pyncheon gone, the question of unstable wealth seems to be settled by the formerly radical Holgrave's conversion into a "conservative" (*HSG*, 315). Prior to his arrival at the Pyncheon mansion, Holgrave was a transient young man—his "career" defined by brief stints as a peddler, teacher, and even a dentist (*HSG*, 181). His preference for the ephemeral further leads him to criticize the permanence of real estate like the House of the Seven Gables itself. But, in its resolution, Hawthorne's text aims (as Michaels writes) to "defuse" its hero's association with tumult in two ways.[69] First, Holgrave's marriage to Phoebe (and the coming inheritance of the judge's estate) insulates this aimless man from the threat of commercial failure.[70] And, second, prior to his proposal to Phoebe, he actually renounces his one clearly stated ambition to appear as an author in "*Graham* and *Godey*," which were popular nineteenth-century magazines, the latter being what Patricia Okker describes as "the most widely read periodical in the United States at the time" (*HSG*, 186).[71] Freed from potential impecuniousness and divested of ambition (to appropriate one of Hawthorne's terms from his romance's preface [*HSG*, 2]), Holgrave can retire to the country. Having seemingly escaped those go-ahead agitations, his only business now will be with contentment.

Except that, after Holgrave's renunciation of the market's affective protocols, the judge's wealth endures—and not just his real estate so frequently discussed by critics, but his paper wealth that is implicated in the financial volatility that the romance supposedly spurns. For Rifkin, *House* presents a "romance of labor," a Jacksonian narrative antithetical to "the speculative dynamics of US political economy."[72] But the risks—and so, too, the rewards—of speculation remain. Hawthorne refers in his preface to the "folly of tumbling down an avalanche of ill-gotten gold . . . on the heads of an unfortunate posterity," but what of the judge's corporate holdings? (*HSG*, 2) His "railroad, bank, and insurance shares, his United States stock, —his wealth, in short, however invested, now in possession, or soon to be acquired"? (*HSG*, 270) Indifferent to the nature of investment—wealth is wealth, this passage makes clear—the novel implies that such returns will be of use for "posterity" after all (*HSG*, 2). Indeed, if the preface draws attention to real estate and hard currency, the conclusion subtly substitutes one form of paper value (a now "worthless" deed to Maine forests) for another (valuable securities) (*HSG*, 316). With proceeds from the latter, each generation will "alter the interior" of the family home "to suit its own taste, and convenience" (*HSG*, 314). Such anticipation is hardly that of the imminently ruined clerk, the ill-fated cotton factor, or even the failed writer. Rather, although left unstated, Holgrave anticipates finance continually making new the "interior" stage of the Pyncheon-Maule home for future dramas of self-making.[73]

With this implied transformation of the wanderer into a capitalist, the romance thus seizes the paradox of capitalist selfhood in which one simultaneously pursues security from, yet vulnerability to, the market's unpredictability. In doing so, *House* keys us into how the nineteenth-century self, scarred by financial distress in the past, will be spurred "to order present economic action toward an uncertain future, as opposed to the mere replication of [that] economic past."[74] These are the words of Jonathan Levy, a historian of risk in the United States, who conceptualizes capital as an ongoing "process" in which "legal property [is] assigned a pecuniary value in expectation of a likely future outcome."[75] Far from escaping uncertainty, then, *House* demonstrates, finally, how the "orientation toward an uncertain future" in which one might realize profit constitutes life under midcentury capitalism.[76] And it suggests, more generally, how literature engaged not just with the investment processes that, together, constitute "capitalism" and all of its "institutional contexts and representational technologies," but also with the styles of subjectivity and the categories of the self that would ultimately help naturalize this mode of production in the first place.[77]

Contemplating Crisis 13

Liquid Selves and the "Task of Modernity"

Hawthorne's integration of finance thus counteracts the premise of the romance as hostile toward capitalist exchange. Although important in and of itself, such integration is an essential context for my study because it further reveals a prominent pattern of the contested naturalization of capitalist selfhood. Midcentury authors, that is, seek freedom from economic and financial institutions only to acknowledge them as boundaries and, with this knowledge in mind, reengage the social world. Such a turnabout is the subject of the historian James E. Block's *A Nation of Agents* (2002). There, he tracks how colonial, revolutionary, and antebellum-era Americans undertook "the very task of modernity."[78] That project was to make the "exuberant, unreflective embrace of economic participation" appear voluntary—to normalize converting unprecedented "freedom effortlessly into agency," seeming "independence . . . relinquished [into] systematic engagement."[79] The desired outcome of this alchemy was to "mak[e] the economy the institutional linchpin of idyllic liberalism."[80] And as this process unfolded in an apparently noncoercive "open economic market," capitalist selfhood fit the bill for smoothing out these changes.[81]

Like foreign observers, including Tocqueville, Martineau, Michele Chevalier, and others, midcentury writers could "recognize [this] regimentation" of the self for economic ends.[82] But more often than not, such self-conscious knowledge of "the internalization of the market agency role as the operational equivalent of economic freedom" compelled integration, not dismantling.[83] The writers I study throughout my book thus often participate in what Block terms a "narrative of reversal," whereby one charts a new, countercultural path "not by continuing the journey toward openness indefinitely but only by in time relinquishing it."[84] We see this backpedaling in *House*'s conclusion when Holgrave and Phoebe temporarily inhabit the House of the Seven Gables with Judge Pyncheon's dead body. The couple worries about how the judge's death will be construed by the villagers. Will Clifford once more be wrongfully accused of murder, as in years prior with a deceased bachelor uncle? Yet Holgrave is in no "haste" to reenter "the precincts of common life," even to clear Clifford's name (*HSG*, 305). "On the contrary," from this desolation "he gathered a wild enjoyment," which he saw as "separat[ing] Phoebe and himself from the world, and b[inding] them to each other" (*HSG*, 305). If such binding leads Holgrave to briefly imagine a prolonged freedom, it frightens Phoebe. In response to his declaration of love, she cries, "you will make me strive to follow you, where it is pathless. I cannot do so. It is not my nature. I shall sink down, and perish!" (*HSG*, 306) A spectral residue of the judge's grasping way of life, the words "strive" and its implied counterpart "sink," as uttered by Phoebe, combine as a defensive tactic. But, Holgrave reassures her, he will "confine himself within ancient limits" and "conform [himself] to laws and the peaceful practice of society" (*HSG*, 306–7). He will leave behind, seemingly, the aggressive go-aheadism typical of the judge. Conquering "the crisis" together through this compromise, they return to the world having "transfigured the earth, and made it Eden again, and themselves the two first dwellers in it" (*HSG*, 307).

We have already seen how this Edenic vision is tacitly framed by anticipated financial returns that will allow the new Pyncheon-Maules to countenance an unknown future. But here the novel implicates financialization at the level of the "transfigured" self as well. Indeed, where Gillian Brown brilliantly reflects on the bourgeois containment of Phoebe's domestic labor, we also see Hawthorne's text chart this character's changed understanding of the self.[85] At first glance, Phoebe's protest of Holgrave seems to eschew the ethos of commerce. In his oft-reprinted "Lecture on Commercial Integrity" (1839), Joseph Hopkinson writes: "The life of a merchant is, necessarily, a life of peril. He can scarcely move without danger. He is beset on all sides with disappointments, with fluctuations in the current business, which sometimes leave him stranded on an unknown bar, and sometimes sweep him helpless into the ocean. . . . To risk much, to be exposed to hazards, belongs to the vocation of a merchant."[86] Phoebe's reticence partakes of this rhetoric. For Hopkinson, the merchant "must have the courage to explore new regions of commerce"; Phoebe worries she will "perish" on the "pathless" main.[87] And yet relying on what Holgrave calls her "poise," she plots a way forward. What once made her "uneasy" about him—his rigorous "integrity . . . amid all these personal vicissitudes"—now reassures her (*HSG*, 177). But, and at the same time, she also discovers in herself an attribute that Hopkinson ascribes to the merchant: she no longer fears peril. So, the romance not only naturalizes hazard-taking, but also expands the domain of its "vocation" into everyday life. Critics have tended to dwell on how *House* taps into an American's fear of "sink[ing] below his order," as Hawthorne puts it in the preface. But, as Phoebe's example makes clear, such concerns over being adrift in the "ocean" equally compelled risk-taking individuals to swim. Reconciling the (stable) self's inner being with its (unstable) external spatiotemporal circumstances, Phoebe embraces risk. In such a frame of mind, she seeks not just to stay afloat, but to build "Eden again."

Evincing what I am calling a paradox of capitalist selfhood, Phoebe's self-dynamism aims at surviving fluctuations, not avoiding them. It expects volatility, rather than ignores it. In running Phoebe through such a crisis, thereby transforming her into this kind of self, Hawthorne portrays the security ("integrity") required to survive insecurity ("vicissitudes"). Modeling a relation between the individual and the structure that limits it, the romance thus stages a compromise between one's desire for freedom and the institutional forces that press on this hope. In doing so, the romance normalizes a self that could map its relation to social forms—and then plan accordingly. (With the right mindset, even one "stranded on an unknown bar" is safe!) In terms of financialized identities, the romance takes for granted that the self is brave enough to risk failure or success.

We will see such assurances tested across the writing studied here. Despite their anxieties about the definition of money, the reliance on debt beyond what Catharine Maria Sedgwick termed during the Panic of 1837 as the "means of actual support," and other financial phenomena that started to restrict the self, then, the authors of these works held their gaze.[88] They looked squarely at the results of the era's economic earthquakes (Emerson's term for 1837 panic) and lesser tremors. In doing so, Cooper and Irving, Sedgwick and Emerson, Hawthorne, Melville and Fern, and Webb and Douglass came to see fluctuations as, paradoxically, regular irregularities of midcentury life. Across literary genres and social identities, what was up for debate was what such booms and busts foretold for the meaning of the self. The determined focus on the self's status amid business unrest that this writing demonstrates would have long-lasting social implications in the United States. Observing the spatiotemporal disorientations of the commodified, financialized, or neoliberal present, literary scholars like Annie McClanahan see in the aftermath of the 2008 crisis cultural texts that struggle to link the self to increasingly abstract financial forms.[89] The problem, as Zygmunt Bauman assesses it, is that twenty-first-century (or late) capitalism poses a "series of challenges never before encountered" by individuals.[90] Among these trials is the evanescence of "social forms (structures that limit individual choices, institutions that guard repetitions of routines, patterns of acceptable behavior)," which "can no longer . . . keep their shape . . . because they decompose and melt faster than the time it takes to create them."[91] Mirroring the hyper-liquidity of modern finance capital, selves and institutions scuffle to avoid (in Briggs's nineteenth-century formulation) "oozing."

As those scholars at the vanguard of the Economic Humanities remind us, and as Briggs's term clarifies, such "cultural understandings of" the self in relation to unstable economic institutions "are not timeless, but have their own histories."[92] And what the authors of twenty-first century "liquid realisms" confront as new givens—the constancy of unrest, the instability of social institutions, the ruthless racket of a now demystified go-aheadism, indeed, the overall violence and precarity of everyday life under late capitalism—the antebellum ones I study saw as contingent.[93] Nineteenth-century financial crises would force these issues into the open.[94] Sure, Holgrave and Phoebe decide to remake Eden with a stout inheritance, but what happens when their investment portfolio plummets in 1857? And what about Clay's observant clerk? What tactics—compensatory or compensation-seeking—would he adopt after the ruckus in 1837? Does he set about "transfigur[ing]" the social world? Or, more likely, does this perhaps "smart young clerk, who gets the taste of traffic as a wolf-cub does of blood," as Hawthorne writes in "The Custom-House" (1850), link the liberal past to the neoliberal future by construing crisis as an opportunity to enact the next financial innovation that keeps the boom-bust cycle churning in perpetual motion?[95]

Project Overview

Bounded by the financial panics of 1819 and 1865, the chapters below move chronologically to expose necessary adaptations to the ideology of an achieved identity amid the reality of a life in which failure is ever threatening. If this chronology of midcentury writing seems to follow a traditional periodization, then, it can also soften the presentism of neoliberalism as a frame. Where the new history of capitalism sees these nineteenth-century business dislocations as linked to the present, indeed, recent literary scholarship on late-capitalist writing can seem to obscure the antebellum era from the picture. Following a 2006 special issue of *American Literary History*, in which David Zimmerman identifies an "economic turn" in Americanist criticism, another special issue of that journal (2019) calls for the Economic Humanities to historicize the neoliberal present.[96] Although this latter volume begins with assessments of the economic resonances of the colonial and republican eras, it all but skips over the antebellum period on its way to the Gilded Age.[97] The story of nineteenth-century capitalism, though, is as much one of evolving personal identities across the antebellum era, as it is of corporate forms consolidating into the postbellum era. In her study of contemporary financial realisms, Alison Shonkwiler previews my point in "suggest[ing] that it is more often than not an individual who (sometimes

Contemplating Crisis 17

bewildered, sometimes not) confronts" the financialization of value.[98] But antebellum American literature defamiliarizes this current reality and reveals that what theorists like Michel Foucault and Wendy Brown diagnose as the entrepreneurial or neoliberal self is neither brand new nor inevitable.[99]

In doing so, moreover, midcentury writers track evolving epistemologies of capitalist selfhood in which an individual's supposed freedom won in the market is always tenuous. What distinguishes Irving at the beginning of the antebellum era from Webb at the end of it, then, is the ability to recognize—and gain the distance to criticize, as in Hawthorne and Melville—the paradoxes that success is ultimately failure, independence always subservience. Irving only faintly recognizes the force of this conundrum in 1819, as he rushes to earn an identity through proximity to commercial swings, rather than safe distance from them. And Sedgwick, more aware of its implications than Irving, must still romanticize this model of selfhood to secure space for women within a topsy-turvy market culture. And so, too, must Emerson idealize commercial identities if only to harness their entropic potential for philosophical strivers. And finally, the Black American writers I discuss in chapter 5 return to Irving's insistence on the viability of capitalist selfhood with the knowledge of the violence that racial capitalism has wrought. In this way, then, fiction from writers like Sedgwick and Webb is not simply a testcase for this book's claims about nineteenth-century writing's textualization of risk-taking. Instead, business turbulence in the midcentury consistently pushed white and Black American writers, men and women, to reflect on the bewildered, non-bewildered self amid a gathering economic storm. And considering this unrest, they saw the limits of the striving self in the damage inflicted by widespread ruin. The progression I chart thus reveals increasing reflexivity among the writers assembled here about the costs of capitalist personhood—as well as the difficulty of abandoning this model of the self once it is entrenched in everyday life.

Chapter 1 turns to two early strivers who embraced go-ahead go-getting, James Fenimore Cooper and the primary focus of my analysis, Washington Irving. The historian of the book William Charvat's influential account suggests how these authors transformed literary production to sustain "professional" authorship in the United States. Subsequent challenges to Charvat's thesis by scholars like Leon Jackson, however, trouble the idea of market triumphalism.[100] My chapter sympathizes with this latter idea that even so-called professional writers saw their practice as multiply economic. And by focusing on Cooper's and, especially, Irving's experiences of bankruptcy, I recast early professionalism as motivated by identity achievement through risk-taking. Although threatened with penury in the late 1810s and early 1820s, they had more at stake than dollars and cents. And in this context of uncertainty, I read Cooper's historical romance *The Spy* (1821) and, to a much greater extent, Irving's personal correspondence and popular literary success, *The Sketch-Book* (1819), as textual registers of—and meta-commentaries on—the psychology of incipient capitalism.

The first chapter's emphasis on how early literature navigated market swings from a masculine perspective, as one feminist critique of the new history of capitalism notes, can omit women's contributions to "the cultural politics necessary for capitalism to prevail among other ethics of exchange."[101] Chapter 2 thus focuses on Catharine Maria Sedgwick's sustained engagement with economic prosperity, panic, and depression across her journals, letters, tales, and novellas from the 1830s and '40s. As an author and frustrated social reformer, Sedgwick looks for opportunities in her writing to integrate financialization into the domestic sphere, even as she wants stringently to moderate the psychological protocols of go-aheadism. She deploys this project with male characters, like Harry Aikin in *The Poor Rich Man and the Rich Poor Man* (1836), who can model successful failure. But she is eager to assess women's relation to these protocols too. And through the normative identities of wives, mothers, sisters, and daughters, she probes how women managed the consequences of risk-taking in a culture that gendered capitalist striving. In doing so, she joins a robust women's panic fiction. But where other writers naturalized "domestic constancy" as a compensatory response to financial unrest, Sedgwick acknowledged the affordances of instability.[102] In her critical relation to capitalist selfhood, she reveals the contradictions of prodding economic growth among men, while at the same time relying on a stability of character among women.

Chapter 3 continues the theme of how the era's major writers reframed go-aheadism for their own ends. Here, I examine business fluctuations as a preoccupation of Emersonian transcendentalism. Living off financial returns from his deceased wife Ellen Tucker Emerson's estate, Emerson played "family banker" in the 1830s.[103] Perhaps because he had skin in the game, the Panic of 1837 shook him as much intellectually as financially. In his *Journals*, he reflected immediately on the wide-ranging aftershocks of this "earthquake." But his subsequent lectures, orations, and essays suggest a thoroughgoing (if at times less obvious) engagement with financial swings. Drawn to the theme of flux, in well-known texts like "The American Scholar" (1837) and "The Poet" (1844), in addition to lesser studied speeches from the late 1830s, he joined a culture-wide debate over capitalist identity. How can

Contemplating Crisis 19

the scholar, engrossed in an arduous mental activity like "speculation," relate to the financial structure?

Chapter 4 turns to more skeptical examinations of ideologies of capitalist selfhood in works by Hawthorne and Melville, which question the desirability of identity achievement under conditions of financial duress. I begin with Hawthorne's *New-England Magazine* tales — precisely the products that, as he would retrospectively opine, haunted him as early failures. And yet these oft-overlooked texts offer important clues for his evolving sense of identity amid a commercial society. In "The Ambitious Guest" (1835) and "Mr. Higginbotham's Catastrophe" (1835), his characters seek a success that transcends the market. But this seeming protest against go-aheadism continually fails, as his characters fall into a financialized model of the self. Like Hawthorne, Melville also studies the psychological features of market culture in a lesser-known text, "The Happy Failure" (1854). But it is his final novel, *The Confidence-Man* (1857), that offers his most potent account of the self's relation to economic flux. Representing an engineered panic, optimistic securities investors, and confused debtors, the novel holds up a mirror to a financialized society. In doing so, it captures the paradox of business turbulence now internalized within the self — once normalized, economic volatility can no longer provide a reliable context in which to distinguish the self.

This is precisely the outcome that, as I argue in chapter 5, some contributions to early African American literature worked against. The financialization of enslavement has been a major research topic for the new history of capitalism.[104] Midcentury African American writers perceive exchange as ruthless, yes — the traffic in human flesh abominable. But, as recent scholars attest, market culture also provided models of the self that would allow African Americans to engage with US institutions. Formerly enslaved writers like Harriet Jacobs, William Wells Brown, and Frederick Douglass each consider the affordances of achieving an identity through finance. It is Frank J. Webb's novel of a clerk on the make, *The Garies and Their Friends* (1857), though, that most fully tests go-aheadism. Exposing the hypocrisy of the urban North's business culture through the experiences of a would-be office clerk, Charlie Ellis, the novel complicates the script of self-directed striving. Webb's ambivalence about capitalist selfhood thus sets the stage for later conflicts about equitable access to the rewards that the era's turbulent economy produced.

The urgency of Webb's project is justified by the fact that, in the everyday experiences of capitalism and figurations of the self, we are still tied today to the antebellum era's go-ahead ethos. And my book's Epilogue considers the extent to which even a writer like Melville, so critical of go-aheadism in the 1850s, presaged this normalization—if also the evolution—of striving. His book of Civil War poems, *Battle-Pieces* (1866), will begin to illustrate my point, as it might lead us to imagine the returning Union troops as clerks who will contemplate future crises from desks, rather than from factory floors or country fields. His volume's subtle attention to office work thus gives way— perhaps inevitably for a study of the midcentury capitalist self—to "Bartleby" (1853), likely the most famous renunciation of ambition in US fiction. Like an episode of the US sitcom *The Office* (2005–13), here I attend to the range of quirky personalities. And the errand boy, Ginger Nut, drawn to the Wall Street law firm as a stage on which to find success, is the star. If Bartleby prefers not to, Ginger Nut seemingly prefers to. Compelled by his father, he naturalizes striving, justifies toil, and chases the example of his boss, the tale's lawyer-narrator. In doing so, Ginger Nut—not Bartleby—joins Irving's banker Roscoe, Sedgwick's investor Beckwith, Emerson's scholar, Hawthorne's salesman Dominicus Pike, Fern's Ruth Hall, and Webb's Charlie Ellis in the march from the antebellum office to the postbellum one: to an era where so many studies of economics and US literature want the story of capitalist go-getting to begin.

CHAPTER ONE

Irving, Risk, and Ruin

Professional authorship in the early United States was born of bankruptcy. Not that the inability to repay outstanding debts was so unusual in the aftermath of the Panic of 1819 and its "increasing harvests of ruined business owners."[1] And yet if insolvency was experienced by unprecedented numbers of people, our sense of how some reacted to it has been limited. No doubt, as one historian of antebellum bankruptcy writes, this social reality "emboldened some residents . . . to resist the incursions of a thoroughly commercial world."[2] Such was the case for the leading "critics of the antebellum financial system," Andrew Jackson and Thomas Hart Benton, themselves erstwhile bankrupts.[3] What *has* seemed strange is that bankruptcy could also "encourage individuals to rethink their place within a capitalist economy."[4] Early professionals, James Fenimore Cooper and Washington Irving, belong to this latter group.

In the fall of 1819, surveying the "very hard" times, one Virginia periodical writer wondered how to resume the "career of prosperity."[5] A few ideas came to mind. First, mend old clothes, rather than buy new ones. Second, drink less imported whiskey. And, third, although "not a very bookish race," Americans should purchase homegrown "books, paper, and stationery."[6] In a similar protectionist vein, the Boston physician Walter Channing lamented that "this country wants literary distinction."[7] The title of his essay, "Reflections on the Literary Delinquency of America" (1815), indeed figured the United States as a kind of artistic bankrupt.[8] Channing argues that the nation must elevate the perception of its literature to the height of its "commercial reputation."[9] And to accomplish this feat, the United States needs an author-merchant. Such a writer will be a "bold man" who "strive[s]" to avoid the humiliation of "dependence."[10] Shirking "listlessness," ignoring the false narrative that "there is no stall for [America's] literary wares, in the whole market of letters," this go-getting figure will fulfill the obligations of the nation's "literary enterprise."[11]

Modern accounts of early American literary professionalism centering on Cooper and Irving have tended to emphasize, first, this "market of letters." "The profession of authorship began in the United States in the 1820s," William Charvat explains, "when Washington Irving and James Fenimore Cooper discovered that they could turn out regularly books which readers were willing to buy regularly."[12] Separate from newer critiques of Charvat's market triumphalism, but still in tension with this materialist line of inquiry, other scholars have focused on, second, the pathological, nervous psychology of fledgling writers seemingly ill-suited to the compulsions of market culture.[13] So, critics from Stanley Williams to Michael Davitt Bell, Jeffrey Rubin-Dorsky to David Anthony see in Irving's turn to authorship a strategy of "repression and control," not a deliberate engagement with what J. G. A. Pocock famously coined the era's "Machiavellian Moment."[14]

This chapter illustrates, however, that financial and psychological contexts cannot so easily be separated. Situating, briefly, Cooper's and, to a larger extent, Irving's literary and nonliterary writing within their experiences of business turbulence, I argue that commercial instability enabled their early work. If each writer faced a stimulating tension between macro- and microeconomic unease in the late 1810s and early 1820s, they did not, in turn, produce escapist fantasies. Rather, Cooper's *The Spy* (1821) and Irving's *The Sketch-Book* are texts that grapple with the relationship between risk and identity. Whether explicitly engaging the era's financial tumult or not, such works function as "capital" (Irving's term) to enact an ideology of selfhood that "depended not only on the chance of success but on the risk of failure" too.[15] In 1815, Channing wanted venturesome writers—he got them in Cooper and Irving.

Cooper's Long Game

Do not invest in war zone real estate. So advises James Fenimore Cooper's first historical romance of North America, *The Spy: A Tale of the Neutral Zone* (1821). One of the earliest fictionalized treatments of the War for Independence, Cooper's second novel examines the social conflicts between loyalists and revolutionaries in the early 1780s. To do so, it recreates the "neutral zone" of Westchester County, New York, a lawless space between New York City encampments controlled by the British Army and Hudson River Valley ones occupied by the Continentals. Here nothing is secure—certainly not identity. Although he works for George Washington, Harvey Birch, the titular spy, is hunted by American soldiers as a British saboteur. Even Washington must navigate this space disguised as Mr. Harper. Nor is property safe. A presumably pro-American paramilitary group, the Skinners, burns Birch's home to the ground. The upper-class Whartons, too, suffer the same fate when the Skinners torch their homestead, the Locusts.

Now, as for buying war zone real estate *after* the conflict? That moral was harder for Cooper to parse. On becoming the administrator of his late father William Cooper's extensive land-based estate in the 1820s, he faced a series of three chancery suits brought forward by Albany, New York lawyer Thomas Bridgen. After the war, Cooper's and Bridgen's late fathers were coinvestors in parcels of the New Military Tract in upstate New York earmarked for Continental Army veterans. The titles to this property, however, were unclear, and the investor group (led by William Cooper) could not realize profits on the deeds. Debts between Cooper and Bridgen remained unsettled throughout the decades. As the Bridgens suffered from the hard times, "the surviving heirs came to view the Military Tract losses as a source of hope rather than regret."[16] And in the 1820s, now seeking a "speedy" financial recovery, Thomas Bridgen moved against the Coopers.[17] Profits gleaned from a sheriff's sale in fall 1821 of Cooper-owned properties, including the family estate, Otsego Hall, finally closed this protracted matter.

Below, I offer a quick reading of *The Spy* as a response to the financial instability that beset Cooper in the late 1810s and early 1820s. I begin here because thematically and formally, this historical romance at the outset of US literary professionalism alerts us to a more complex engagement among early authors with market culture than critics have allowed. Cooper has been seen as either aloof from trade or slavishly devoted to it. On one hand, with reference to his first novel, *Precaution* (1819), Robert E. Spiller, hewing to a theory of literature as a gentlemanly avocation, remarked that "Cooper's venture into literature had no commercial intent."[18] On the other one, critics blame his novels' flaws on "the over-rapid writing of a mercenary author."[19] The fact is that, for Cooper, authorship was a capital investment: he needed future cashflow.[20] And in viewing novel-writing as a financial enterprise, he embraced the identity protocols—and risk-taking—then displacing republican values. In practice, his writing might look like hasty job-work undertaken for short-run gain. At its core, though, his approach was undergirded by a long-run faith in commerce.

This faith, which helped Cooper survive his chancery ordeal, most explicitly informs an unsigned review he published in 1821 of an anonymously authored economic pamphlet.[21] The text that Cooper assessed was a free-trade critique of a protective tariff proposed by Pennsylvania US representative Henry Baldwin.[22] For Baldwin, like the Virginia periodical writer cited above, tariffs were the solution to the nation's depression. In his review of the tract, Cooper gently chides protectionism and, thereby, wades into an explosive policy debate. For my purposes, what is interesting about Cooper's essay, though, is the extent to which it focuses more generally on commerce than on any one doctrine.[23] Free trade or protectionism? "No American economist," one historian tells us, "completely avoided" this debate.[24] But for Cooper, such a dispute was secondary to the importance of focusing attention on future capital gains.

This is not to say that his review avoids the "present distress."[25] Indeed, he situates the downturn within a compelling macroeconomic context. Following the War of 1812, Cooper explains, US manufacturers exported their wares "at war prices," and Americans imported goods at large expense too.[26] This situation was fueled by "obtaining credit," and it "was so protracted as to make it the basis of all our calculations of wealth and gain."[27] Such an environment made individual risk assessment among merchants paramount and, thereby, provided the parameters for self-making. As the historian Edward J. Balleisen writes, "The new republic was . . . a developing economy, richer in potential than actual stores of wealth."[28] Cooper would sympathize with this point, but he would insist that for this potential profit to be realized, individuals undertaking business analyses would take the lead. The United States is "a nation of debtors and creditors," he writes, so let the "prudent man . . . invest his fortune" where he deems fit.[29]

The most recent Cooper biographer, Wayne Franklin, finds in the author's policy-tract review "a disconnect between [Cooper's] opinions as an essayist and his realities as a private citizen—indeed, as an author."[30] Franklin's point is twofold. First, the sentiments Cooper expresses seem at odds with an aspiring author-merchant who likely would have favored protection from cheap imports into the United States of English literature. Second, Cooper's optimism in one's ability to navigate the US financial system would not seem to square with the lessons he learned from the chancery suits about *imprudent* risk-taking. And yet, from my perspective, the review is entirely consonant with Cooper's attempt to naturalize business fluctuations as a context for self-making. In his conclusion, he quotes approvingly—and lengthily—from the unsigned tract, some of which bears repeating here: "Let us have a little patience, and we shall have something better to do than to croak about the times. If men would but pay more attention to these changes in the world, as natural as day and night, and trouble their brains less for discoveries of financial causes and new systems, we should all make better farmers, better merchants, better manufactures and better legislators."[31] The paragraph that follows Cooper's extended block quote dwells on the physical details of the tract qua book. The implication is, perhaps, clear: Cooper would like to add "better authors" to the grammatical series above too.[32] No systemic economic

Irving, Risk, and Ruin 25

reformer, he wanted to find a career within "natural" financial turbulence, rather than "croak" about the times. Instead of wracking his "brain . . . for discoveries of financial causes and new systems," that is, he would get down to business.

Literature would operate here as capital for Cooper to invest. Rather than pine for his boyhood home lost to speculators in the sheriff's sale, he saw "literary success" as a path on which to achieve "independence" from his father's wealth and, thus, "some new identity, a new grasp on the world."[33] This risk-taking posture connects his early fiction to the 1821 essay discussed above. It is a commonplace of criticism to observe Cooper's artistic debts to Sir Walter Scott's historical novels.[34] Indeed, modern readers of *The Spy* see the theme of the "neutral ground" as "a metaphor for the conflicts and ambiguities that flourish in the absence of clear-cut authority."[35] If Cooper was drawn to the "neutral ground" as a site of combatants' "fluctuating power," though, I argue that its resonance with *business* fluctuations appealed to him as well.[36] Taking on a new venture, writing for money, while concluding the chancery suits, Cooper "directed [his 'capital employed'] to new channels."[37] In doing so, in a historiographical insight I cite in the Introduction, he "kept revising [business culture's] premises and practices in a ceaseless effort to negotiate a better deal."[38]

What one of the era's prominent reviewers, W. H. Gardiner, found exasperating about his literary venture, *The Spy*, makes it difficult to summarize the novel efficiently. Along with the common peddler, Harvey Birch, the aristocratic Whartons live in the neutral zone. Young Henry Wharton fights for the Redcoats, while his sister, Frances, ardently supports the colonists' push for independence. Frances's fiancé, Major Dunwoodie, too, is an officer in the Continental Army, while Henry and Frances's sister, Sarah, is sought after by the British Colonel Wellmere. What seemed so strange to Gardiner was that Cooper would further complicate his plot by introducing yet one more character, Isabella Singleton, who joins Frances in vying for Dunwoodie's hand. Here is an extended passage from Gardiner about this "folly":

> Our author, with that unaccountable perversity with which young men will sometimes indulge a whim—a freak—a folly—against all sober judgment, does not merely stop short in his bright career, and fall into a profound slumber—we could forgive him that—does not move on more drowsily, or meander a little in his path from ignorance of the way, or a slight bewilderment of his senses—we could forgive him that too—but suddenly, with his eyes open, and without any manner

of provocation, wheels off at a right angle, and walks entirely out of a plain road, to bring in for no conceivable purpose but to create confusion, the least agreeable of all disagreeable "bundles of sensibilities" we ever remember to have met with in print—or out of it.[39]

The historian Jonathan Levy has linked this diction—"a freak"—to transatlantic risk culture in the antebellum United States.[40] What so galls Gardiner is the fact that Cooper seems to deliberately take such an ill-timed risk. Prior to the introduction of Isabella Singleton, the novel's "career" enjoyed a "prosperous state of things." To Gardiner's chagrin, such manufactured twists pushed the vehicle to "wheels off at a right angle."

Gardiner's diction implies that the novel's instability is as much financial as literary. The text dwells on insecure real estate, as mentioned above. When Birch is forced to sell his paternal home to a speculator for below market value, perhaps we can glimpse a biographical motivation in Cooper. When that same home burns before the speculator can realize the profits on his maneuver—there we can surmise, indeed, a compensatory strategy for the Bridgen affair. But, beyond such reactions, the novel develops its theme of long-range economic thinking in the spy Birch himself. In fact, what initially impelled Cooper toward this historical tale was an anecdote from John Jay, the first Chief Justice of the United States Supreme Court, about a revolutionary-era spy who deferred payment for his services for the sake of the fledgling nation (*The Spy*, 19). When Birch and Washington meet for the final time in the novel's penultimate chapter, the grateful general tries to "pay [him] for these services—[since] hitherto you have postponed receiving your reward." He offers Birch 100 gold doubloons, to which Birch retorts: "Does your Excellency think, that I have exposed my life and blasted my character, for money?" (*The Spy*, 415)

Worded so, this refusal of filthy lucre strikes a republican chord. According to one historian of the early republic, this would be a classic example of civic virtue, which entailed a "willingness of the individual to sacrifice [one's] private interest for the good of the community."[41] For John Lauritz Larson, this was "the ethical conundrum at the core of republicanism [that] lay at the heart of people's experience of the market revolution."[42] Birch clearly chooses the republic over individual gain, but an acquaintance of Cooper's sketches the other side of this conundrum. "A prominent merchant, well known in Wall Street," indeed, could not countenance such risk-taking from Birch without remuneration. As told later by the author's daughter, Susan F. Cooper, this banker saw "one capital mistake in drawing Harvey's character!"

"But just as I expected to see it all settled," the banker reportedly said to Cooper, "he refuses the gold. There was your great mistake; you should have given Harvey some motive."[43]

The Wall Street banker's narrow emphasis on an immediate payout misses that Birch's refusal suggests a larger "motive" to weave commercial exchange into the fabric of early American social life. Earlier, I stated that, for Cooper, the distinctions between free trade and protectionist policies were less important than America's long-term economic prospects. Something similar is happening here at the conclusion of *The Spy*. The contours of the imagined horizon are uncertain, as Cooper gives us in Birch an image of the republican yeoman. When he refuses the gold, Washington asks, "what have you to subsist on?" (*The Spy*, 415) "These!" Birch replies, "stretching forth his hands, that were already embrowned with toil" (*The Spy*, 415). Critics have pointed out that, because of his lowborn status, Birch could not be the hero of the novel's romance plots. Rather, his republican, self-sustaining economic labor ("toil") will take the place of sexual reproduction in the new nation. But, as we have seen in his 1821 economic review, Cooper is not content to imagine a polity of such limited commerce. And what looks like Birch's refusal to commodify his identity by sustaining himself instead with his own labor gives way to the compulsion to extend trade. For, in the end, what is Harvey Birch but an agent of the market itself?

James E. Block's *A Nation of Agents* (2002) points me to this question, as his historical synthesis can illuminate antebellum literature's contribution to the project of making economic exchange seem inevitable. The ideology of market voluntarism responded to the perceived loss of social cohesion after the War for Independence.[44] But where some contemporaries worried "of agitation and instability spreading everywhere," Cooper sees a salutary commerce "springing up in every direction" (*The Spy*, 417).[45] In the novel's final paragraph, we learn that Washington would sometimes try to locate Birch. Through such inquiries, "[Washington] learnt that a pedlar of a different name, but similar appearance, was toiling through the new settlements that were springing up in every direction, and that he was struggling with the advance of years, and apparent poverty" (*The Spy*, 417). The reviewer Gardiner might complain about Cooper's plot "springing up in every direction." For Birch, however, in an economic context, such proliferation is a desideratum of "toil." If he initially looks like a republican yeoman, his identity becomes obscured within a web of exchange relations. Unrecognizable even to his symbolic father, Washington, Birch is an ethereal force that exists at the boundaries of trade. And his traffic will allow others to seek selfhood in this "open economic market."⁴⁶ Birch's patient, plodding labor has enabled economic development—his seeming Jeffersonian ethic giving way to a surging Hamiltonian network of trade.⁴⁷ He played a long game, not for the political form of freedom (the republic), but for the abstraction with which it would be conflated—and naturalized—by future generations: the economy.

With steady sacrifice, Birch seemed seamlessly to institute patterns of exchange that would define life under capitalism for subsequent strivers, but Cooper's career trajectory hardly went so smoothly. It was one, rather, of jagged peaks and valleys. By the time of the publication of *The Last of the Mohicans* (1826), the *North American Review* could report with considerable chagrin that "Mr. Cooper . . . has the almost singular merit of writing American novels which everybody reads."⁴⁸ Soon enough would come the vociferous criticisms in the 1830s of his "all-too-brisk pace of publication," which, in turn, would cede in the 1850s to accolades for this firmly fixed "literary star."⁴⁹ And yet if one can compellingly apprehend Cooper's career, as Susan M. Ryan has in her recent study, with the metaphor of a "rise and fall," that fact alone attests to his long success in the go-ahead age.⁵⁰

The Ruin of P. & E. Irving

Like Cooper, Washington Irving entered, and would transform, the literary marketplace during the nation's first major depression. Cooper controlled his father's estate during the turbulence. Not so in Irving's case. While his older brothers, William, Peter, and Ebenezer, worked in the import-export hardware business, eventually running the firm P. & E. Irving, Washington plied a literary avocation as a dependent of his ambitious family. After James Madison repealed Thomas Jefferson's Embargo Act of 1807, American business thrived. The Irvings prospered too, so much so that they made their literary brother a silent partner in the business: he would receive one-fifth of the firm's profits to write.⁵¹ If this deal sounds like a sweet one, it was too good to be true—as we will see, the economic context would drive Irving to shift his sensibility from dependence to independence.

This biographical-financial context has not featured prominently in accounts of early male professionalism. Yet the question of Irving's supposed inauguration of professional literature in the United States has generated no shortage of responses. As discussed earlier, Charvat offers a purely market account of the phenomenon: Irving wrote because he finally had a paying audience. The public's willingness, to quote from Irving's correspondence, "to pay for the support of authors" was well timed, as it coincided with P. & E. Irving's bankruptcy proceedings in England in 1818 and, hence, the end of his brothers' patronage (*L*, 23:554). No longer supported by business revenue, Irving needed to employ (again, to quote from his letters) "a little capital" of his own (*L*, 23:540). He needed, that is, to turn his literary avocation into a vocation.

Other scholars have turned to psychology to understand the relation between the demise of P. & E. Irving and the "crucial issue of vocation."[52] While Jeffrey Rubin-Dorsky acknowledges Irving's pressing financial need during *The Sketch-Book*'s "prenatal period" (1816–18), he reads the text as a "map of [Irving's] psychological pilgrimage," as a sign, that is, of Irving's repression of anxiety incited by financial tumult.[53] In this account, the equipoise of Irving's persona Geoffrey Crayon "derives from the working out of this [market-based] anxiety."[54] Indeed, for Rubin-Dorsky, "anxiety" emerges as the shibboleth that unlocks the whole of *The Sketch-Book*, a text that exists as the product of Irving's need for emotional calm after the firm's collapse left him as "traumatize[d]" as those victims of the new economy chronicled in the era's sensationalist texts about (in David Anthony's term) paper money men.[55] In a more recent examination, indeed, Anthony synthesizes the materialist and the psychological approaches. He argues that Irving writes in the late 1810s in response to the erosion of a mercantilist economy and the subsequent rise of a paper money one. He identifies *The Sketch-Book* "as reflecting a nostalgic longing for a period predating the modern period of commerce and credit, one that found an anxious Irving financially embarrassed and decidedly out of place."[56] Building on Pocock's insights, Anthony argues that Irving's "nostalgic" but "nervous" sketches "reflect" anxiety over the fact that, in the brave new economic order, identity was not static but fluid, not given but achieved.[57]

What unites the approaches to Irving and the rise of professional authorship sketched here is the assumption of an antagonistic relationship between the author and the market, a form of economic organization that began to discipline the individual through an ideology of achieved identity in the nineteenth century. This ideology held that "with few exceptions, the only identity deemed legitimate in America is a capitalist identity: in every walk of life, investment and acquisition are the keys to moving forward and avoiding stagnation."[58] A different way of accounting for Irving's turn to professional authorship, the remainder of this chapter argues that *The Sketch-Book* represents Irving's deliberate turn toward financial unrest as he sought to achieve a socially sanctioned identity. Through a reinterpretation of Irving's correspondence from this era, as well as his tenuous involvement in the ruin of P. & E. Irving, I show that Irving felt anxiety not because of his culpability in the firm's demise, but precisely for the opposite reason: his brothers' ruin threw into relief his own lack of ambition during an era in which striving was "an obligation."[59] As a silent partner in the company, Irving had shown no ambition in that he had risked neither success nor failure. *The Sketch-Book*, then, became his "plan" for achievement (L, 23:487).

Early in his career, Irving's literary wins suggested he had overcome (in his phrase about Rip Van Winkle) the "habits of idleness."[60] His 1809 satire of the Jeffersonian era, *History of New York*, proved to be a "widely read and lucrative book."[61] Belying this portent was Irving's failure to capitalize on the *History*'s appeal and his stint as the editor of the *Analectic Magazine* (1813–14). In fact, he wrote little under his own name from 1809 to the end of his patronage period in 1816. Things got so bad that his brothers pressed him into the firm's service in Washington, DC, since new legislation that replaced the Jeffersonian embargo allowed international commerce with England and France to resume, "but under a watchful eye."[62] Modern biographers indicate that Irving did not treat his new responsibilities as lobbyist seriously. Stanley Williams quips, "How much the 'silent partner' was accomplishing is suggested by the fact that it cost him nineteen days to reach Washington." Williams depicts Irving as reveling in DC society and finds it "difficult to imagine what the firm of P. and E. Irving and Company" gained "from sending this irresponsible fellow" to look after its interests.[63]

Business fluctuations would temporarily disrupt Irving's complacency. In July 1815, with P. & E. Irving spiraling toward bankruptcy, Irving suddenly left New York for Liverpool.[64] He took a bookkeeping class in September 1815 to try to solve the problem of the firm's accounting, a problem that left him too busy to write. "I will certainly write to you amply," he tells his close friend and eventual literary agent, Henry Brevoort, Jr., in October 1815, "but for several weeks past I have been more *really* busy than I ever was in my life." "I am a complete novice in business," he laments, while hoping soon to "shake off the sordid cares of the Counting House."[65] In reality, Irving did not stand a chance to save the firm. Its "special corruption" was Peter Irving's "imprudent overpurchase in English goods" in autumn 1816.[66] The least savvy of Irving's elder brothers, Peter miscalculated in the aftermath of the War of 1812. At this conflict's conclusion, firms like P. & E. Irving resumed importing British wares to the American market. Yet, as we saw Cooper detail in 1821, during the war, American manufacturing grew to fill the void created by nonintercourse with Great Britain. Whereas Americans formerly needed to buy British glassware, hardware, and textiles, they could now buy domestic goods. Even still, "in the convalescence of 1815, many firms recovered their health."[67] Thus, while P. & E. Irving's Liverpool competitors renewed business activities to satisfy demand, the Irvings found the "times so hard that they sicken my very soul" (L, 23:446). And as its stock languished in Liverpool, the firm died a slow death.

A bit player in the firm's ruin, Irving saw up close the complex ideology of failure governing business culture in the Early Atlantic. Failure struck at the core of one's identity.[68] Yet as the marketplace became more intensely globalized, people began to understand ruin as the consequence of a host of issues largely outside one person's control.[69] Eager to limit any collateral damage to the family's reputation, Irving thus explains to Brevoort in the days before the firm would "pass through the Bankrupt act": "Above all, the situation of my poor Brother Ebenezer and his family distresses me. . . . His ruin has been occasioned by circumstances over which he had no controul" (L, 23:517). Aware of the fact that Peter Irving would be indicted for violating the ideology of failure nevertheless, Irving sought to ease his brother's guilt over the affair. Yet, ironically, it was just this causal relation to ruin that Irving would now seek.

"My Future Career Must Depend Very Much on Myself": Irving's Failure

The firm's failure, as Irving's correspondence from the period attests, seems to have left him traumatized—wrecked by financial clamor. After landing in Liverpool, he complains of "a constant load of anxiety on my mind" (L, 23:431). In spring 1816, he further laments how the "hard times make every body dismal" (L, 23:442). "The cares of business, in these gloomy times," he tells Brevoort a few months later, "harass my mind & unfit me for society" (L, 23:446). And, by summer 1816, he complains (again to Brevoort) of having "been so harassed & hagridden by the cares & anxieties of business for a long time past, that I have at times felt almost broken down in health and spirits" (L, 23:449). Watching the firm's inevitable ruin thus left his "mind . . . in a sickly state and my imagination so blighted that it cannot put forth a blossom nor even a green leaf" (L, 23:449).

This portrait of imaginative blockage implies a contrast between business and art, commerce and nature. Such oppositions have enabled critics to adduce *The Sketch-Book* as Irving's romantic triumph over despair.[70] The problem with this interpretation is that it exaggerates Irving's involvement in the business affairs of P. & E. Irving. Anthony rightly suggests that the modern economy left Irving "decidedly out of place."[71] But Irving found himself out of place because by the period of *The Sketch-Book*'s gestation (1817–19), he had neither failed nor succeeded on his own. Put otherwise, although Irving witnessed the ruin of P. & E. Irving—and even, as his correspondence suggests, suffered because of it—he in no meaningful way precipitated the firm's bust. Thus, in accordance with the era's ideology of failure, if to fail was to indict oneself, he had not yet established a self through commerce to indict. It is no surprise to find, then, that Irving's correspondence illustrates his anxiety over a *lack* of culpability in the firm's demise. In addition to declaring himself a "novice in business," Irving further admits that he "was no man of business; I knew nothing about it & disliked the very name; to such a one the horrors of commercial embarrassments and ruin are strange, and frightening and humiliating."[72] If he imagined that what he called "the Detestable ordeal of Bankruptcy" sullied his name, this further supports his sense of embarrassment in the aftermath of ruin. Williams puts it this way: "In view of his tenuous connection with the firm's formative policies—he was only technically a partner—this sense of dishonor appears squeamish, born of his excessive sensibility. He was blameless, but the illusion of his own guilt pulled on his sick nerves and deepened his despair."[73]

Irving's "blameless[ness]" in the face of ruin more properly generates his anxiety during this period. Realizing his powerlessness to save the firm, in summer 1816 he complains to Brevoort of the "hardships of these disordered times." Parrying his friend's attempts to establish a firm return date, Irving exclaims, "As to my return to America . . . I must wait here a while in a passive state, watching the turn of events, and how our affairs are likely to turn out" (*L*, 23:450). Subsequently describing himself as "vegetating for the present," Irving indicates that he is compelled to stay in Liverpool, but only as an observer of the bankruptcy. Writing a "sad, lackadaisical scrawl" to Brevoort, Irving depicts himself as a man with nothing to do (*L*, 23:452). Complaining of Liverpool, "a bustling busy town," Irving declares in spring 1817, "I have received attentions from some people who seem both amiable & intelligent; but the good folks here are too busy & too dissipated to be social, and a Stranger who has not business to employ his time will find it a dead weight on his hands" (*L*, 23:474). (So much for the romance of the Old World!) And, to cite at length yet one more instance, we find Irving confessing to Brevoort in summer 1817: "I have felt the correctness of your advice that I should return home & had prepared to do so, but troubles have thickened upon us & I cannot leave Peter to buffet them alone. I do not pretend to render any active assistance. I have long been utterly passive in respect to business; but my company is of importance to keep up his spirits in these trying times" (L, 23:482). Not just pretensions of guilt, here Irving's writing acknowledges his inability to do much of anything, let alone stave off ruin. "Utterly passive in respect to business," Irving was going nowhere in the go-ahead age.

Irving thus denies himself status as a subject. Such a tack in his correspondence with Brevoort, a man of business *par excellence*, departs from the usual mode of self-presentation among urban acquaintances. Indeed, modern historiographers suggest that male correspondents carefully controlled their image, especially in the aftermath of financial ruin. Such scholarship has sharpened our sense of male identity formation in the early United States by analyzing letter writing as a key technology.[74] Given the high stakes of private communication among merchants, Irving's letters seem especially disjointed. Yet, in the aftermath of financial ruin, Irving less managed his reputation to business colleagues than revealed his desire to earn one. Michael Davitt Bell theorizes that Irving "pretty clearly turned to writing as an escape from, even a defiance of, the 'real' legal business for which [he was] being trained." And he explores Irving's "paradoxical hope . . . that literature itself, the symbol of his alienation, might secure the very status it seemed to deny him."[75] Although Bell's paradigm articulates Irving's efforts to achieve "control" within an increasingly hostile commercial culture, it obscures how Irving sought out turmoil that could lead to success or failure. Irving's flight from the law to literature, therefore, was no escapist retreat, but a flight toward the literary marketplace as the matrix of identity. He sought the orthodox (success or failure) with unorthodox means (literature).

Determined to achieve an identity through his own efforts, in summer 1817 Irving tells Brevoort, "I have a plan" (L, 23:486). That plan, *The Sketch-Book*, was crafted to "extricate myself from the ruins of our unfortunate concern after which I shall turn my back upon this scene of care & distress." He hopes it "will yield me for the present a scanty but sufficient means of support" (L, 23:486). With this emphasis, Irving reveals to Brevoort his abhorrence of "destitution or the more galling mortifications of dependence" (L, 23:487). The historian of bankruptcy Balleisen reminds us how antebellum Americans "inherited intense fears of economic dependence." Such a prostrated state might result in the loss of "one's capacity for self-direction."[76] Irving seemed determined to avoid such a state—he even rejected a government position secured by his brother William. He would insist, "let me take care of myself" (L, 23:515). One year later, determined that "my future career must depend very much upon myself," Irving refused yet another of William's offers, this time for a Navy clerkship in late 1818. "I do not wish to undertake any situation," he implored, "that must involve me in such a routine of duties as to prevent my attending to literary pursuits" (L, 23:536). With these chants of the entrepreneurial self, Irving cements his commitment to achieve an identity on his own terms.

"From the Wrecks of Our Concerns": *The Sketch-Book*

Irving's letters make his strategy of capitalization explicit. As early as spring 1818, he spoke of his new work as if it were a financial speculation: "I feel confident that I shall be able to rub along with my present means of support; and in the mean time am passing my time advantageously by attending to some studies that will be of future service to me" (L, 23:522). No doubt meant to reassure his brother Ebenezer as to his well-being, Irving here sees his "studies" in terms of future value. This fluency in what Ian Baucom terms "speculative discourse" governing transatlantic exchange informs an oft-cited passage in discussions about Irving and money.[77] In a spring 1819 letter to his brother Ebenezer, Irving writes: "I have been for some time past nursing my mind up for literary operations, and collecting materials for the purpose. I shall be able, I trust, now to produce articles from time to time that will be sufficient for my present support, and for a stock of copyright property, that may be a little capital to me hereafter" (L, 23:540). Historians of publishing have demonstrated the crucial role copyright played in the formation of modern authorship in Anglo-America.[78] But here I emphasize Irving's theoretical sophistication, as he undertakes what he elsewhere terms his "scheme" to realize future receipts on his investment. This rhetoric seems to be at odds with his previous disavowals of labor. He indicated to Brevoort, for instance, that "indeed I have been so completely driven out of my usual track of thought and feeling by 'stress of weather' in business, that I have not been able to pen a single line on any subject that was not connected with traffic" (L, 23:432). Yet, moving from passivity to activity in 1819, Irving directly thematized his imaginative work as generative of "property" and "stock": as capital assets that, as the historian Levy puts it in work I cite in the Introduction, will "yield future pecuniary income."[79]

I want to note that the premise of Irving as a speculator who emerges from the bankruptcy ordeal can be taken too far, since he favored calculation over headlong risk-taking.[80] Irving's attitude here was normative. *Niles' Weekly Register* attributed the inflation of values in the late 1810s to the "spirit of speculation" and opposed this phenomenon to "real sales."[81] In short, the newspaper aligned speculation with irrationality—the people were "delirious"—and opposed it to "reason."[82] *The Sketch-Book* was Irving's reasoned hazard. Moving from editing the *Analectic Magazine* to hopeless business activities in Liverpool, "Irving spent the better part of five years priming himself to make a full commitment to professional authorship." Such "priming" was more than an extended "pep-talk," but rather, "these [1815–1818] were years of self-appraisal," as William Hedges writes—cycles "of anxious tinkering followed by fits of inspiration, of restless searching for material and scrutinizing of prices current in the literary marketplace."[83] Irving viewed risk in the literary market as inevitable, but he also realized he could navigate it deliberately for the purposes of future success.

When read through the lens of Irving's engagement with business swings, *The Sketch-Book*'s preoccupation with the themes, sites, and occasions of ruin takes on new meanings. And the tension between security—financial and/or psychological—and uncertainty pervades the first of seven installments of *The Sketch-Book*, which appeared in the United States in June 1819. Thinking of America in the opening sketch, "The Voyage," Crayon wonders "what vicissitudes might occur in it—what changes might take place in me, before I should visit it again. —Who can tell, when he sets forth to wander, whither he may be driven by the uncertain currents of existence . . . ?" (*SB*, 8:11–12) Here Crayon rhetorically dwells in "uncertainty." In doing so, he seeks to unmoor himself "from the common-place realities of the present"—to risk an identity that had so far eluded him (*SB*, 8:9).

What so often constitutes Crayon's spectatorship "of other men's fortunes and adventures" in this meditative state are the "vicissitudes" of finance. No sketches display this obsession with the linkage between finance and identity better than "Roscoe" and "The Wife." In "Roscoe," Crayon recounts his first few days in Liverpool, the very city in which P. & E. Irving declared bankruptcy in 1818, and the home of William Roscoe, an abolitionist, writer, rare book collector—and famously failed banker. He observes Roscoe in Liverpool's Athenaeum, a private club with a renowned library devoted to the education of the city's merchants. The occasion produces in Crayon an immediate sense that "there was something in [Roscoe's] whole appearance that indicated a being of a different order from the bustling race around him" (*SB*, 8:16). This romantic interpretation sets Roscoe apart from the world. But even if Crayon views the merchant as untainted by the "trivial or sordid paths of life," he soon collapses this opposition, and the story "turns into a particularly pointed integration of aesthetics and economics."[84] Crayon accomplishes this junction by framing Roscoe's failure in business as an opportunity for this "gifted individual" to clarify the parameters of his identity. In this way, Irving presents the historical Roscoe, paradoxically, as a successful failure.

This integrative approach is different than longing, nostalgically and anxiously, for a stable model of subjectivity removed from market structures. As implied above, such a model seemingly inflects Crayon's apprehension of Roscoe's financial destruction as transcendent: "I could not pity him as I heard some rich men do. I considered him far above the reach of my pity. Those who live only for the world and in the world, may be cast down by the frowns of adversity; but a man like Roscoe is not to be overcome by the reverses of fortune" (SB, 8:18). But if Roscoe becomes "independent of the world around him" and if his prized book collection, as Crayon impishly envisions, will "baffle . . . some knot of speculators debating with calculating brow over the quaint binding and illuminated margin of an obsolete author," this lofty idealism emerges through being "unfortunate in business" (SB, 8:18, 19). "In America," Crayon writes, "we know Mr. Roscoe only as the author; in Liverpool he is spoken of as the banker" (SB, 8:18). When combined through Crayon's sensibility, these opposed national perceptions represent the more general idea that the modern self can define itself neither solely in business terms nor purely aesthetic ones. This sketch thus aims to accomplish what Walt Whitman's ode to failures in 1888, as discussed in the Introduction, refuses: it romanticizes Roscoe as a noble business failure whose "genius" shines through not despite but because of bankruptcy.

Such optimism for commercial ruin as a pretext for self-realization wanes in Irving's subsequent sketch of business failure, "The Wife." The first installment of *The Sketch-Book*'s most explicit intervention into the culture of the depression-era United States, the tale seems to find a straightforward solution to economic fluctuations in what the cultural historian Barbara Welter famously termed "true womanhood." The titular wife Mary embodies the ideals of "piety, purity, submissiveness, and domesticity."[85] Such attributes were perceived to oppose the endlessly changing values of finance. Indeed, Leslie, Crayon's friend and Mary's husband, opines that "Providence" has "ordered" that "woman, who is the mere dependent and ornament of man in his happier hours, should be his stay and solace when smitten with sudden calamity, winding herself into the rugged recesses of his nature; tenderly supporting the drooping head, and binding up the broken heart" (SB, 8:22). When a husband loses his market-based status, as Leslie does here, the woman, normally a "mere dependent," reverses her position in this dyad: she props up the failed man.

When considering Irving's correspondence from the period, this language of dependency points to the implicit gendering of the ideology of achieved identity. I return to this theme in chapter 2, but I want to emphasize here how, as Leslie continues, "sudden calamit[ies]" in the public sphere are therefore negated when "there is still a little world of love at home, of which he is the monarch" (SB, 8:23). The sketch thus implies that women who can "sustain the most overwhelming reverses of fortune" provide affective barriers against the tidal waves of finance. Brevoort alludes to this gender ideology in his puff review of *The Sketch-Book*, No. 1. He declares that "'The Wife' is beautifully pathetic, and in these times of commercial disasters will be read with interest, and, it is to be hoped, with *benefit*, by many."[86] Brevoort frames "The Wife" as a didactic sketch well-suited for hard times, as it instantiates unchanging womanly virtue as the salve to commercial ills. More specifically, "The Wife" imagines a woman's constancy as a corrective to male speculative excess. "It was the misfortune of [Leslie]," Crayon tells us, "to have embarked his property in large speculations, and he had not been married many months, when, by a succession of sudden disasters, it was swept from him, and he found himself reduced almost to penury" (SB, 8:23).

A magazine article from 1820 entitled "On Fluctuations of Property," a typical screed against speculation as the "wild pursuit of wealth," questions what impels this risky financial behavior. The writer concludes that "the instability of fortune" leads men to take extraordinary risks. By "instability," the writer means that wealth, from the long view of Christian salvation, is ephemeral, yet man irrationally desires it even still. In tandem with property rights, in this view, the lack of a caste system in the United States encourages one always to seek more wealth.[87] But "The Wife" shows no interest in such anti-speculation polemics. Instead, Irving wants to define the boundaries of an identity achieved within the market. Crayon signals this project in questioning the extent to which Leslie's speculations even register as such in the first place. For this investment strategy loses its relation to risk when underwritten by the eternal "spark of heavenly fire which lies dormant in the broad daylight of prosperity" of "every true woman's heart" (SB, 8:25). The constancy of Mary's love thereby threatens the meaning of Leslie's "large speculation" because it strips the act of risk. Indeed, Leslie's "fairy tale" becomes Crayon's nightmare, as the former's hazardous financial behavior yields not an assertion of identity but its erasure. The title of the sketch—"The Wife"—gestures to this fact, as Leslie's failure in business leads to *his* dependency on his wife: not a *femme covert*, but an *homme covert*.[88] Mary Templin's scholarship shows how panic fiction by nineteenth-century American women writers challenges the fact that women had "little direct control over family or personal finances."[89] The source of Irving's anti-feminism therefore lies as much in his sketch's naturalization of true womanhood as its ambivalence about it in a specific commercial context. In "The Wife," a woman threatens her husband's identity: if one succeeds in his speculations, the woman remains "the mere dependent and ornament." If, however, one fails in his speculations, this domestic situation is catastrophically reversed, as a wife's constant values "support the drooping head, and bind up the broken heart" (SB, 8:22). In a misogynistic conclusion, which we will see Catharine Maria Sedgwick challenge in chapter 2, marriage, hence, can signal a potential destructive stability for the striving self.

Dame Van Winkle, in the final sketch of the first serial installment of *The Sketch-Book*, "Rip Van Winkle," will certainly not "bind up the broken heart." She would rather "bind" her idling husband to an identity rooted in profit-seeking labor, a nearly impossible task given Rip's indisposition to hazard. Noting this story's misogyny, literary scholars present Dame Van Winkle as infamously annoyed—and ambitious.[90] The source of her ire, indeed, is her husband's "insuperable aversion to all kinds of profitable labour" (SB, 8:30). As Howard Horwitz has noted, Dame Van Winkle's economic competitiveness—her demand for profit—implies a continuity between the pre- and post-Revolution economies that Irving's New York villagers wanted to repress. Hence, the tale kills her off while Rip sleeps through the war.[91] In terms of capitalist identity, what the tale seems to dispense with, more specifically, is the go-ahead determination that Dame represents. And when Rip finally awakens, "he now is entirely idle" and seems to have no relation whatsoever to the agitations of go-getting so stridently endorsed by his wife.[92]

Except that Irving's fictional historian Knickerbocker cannot so easily excise the profit mandate from the Hudson River Valley. As observed by previous critics, Rip's retelling has two economic implications for the outset of the antebellum era. First, for Jennifer J. Baker, the lazy, dreaming Rip indexes through his imagination a romantic bent akin to the speculators then crashing the economy.[93] Second, along with the expulsion of Dame Van Winkle's competitiveness, the repetition of his tale underwrites the idea of the "new nation's evolved commercial economy as mutual cooperation."[94] With Block's integrative thesis in mind, we can entwine these seemingly contradictory thoughts. Doing so lets us see how Rip continually "retell[s] his fabulous tale" of bowling with Henry Hudson in the Catskills to warrant the village's business enterprise.[95] For Block, the "drive into assimilation" that transpired across the early 1800s "rendered all institutions and authorities that resulted equally voluntary, tangential, erasable—hence by definition unauthoritative and uncoercive."⁹⁶ Rip's storytelling/speculating melds the villagers together, even as the protocols of financial capitalism threaten to "rip" their association asunder. This tension manifests in his tale's status as the property of all—everyone "knew it by heart" (*SB*, 8:41). But this collective hymn also, as observed more generally by the anti-speculation discourse cited above, requires a suspension of disbelief to be effective: where some "pretend," others issue "full credit" (*SB*, 8:41). The tale, then, does not eliminate the regime of "profitable labor" that the story misogynistically calls a "petticoat government," but rather normalizes it (*SB*, 8:40). Allowing the community of "free citizen[s]" to reimagine a story of competitive commerce as a republican idyll in which everyone holds an equal stake, the story defangs capitalism by making it seem (in Block's words quoted above) "unauthoritative and uncoercive" (*SB*, 8:40). For "Rip Van Winkle," finally, it is one thing to be henpecked into go-getting—this can drive a man into the woods with his dog for a long nap. It is another one entirely, though, to *choose* to be henpecked— this can spur a man (and even his drinking buddies) to leave behind idle habits and get to work.

In his correspondence, as we have seen, Irving wanted his attempts at independence to be entirely self-directed. These early tales of *The Sketch-Book*, however, complicate this desire by revealing how identity rises and falls dialectically within business culture. Here, the self that Irving projected as the outcome of his "plan" is variously—and increasingly—*subjected to*. So, the optimism of "Roscoe" for an identity that integrates art and commerce hits a roadblock in "The Wife" and "Rip Van Winkle" in the form of a woman's constancy and then her inescapable domination, respectively. A product of Irving's simultaneous eagerness to thwart a humiliating dependence and his intuition of the enterprising self's inability to do so, *The Sketch-Book* is thus a fair representative of early professionalism in the United States. That is the case not only because it was a book that some were willing to buy. It is also a book that imagines what could happen to the self if no one did.

Coda: John Law and the Romance of Trade

A Rip Van Winkle nap—twenty years—would pass until the next economic depression in the antebellum United States. And, like many other profit seekers in the 1830s, "the panic had caught [Irving] with much of his capital invested in unprofitable land speculations" in the West.⁹⁷ Needing money, and (in Irving's words) "growing too indolent and unambitious for anything that requires labor or display," he "thought, therefore, of securing to myself a snug corner in some periodical work."[98] His historical sketch of John Law, the eighteenth-century Scottish financier and engineer of the Mississippi Bubble in colonial Louisiana in 1720, exists as one result of this labor regularly performed for *The Knickerbocker* magazine from 1839 to 1841. This turn to what Charles Mackay in *Extraordinary Popular Delusions* (1841) would call France's "Mississippi madness" might seem the compensatory escape to history prompted by succumbing to what Irving calls "one of these delusive seasons" in the present of the late 1830s.[99] And yet, although one can comprehend this essay in psychobiographical terms, Irving's work on Law also resonates as an attempt to further understand the logic of financial modernity. How did the daily grind of go-getting—the mandate to "labor or display"—become normative amid "the romance of trade"?[100] And how does the "windy superstructure," on which that romance transpires, withstand such catastrophic systemic shocks?[101]

Irving's article, "'A Time of Unexampled Prosperity': The Great Mississippi Bubble" (1840), critiques a damaging market epistemology, but it quickly routes this approach through the lens of selfhood. The speculative frenzy in colonial France transforms the clerk of the "dusty counting-house," seeking "the slow but sure gains of snug per centage," into a "kind of knight errant, or rather a commercial Quixote," who seeks "an immediate fortune."[102] Of course, such "dreams and projects" of "idlers [turned] men of business" "leav[e] scarce a wreck behind."[103] In an impressively detailed piece, Irving focuses on "the individual who engendered" this catastrophe, John Law.[104] For the literary scholar Peter Knight, such an "account of individual manipulation of the market" would seem "outdated" by the Gilded Age and Progressive Era.[105] And yet, although Irving puts Law, as "the originator of the scheme," at the center of his account, he ultimately refuses to indict him as a failure—or, in the first place, even blame him for the severe social dislocations.

The target of Irving's essay, then, is not actually financial capitalism as such, but the old order that it threatens. As I discussed in the Introduction, the US political economist Daniel Raymond claimed in 1820 that an individual failure is meaningful only in the aggregate—that is, when a mass of failures negatively "affect[s] the energies of the nation."[106] This piling up of wreckage is precisely the scenario that Irving documents at the end of his essay, with "thousands of meritorious families . . . reduced to indigence."[107] But he blamed "too great confidence in government" for this stern reality, rather than Law's chicanery.[108] The French Regent, Duke Orlean—abetted

FIGURE 1.1 1833 lithograph that depicts President Andrew Jackson as a despot after his order to remove federal deposits from the Bank of the United States. Courtesy of the Library of Congress.

by the grasping nobility—promoted "the evil spirit of the system, that forced Law on to an expansion of his paper currency far beyond what he had ever dreamed of."[109] Where Law exhibits "imperturbable assurance and self-possession," the "old noblesse" financialized every aspect of their social intercourse: "Rank, talent, military fame no longer inspired deference," and "all respect for others, all self-respect, were forgotten in the mercenary struggle of the stock-market."[110] The pillars of the ancient regime are no match for the speculative mania of new world capitalism.

Those invested in the old order, rather, present institutional obstacles to Law's financial innovation. Consistent with his turn to financial instability in the late 1810s, Irving does not react anxiously to this loss of social cohesion, but laments past institutions' obstructionist elements. He argues that the French Regency imprudently interfered with Law's scheme—if his "bank had been confined to its original limits, and left to the control of its own internal regulations, [it] might have gone on prosperously, and been of great benefit to the nation."[111] This bank, he adds, "was an institution fitted for a free country."[112] It is hard not to read into this passage a critique of President Andrew Jackson's hostility toward the Second Bank of the United States, a "despotic" bellicosity popularly seen to have resulted in the 1837 panic and ensuing depression (see fig. 1.1).[113] But what stands out to me is how Irving sees the financier Law as a study in the relationship between the individual and the economic context in which he operates. Business fluctuations do not overly bother Irving here—as revealed in his insistent use of meteorological metaphors at the outset of the essay, they are natural.[114] Nor, really, do the severe social dislocations irk him. Finally, he seems drawn to this topic because he believes that, historically, speculative finance produces memorable selves—those paradoxically solvent bankrupts. He once sought this kind of self through storytelling, and he had started to represent it in fiction with Roscoe and Rip Van Winkle. By 1840, though, he realized with certainty that such a self like Law, plucked from history, ever in conflict with economic institutions, will always make for—and not just make—"interesting and salutary" tales.[115]

CHAPTER TWO

Sedgwick, Failure, and the Romance in Real Life

If Washington Irving was playing a long game with his story from *The Sketch-Book*, "The Wife," it paid off during the depression of the late 1830s. At least six literary magazines reprinted the sketch between 1837 and 1838. It even resonated in the commercial press when an article entitled "Morals of Trade" from an 1842 issue of Freeman Hunt's *The Merchants' Magazine and Commercial Review* put forth the story as one "that every merchant may read with advantage."[1] Through the ruined Leslie "retrench[ing] his expenses," Irving "painted the struggle of a highminded man, in his hour of mercantile adversity."[2] But "The Wife" appealed to more than the hosts of ruined American men in the early 1840s — it found a ready audience among women's magazine readers too. And gleaning a related but different lesson in 1838, the *Ladies' Garland and Family Wreath* elevated the titular wife's "cheering and consoling attributes" that "played in all seasons of trial, of commotion, of calamity and wo."[3]

In his oration, "The Character of Woman" (1838), which *Ladies' Garland and Family Wreath* reprinted and from which I quote above, James Hoban, Jr., avoided any specific reference to the depressed economy. He emphasized, rather, that "calamity" as such exposed the "peculiar disposition of woman, seemingly so incompatible with the mild tendency of her nature."[4] For Hoban, Irving's "The Wife" exemplifies the transhistorical doubleness of woman — on one hand, her "patien[ce] . . . under the most cruel sufferings" and, on the other hand, her "sensitiv[ity] . . . when others endure them."[5] The same can be said, Hoban finds, for the writings of Catharine Maria Sedgwick. "Others of the distinguished sex crowd upon the memory, and seem to demand notice," but he singles out "Miss Sedgwick" as a writer "whose stories are full of truth, full of effect, eloquent with morality, and lessons of practical good sense."[6] Like Irving, Hoban reasons, Sedgwick, too, is a writer for the times.

Modern scholars have tended to agree with part of Hoban's premise — that Sedgwick's work occupies itself with practicality. To make this point, they associate her fiction not with breezy, apolitical romances, but (as Nina Baym once put it) with a "new kind of American woman's fiction."[7] Part of this project entails separating Sedgwick from a "paradigm" (romance) that has "completely marginalized [her] and the school of women writers she started."[8] Alternative frameworks include ones more obviously tied to reality like the historical novel, the novel of manners, the literature of benevolence, and even the urban novel. Continuing this trend, more recent scholars have aligned Sedgwick with nineteenth-century women's economic fiction defined as "self-conscious responses" to issues ranging from business volatility to literary genre to class inequality.[9] In this chapter, I contribute to this latter project by considering Sedgwick's engagement with categories of capitalist selfhood—failure and success. For Patricia Okker, Sedgwick, embodying a feminine mode of literary professionalism in the early-to-mid nineteenth century that was distinct from that of Cooper and Irving's, wrote works that are "both realistic and essentially moral—and thus both pleasing and beneficial."[10] And yet, if Sedgwick's career encapsulates a different version of professionalism, she embraces in her work similar themes of financial unease. In doing so, I argue, Sedgwick's writing explores, in the words of one feminist historian already cited in the Introduction, "the cultural politics necessary for capitalism to prevail among other ethics of exchange."[11] Her fiction lets us see how women could pursue, while also moderating, the ideology of achieved identity that Irving and Cooper sought through their own practices.

As I show in the first part of this chapter, Sedgwick developed a normative view of exchange that could be threatened by crises, natural and commercial. And yet she was less interested in what led to those economic disruptions than how to return people and societies to an ideal state that, as she routinely imagined it in her work, was premised on the seamless integration of the market into everyday life. Like other popular women writers responding to commercial turmoil in the antebellum United States, Sedgwick "seek[s] an economic system marked by slower growth, less greed, and less vulnerability to periodic downswings."[12] Yet lumping her work in with midcentury panic fiction can shadow the full extent to which Sedgwick was preoccupied with those "periodic downswings." In a popular novel like *Riches Without Wings* (1839), Elizabeth Oakes Smith critiqued the people of the "go ahead" age as too "enterprising."[13] Across several works and different genres, though, Sedgwick revealed a sustained thought about commercial culture, rather than a topical interest. She wondered if success (economic or moral) was possible without the risk of loss. Was the security of tradition (in her view, the "real") achievable without the stimulus of the "romance" and, hence, the risk of failure? What of women and their economic agency? Hoban was right to link Irving and Sedgwick to the same cultural impulse in the 1830s, but whereas "The Wife" cannot countenance women's business acumen, as we see at the end of this chapter, Sedgwick begins to give this fact due consideration. In doing so, she would come to accept mercantile unrest as inevitable—even, surprisingly, inviting. As if selfhood and business swings were coextensive, her work thus wanted to normalize, for both men and women, acting with both "practical good sense" and "eloquent morality" amid a clamorous economic context.

"Suspension of Business": The Romance and Risk-Taking

The didacticism Hoban observed in Sedgwick's fiction was, according to the historian Block, part of a secular movement in the antebellum United States in which "spiritual strenuosity had to be replaced with consistent rules of practical behavior."[14] Such consistency was necessary to navigate the era's economic environment, including a "multifarious monetary system" riddled with counterfeit currencies that could "baffle the uninitiated," as the historian Stephen Mihm has written.[15] Indeed, if fictional "characters . . . cultivated the virtuous self-discipline for social and family engagement and for productive careers," this training entailed the expectation of murky, uncharted financial waters in which one would either sink or swim.[16] The tension between order and unrest as a context for self-making registered for Sedgwick as a generic contest between the ups and downs of what she called "romance" and the stability of a rule-bound reality. Thus the appeal for Sedgwick of the "romance in real life" genre. An attempt at synthesizing the vacillations of the romance and the stolidity of realism, as Michael Gamer explains, the "romance in real life" emerged in England during the late 1700s and gelled into a commercially successful mode by 1825.[17] Popularized by the Anglo-Irish author Maria Edgeworth, to whom Sedgwick dedicated her first novel, *A New-England Tale* (1822), and to whom Hoban also refers in "Character of Woman," the genre reconciled the seemingly incommensurate categories of salutary realism with entertaining stories derived from the imagination.[18]

In a US context, it aimed to redress the social effects of economic turbulence by moderating the acquisitive urges that a market society demanded.[19] In what is ultimately an integrative project, Sedgwick contributed to this genre in a tale entitled "Romance in Real Life," first published in the annual *The Legendary* for 1828 and later included in her *Tales and Sketches* (1835). The tale is not explicitly about finance—rather, it follows the fate of Marie Angley, a fictional orphaned daughter of J. Hector St. John de Crèvecœur, the famous French nobleman known for his *Letters from an American Farmer* (1782). And yet it adheres to a literary pattern relevant to midcentury capitalism, as described by María Carla Sánchez, in its seeming ethico-affective opposition between romance and reality, which the tale establishes early in the narrative discourse with reference to business activity.[20] At the outset, the narrator associates "real life" with "modest graces as faith and temperance," "downright honesty," and "simplicity and respectful courtesy."[21] Alternately, the discourse links the romance to "enterprise," "speculation," "subscri[ption] to a country bank," "lofty aspirations," and "desire [that] passed the bounds of [one's] premises" ("RRL," 237–38).

The priority of "real life" over "romance" is presented to the reader as self-evident. But, compelled to calm the market ethos, rather than reject it, "Romance in Real Life" cannot sustain this formulaic aversion to the implied financial ethos of the romance and comes to begrudgingly accept it in two ways. The first hint, which shows up early in the tale, has to do with the suitability of characters for narrative. The narrator assures the reader that the "passive, . . . content" man, Reliance Reynolds, who would never own bank stocks, will not suffice as a "subject for a storyteller," for his "life" presents "the same monotonous harmony" as observed in "the colours in a ray of light" ("RRL," 238). The second hint comes at the tale's conclusion; here, the narrator explicitly borrows a concept, *indemnity*, from the capitalist institution perhaps most associated with risk—insurance. Apologizing to the reader for the tale's "dullness," the narrator states, "There is nothing in the termination of our tale to indemnify the lover of romance for its previous dullness; but it is a true story, and its materials must be received from tradition, and not supplied by imagination" ("RRL," 277).

This is a strange fixation on indemnity, for it seems possible that the "lover of romance" would have felt fully indemnified—that is, secured against loss—at this point in the story. After all, they would have just read a tale in which Marie Angley, improbably, reconnects with her long-estranged family after marrying a recent widower who had become enchanted with her during a chance meeting on a sylvan walk! Indeed, for one reviewer of Sedgwick's *Tales and Sketches* in the *Southern Literary Messenger*, "Romance in Real Life," while "not the best thing we have seen from the pen of Miss Sedgwick," "is a tale of striking vicissitudes."[22] Given the circumstances, then, it is entirely possible that such a statement by Sedgwick's narrator is a misdirection. As generations of feminist scholars have taught students of eighteenth- and nineteenth-century literature, we should be suspicious about "fiction's conventional dismissal of its fictitious state."[23] But I want to suggest that this downplaying of romance implies a theory of risk that installs it (risk) as a necessary precursor to order. The critical point is that, for Sedgwick, reasoned (not reckless) risk-taking ought to "terminat[e]" in a *non*-"monotonous harmony." (So, Reynolds's utter risk aversion excludes him as hero.) With its "striking vicissitudes," such a tale will indemnify a certain kind of reader, but it must always act as if it cannot. Premised at once on the necessity and the eventual invisibility of risk-taking, Sedgwick's literary idealism thus performs a kind of insurance project of its own—to guarantee the stability of everyday life through the seamless integration of risk therein.

In pursuit of this project, "Romance in Real Life" controls risk through its near erasure. This entwining of literary and financial concepts lets us generalize further about Sedgwick's sense of commercial exchange in the antebellum era. How durable is this quietly integrative outlook in an era of "everlasting uncertainty"? Some events, like the Great Fire of New York in 1835, when "Romance in Real Life" appeared in book form, would prove uninsurable and thus challenge a worldview that requires but, at the same time, invisibilizes risk. So, in her private responses to the devastation caused by the fire, we see Sedgwick adapt her goal of naturalizing finance in response to catastrophe. The tragedy struck just as she arrived in the city that winter. Visual artists such as Nicolino Calyo captured the destruction of the fire (see fig. 2.1). The conflagration also held the attention of the era's diarists. In addition to the oft-cited former mayor of New York, Philip Hone, Sedgwick attended to the event in an extended passage from December 17, 1835. There, she focuses on the financial aspects of the fire and notes this day as one of "the most sudden and overwhelming calamity." She continues:

> When we went to bed . . . the fire appeared to us going down, but it still raged; the extreme cold . . . accelerated the flames. The hose froze, the firemen were impotent, the flames spread through the packed warehouses of the wealthiest portion of the city. It was a scene of helplessness, bewilderment, and dismay. The flames were only arrested by blowing up houses—they are not yet extinguished. It is a scene of desolation, from the ruins of the noble exchange to the water's edge. There is no calculating the extent of loss—the direct loss—the loss from suspension of business, and payments, and interruption of industry, and the failure of moneyed institutions. All the fire-insurance companies being bankrupt, the city is at the moment uninsured.[24]

FIGURE 2.1 An aquatint by Nicolino Calyo showing the disarray, as seen from Exchange Place in New York City, of the Great Fire of 1835. Courtesy of the New York Public Library.

Awed by this "scene of helplessness, bewilderment, and dismay" unfolding in Manhattan's financial district, and fixated on the "loss" (repeated three times), Sedgwick confronts a demystified commercial order.[25] And what is laid bare is the utter ruin of the city's merchants and financial institutions, which defies tabulation ("no calculating") and reveals, in short, the contingency even of orderly risk-taking. With the "insurance companies being bankrupt," some losses, it seems, cannot be indemnified, even if they are insured.

For Sedgwick, the exigency of the fire registers as two problems, one macroeconomic and one microeconomic. First, at the structural level, what she notices about the event is how it has disrupted the tidy flows of goods and services that, typically, regulate on their own, without any worry given to indemnity. In a tableau of *non*commercial intercourse, she dwells in her private writing on a "curious spectacle" that follows the "suspension of business."[26] Indeed, "churches and private houses [are] turned into receptacles for merchandise; carts, coaches, going in every direction filled with boxes, cans, and every species of commodity; the sidewalks filled, guardians stationed over them."[27] Clearly defined boundaries between (for example) church and market have blurred, and shopkeepers are now "guardians" of goods, not sellers of them. She observes, in the final analysis, a jarring aimlessness—"carts, coaches, going in every direction"—rather than cohesiveness.

Here, Sedgwick struggles to apprehend a situation that is like, from Marx's perspective, a crisis of nineteenth-century capitalism. When writing about financial crises, he points out: "The *possibility* of crisis . . . is once more demonstrated, and further developed, by the disjunction between the (direct) process of production and the process of circulation. As soon as these processes do not merge smoothly into one another but become independent of one another, the crisis is there."[28] And yet what Marx sees as a contradiction within capitalism—the apparent "disjunction" between production and circulation—Sedgwick, in writing about the Great Fire, sees as a mere hiccup in the system's natural orderliness, even though she is bothered by the fire's jagged upheaval of the spatiotemporality of commercial exchange. She is impelled not toward questions about the necessity of exchange. Rather, the fire leads her to a variation of a familiar question for the authors I study in this book: How to let order reign again? How to reinstate the "romance in real life" of the midcentury economy? How to return "business . . . payments, and . . . industry" to their precrisis states?

Such questions bring her, second, to the equally vexing one of individual identity achievement amid a market in ruins. In "Romance in Real Life," Sedgwick was eager to withhold insurance from those seeking the romance. Here, however, "uninsured" is the fate of the men of the "noble exchange" as well. And to conclude her journal entry she draws (as we will see Emerson do "after the earthquake" in chapter 3) "some fine morals [that] may rise the phoenixes of this fire."[29] The fire warns "the poor," especially, against ambitions for the "wealth" of the "individual rich man." For "the *millions* of yesterday, the *ashes* of to-day," a "striking manifestation of the instability of human possessions."[30] Here, she wants to make a conventional point about the ephemerality of worldly possessions lost in flames familiar to students of American literature from the Puritan poet Anne Bradstreet to midcentury domestic fiction—to do so, perhaps, she checks the aspiration of people on the make. But, consistent with Block's observation above regarding domestic fiction, she issues this warning in the context of finance. Indeed, in noting the intersection of the structural (the "failure" of the city's "moneyed institutions") and the "individual" as a problem, she thus reduces the solution of crisis to a matter of one person's affective orientation toward the market. The fire cannot quench the compulsion to exchange—nothing can do that, nor should it, in Sedgwick's view. And yet it can caution against unrestrained grasping, which becomes here the true cause of the mercantile disruption—see the fate, she reads the waste of the Great Fire implicitly to ask, of the "vulgar pride of the mere merchant"?

"Lying Idle on a Book-Shelf":
The Poor Rich Man and the Rich Poor Man

The fire drove Sedgwick toward a more searching economic analysis than she had previously undertaken, and this question about the "vulgar pride of the mere merchant" previews her series of novellas from the mid-1830s. These works were the brainchild of Henry Ware, Jr., a Unitarian minister and former mentor to Ralph Waldo Emerson. Writing to Sedgwick in 1834 from Cambridge, Massachusetts, Ware wanted to bring morally sound books into the hands of impressionable readers. He sought Sedgwick's "aid" in "a scheme for offering to the public an exhibition of the practical character and influences of Christianity"; "This may be done," he continued, "in a series of narratives, between a formal tale and a common tract."[31]

The results, including *The Poor Rich Man and the Rich Poor Man* (1836), which I analyze below, have drawn increasing critical interest.[32] Sarah Robbins finds in the cluster of books that grew from this partnership a "fluid literary form," which (in Ware's terms) would illustrate Christianity's "principles, its modes of operation on the heart and character, and the manner in which men may avail themselves of its power."[33] For Robbins, these "didactic texts" are valuable partly "for what they reveal about the intersection of literature and literacy-based educational programs of uplift."[34] For Joe Shapiro, in an analysis most relevant to this chapter, such "programs of uplift" perform the ideological work of naturalizing class inequality. Shapiro reads *The Poor Rich Man* as evidence of how sentimental texts from the 1830s "refuse to deny what we can call the reality of class in the US."[35] And from this angle of vision, Sedgwick's novella justifies the economic structure in "her ideal nation," in which "there will always be poor families and individuals who must sell their labor to the rich in order to survive."[36]

To Shapiro's class-based analysis I would add that the political economy of *The Poor Rich Man* also hinges on appeals to ideologies of achieved identity.

And Sedgwick's "binary class lexicon in which the US forever consists of 'rich' and 'poor'" can be further articulated as one between winners and losers, successes and failures.[37] Grappling with the ethos of go-aheadism is foundational to the novella's efforts to normalize prudent risk-taking in commerce. The text thus polices the affective boundaries of the "mere merchant" by installing as transcendent a matrix of possible capitalist identities: as the novella concludes, there can be "rich" failures and "poor" failures, "poor" successes" and "rich" successes, these labels saying as much about one's orientation to the market as one's bank account. In her idealist vision, midcentury capitalism accommodates class inequality, as Shapiro argues, but it softens this reality by asserting, further, an equality of individuals striving across the United States' social landscape.

The Poor Rich Man contrasts a materially poor but spiritually rich family, the Aikins, with a materially rich but spiritually poor one, the Finleys. Sedgwick developed this simple tale, which she described as an "image, a portrait," during a time of rapid economic growth in the United States.[38] Both banks and the currency in circulation grew during an expansionary phase of the economy. By 1836, the year of the novella's publication and a pivotal year in President Andrew Jackson's "war" on the national bank, the nation's supply of money had increased to $140 million, from $59 million in 1832, as state-chartered banks proliferated.[39] With money seemingly plenty, "the nation had taken on the aura of boom; the prosperity seemed limitless and without a flaw."[40] The eminent historian of US banking, Bray Hammond, in describing the "prevailing enthusiasm" of 1836, puts it this way: "men's eyes were turned from the swelling volume of their liabilities to gleam with satisfaction on what the assets were doing."[41]

As "men's eyes" were turned to growing asset values, Sedgwick's novella sees a problem with money "so abundant," as Jackson put it in his 1832 veto of the Second Bank of the United States.[42] Although it does not explicitly wade into the era's monetary politics, the novella construes the belief in illimitable growth—be it in the form of paper money or the institution of the bank or whatever—as a precondition to loss.[43] Pursuing money as the "representative of power—the means of extended usefulness," in the words of one character from The Poor Rich Man—Sedgwick's truly "rich" characters operate within carefully contained moral *and* fiscal bounds (PRM, 112). Michael Germana has observed that the era's "monetary politics and the cultural politics of identity are not just analogous but interdependent"; as he writes, "the discourses that give value to money [also] shape the mind."[44] If money earned through individual enterprise can be one valid sign of success in this historical moment of plenty, for Sedgwick it is best apprehended as a sign of the restraint of one's desire for lucre. Irrespective of class identity, one's sense of cash, in other words, indexes how well one regulates the desire to go ahead.

So, from the outset of its plot, *The Poor Rich Man* demonstrates Aikin and Finley's characters as young boys through their respective relationships to money and finance. On one hand, Morris Finley, "the son of the only man in Essex who had not any regular business [but] was what our rustics call a schemer and a jockey," learns to view "money, not as a means, but as an end." Finley's father "in a larger sphere would have been a speculator," and he "infused his ruling passion into his son" (*RPM*, 23). The mandate to strive without end, then, was a constant of the Morris home, since his "keen-sighted" father "often succeeded, but sometimes failed" (*RPM*, 23). But if his father stood out in Essex County as being the only man without "any regular business," Morris Finley would not reject the uncertainty this career entailed, but would rather seek to control it. Indeed, he would make a study of commercial risk—"being better educated than his father, and regularly trained to business," he "had a far better chance of ultimate success" (*RPM*, 23). In the space of a single paragraph about the Finleys, then, Sedgwick sketches increasing financial savvy from generation to generation as a byproduct of individual choices, in which a kind of oedipal drama produces a greedy but now "regularly trained" businessman.

If the novel sees the result of this character development as generational, it is eager to examine how training for the psychology of midcentury capitalism plays out in institutions beyond the home. In school, for example, when the children's teacher, Mr. Reed, gives the students books as gifts, Finley receives *Bewick's History of Birds* (1797–1821), a beautifully illustrated series of volumes that, because of its elegant wood engravings, was much admired by transatlantic readers in the eighteenth and nineteenth centuries. But all Finley can see in this book is money, and he invidiously boasts: "My book cost twice as much as [Aikin's] Bible" (*RPM*, 13). Determined to turn a financial profit, Finley continues further: "When one knows the value of money, one does not like to have so much lying idle. Money should work, as father says. If you could reckon interest and compound interest as well as I can . . . I guess you would not like to have your money lying idle on a bookshelf!" (*RPM*, 13) Schooled in the language of finance, Finley distorts the text. He turns an ornamental book into something like an interest-bearing security—an investment that grows, rather than lies "idle," an object that accrues financial interest, rather than a moderate appreciation of nature. And on the other hand, there is Harry Aikin, whose "father was a farmer—all his property . . . might have amounted to some five or six thousand dollars" who, with this meager lot, cared for "his dozen children" (RPM, 22). Here, Sedgwick is interested in how "excellent lessons in the economy of human life" are conveyed within "such a family, well regulated" (RPM, 23).

The key word here, again, is "regulated," which reinforces for the reader how the novella's distinction between rich and poor will turn on it. This term makes sense; after all, as Block puts it, "overarching regularity and stability" is the "collective goal" of an "agency civilization" that sees the market as the meritocratic arena in which one earns an identity.[45] Sedgwick's reliance on binary oppositions, then, is a convenient tack for the didactic writer, but it also allows her to consider these men to represent two viable but opposed paths one can take within the "single master authorizing system" of liberal capitalism, an institutional framework that Sedgwick's writing sees as nonnegotiable.[46] Whose style of regulation, her novella asks, should be emulated—Finley's, geared toward financial profit and the explicit management of risk? Or Aikin's, geared, more vaguely, toward "the economy of human life"?

Finally, the obvious place to test these styles against one another is neither the home nor the school, but the market itself. So, the novella unites the young men Finley and Aikin as partners in a business enterprise—a joint "shoe concern" (RPM, 69). What is most interesting to Sedgwick about this partnership is precisely its failure. The "partnership" lasts two years, and, "at the close of" it, Aikin learns that the firm's bust is imminent (RPM, 64). How will each man handle this outcome? The results are predictable. As Aikin writes to his childhood sweetheart and eventual wife, Susan Mays, "As soon as I found we could not meet our notes, I made a thorough examination into our affairs, and found we could just pay our debts and no more" (RPM, 64). Through a sober, deliberative account of their business, Aikin becomes "determined to stop short, and not, as many do, put off the evil day, plunging deeper and deeper, making enemies, and making plenty of work for repentance" (RPM, 70–71).

One historian of bankruptcy explains how credit markets finally started to tighten in late 1836, with "short-term interest rates offered by banks and brokers [shooting] up."[47] This sign of trouble in the buildup to the Panic of 1837 is absent from Sedgwick's discourse, and the reader knows nothing about whom the partners might anger and to whom they might "work for repentance" in the wake of their bankruptcy. Contrary to Aikin, Finley puts this issue to the side and "affect[s] to see, flattering prospects ahead" (RPM, 64).

This style of response could be "shrewd" business, and Finley's education might well have helped the firm navigate through this storm to calmer waters. Who knows? What is important, instead, is the novel's contest between individual framing, and although Finley would dishonestly determine to go ahead, Aikin knows when "to stop short." If the typical antebellum debtor "cared more about the fortunes of people close to them" than not, Aikin bucks this trend—he wants to indemnify all, expressly at the expense of his own movement forward.[48] And when he persuades Finley to follow his lead, the firm's individual failure becomes significant in its safeguarding of widespread success.

This fictional failure of a business partnership, which proceeds with the wellbeing of faceless market agents in mind, marks the possibility of a reformed perception of any one firm's ruin. Two ideas further stand out about how Sedgwick portrays Aikin's successful failure. First, his controlled reaction complicates the era's dominant construal of going under. With Aikin in charge of the firm's bust, we witness a kind of orderly undoing, not the melee portrayed in Clay's lithograph, *The Times* (see Introduction). Indeed, as David Anthony has written of the era's sensationalist literature, typically, professional men gained "self-possession *through* the loss of affective and bodily control brought about by financial humiliation."[49] But the broken Aikin instead gains self-possession through the moderation of affective intensities. What warrants further attention, second, is that Aikin develops this affective control in a letter to his intended spouse, Susan, rather than to other men, as in the cases of Irving, Cooper, and (as we will see) Emerson. If the threat of bankruptcy presents itself as an opportunity for Aikin to reflect on his relation to the financial structure, Sedgwick's protagonist approaches this deliberation via a different kind of partnership, one between husband and wife.

This collaboration is possible not because of Susan's transcendent sympathy, the kind we saw Hoban laud at the outset of this chapter, but because of hers and Harry's shared business intelligence. He explains to Susan, adapting the vernacular of go-aheadism: "When our affairs were settled up, I [had to] determine on what business I should follow," and he decides on the cab business: "A sure and regular business . . . They go slowly but surely ahead" (*RPM*, 71). He admits, "some persons think it is going down a step to go from shop-keeping to carting . . . but you and I, Susan, have our own notions about going up and down, and both think it is in a man, and not what is out of him, that humbles or exalts him" (*RPM*, 72). The Aikins are in step with the era's individualist ethos and they see exchange, the determinant of self-worth, as compulsory. But where go-aheadism strictly defines value through the imperative of a relentless ambition, the Aikins counter with their own homespun "notions about going up and down." That is, they want to meet this compulsion through regular business activity of their own contriving. So, Aikin's carting business goes "surely" and "regular[ly]." So, too, goes Susan Aikin's seamstress work. "Susan Aikin," we learn, "could at all times command work from the most respectable houses, was sure of the highest wages, and incidental favours that she knew how to turn to account" (*RPM*, 84). A keen reader of the market like her husband, Susan is confident in the value of her work and, by extension, the economic stability of her own home.

Together, the Aikins, then, evolve their market outlook through the travails of business failure. And their valuing of honesty and slowness, rather than subterfuge and breakneck chasing after profit, leaves the structures of Block's "agency civilization" intact. So, even with this "class-based humility" (to borrow one of Robbins's terms from her analysis of a different Sedgwick work), capital's profit imperative still abides.[50] The problem is that the moderate mode of the Aikins is unlikely to meet the full requirement of capitalist profit. And, as in "Romance in Real Life," Sedgwick's novella concludes by subtly acknowledging the need for investment beyond the Aikins' comparatively meager means. The solution to this dilemma emerges in the character Mr. Beckwith, aptly dubbed by Shapiro as the novella's "rich rich" man.[51] Just as Aikin might have been before failure reset his ambition, Beckwith is a partner in a successful mercantile house. He is also a client of Aikin's who is eager to install the reliable cartman's family as his tenant. Beckwith offers them a great deal, as Aikin explains to Susan: the rent will not "exceed more than we now pay," but will improve their living conditions (*RPM*, 177).

The rich poor man's modest model of success thus guarantees the rich rich man's capital scheme. It ensures Beckwith's risk-taking in the residential real estate market against loss and, thereby, provides a lucrative check on the vulgarity of the "mere merchant." Neither man spurns the market, certainly, but neither man seeks hasty returns therein. Beckwith can charge the Aikins a rental rate that will still "yield him eight per cent, for the money he has invested." According to Aikin, "He says he can afford the house lower to me than to some others, for he is sure of being punctually paid" (*RPM*, 177). That means that if Beckwith's shrewd business sense is rewarded, so too is Aikin's regularity. In handling the failure of his "shoe concern," in which he protected his creditors, he avoided personal bankruptcy *and* recalculated what it meant for him to go ahead. Similarly, here he succeeds again in renegotiating his rent; as he explains to his children, "So, you see, that virtue, and good habits . . . are not only in the highest sense treasures, they are *money to you*" (*RPM*, 177; emphasis original).

In Aikin and Beckwith's overlapping self-protocols, *The Poor Rich Man* finds safeguards for risk-based investment. If the ruin of the Finley and Aikin partnership is the catalyst for these successes, it is perhaps unsurprising that Finley's lucrative response to his near bankruptcy earlier in the novel equally ensures his spiritual ruin. For Edward J. Balleisen, bankruptcy could demonstrate a merchant's "adaptability"—"Perhaps the greatest flexibility resided in those bankrupts who responded to their failures by seeking opportunities within the world of bankruptcy . . . to reestablish solvency and social position."[52] This is certainly the case for Finley, who rights his wealth-seeking ship and ends the novel materially rich, a further sign that the novel cannot dispute the institutions of US capitalism. But Sedgwick cannot accept a world in which single-minded enterprise leads to more and more material riches. Accordingly, the lessons Finley learned from his father will end with him— Finley's "only son" had "died suddenly," a victim of his household's baleful indulgences (*RPM*, 171). There are "opportunities within the world of bankruptcy" to reestablish the self, Sedgwick would agree. The opportunities will be ever-present because, from the view of the novel, capitalist exchange must be assimilated into everyday life. It is rather the content—and regulation— of those failure-induced reflections with which her novel—finally, a training manual for failure in the go-ahead age—quibbles.

"Independent of This Bank-Note World!": Sedgwick and the Panic of 1837

Sedgwick's confidence in failure was more plausible in 1836 than in 1837 when the theme would nearly overwhelm her while the Panic of 1837 "cut a wide swath of injury" across the nation.[53] Indeed, "panic pervades the community," as she would flatly state.[54] If the political economy of *The Poor Rich Man* is premised on the mutually assured restraint of the "rich," what happens when Aikin's carting business—or, perhaps more likely, Beckwith's mercantile house—goes belly-up? In language that resonates with her sense of dismay over the ruin of New York City's financial district by the Great Fire in 1835, Sedgwick noted the upheaval in 1837 in her private writing. What strikes her in a letter from New York in late April to her niece Katherine ("Kate") Maria Sedgwick is the fact that the "drygoods' shops are almost

NEW EDITION OF MACBETH.   BANK-OH'S! GHOST.

FIGURE 2.2 Edward Williams Clay's satirical lithograph from 1837 targeting President Martin Van Buren for continuing the hard money policies of his predecessor, Andrew Jackson. Courtesy of the Library of Congress.

deserted . . . and you will see the line of counters, with clerks on one side walking up and down . . . and no buyers on the other."⁵⁵ Distressed by the uncanny return of goods without customers, she laments that the store clerks can do nothing but pace "up and down like so many ghosts" (see fig. 2.2). This spectral scene could mean but one thing: business had been suspended once again.

Following on the heels of her engagement in 1836 with the ideologies of capitalist selfhood, it is no surprise that this mass failure event struck a nerve. Like many cultural commentators who (in the words of one correspondent to *Niles' Weekly Register*) blamed the panic on "the idleness, and extravagance in which too many have indulged," Sedgwick faulted personal failings.⁵⁶ "You can have little idea," she writes to her niece, "who are surrounded by those who have been accustomed to live upon the fruits of their labor, of the confusion and dismay produced here by the general bursting of bubbles, and the consequent failure of the means of actual support."⁵⁷ Here, Sedgwick partially laments the prior causes of the panic, no doubt, but she is more critical of its effects in the present tense. If "panic pervades the community" (as I quoted above), it perverts, first, nature. "This is the season, you know, of spring butterflies . . . but now it is almost as dingy as it was in the cholera season."[58] And, second, it distorts social intercourse. "Even Broadway, to use the slang phrase, *feels* it," she writes, and goes on to further denounce the fact that "nothing is talked of but 'who has failed to-day.'"[59] What should be a vibrant natural and social season, then, is overshadowed by death, a point she figures graphically by describing the panic's ever-growing pile of metaphorical dead bodies: "The buried carcasses of to-day are covered by the fresh ones of to-morrow."[60]

With this figuration of the panic's "dead," we might want Sedgwick to levy an incisive critique of the necropolitics of midcentury capitalism. But, in her view, the problem with catastrophes—fires or financial crises—is less in their past causes or their structural violence. It is, rather, in their inconveniences—their disruptions of spring in the city, of polite conversation, and so on. Eager to resume the "romance in real life" once more, she would struggle to get beyond individual solutions to this pressing financial problem. As she later writes to Kate Sedgwick, she spends "her spare time . . . in concocting a report for a remodeling of our society."[61] But this project proves "more difficult than writing a 'novel booky.'"[62] "It is easier to get a heroine into a dungeon, and not more difficult to get her out," she writes, "than to decide how to impersonate persons and personify abstractions."[63] Whereas a romantic adventure plot can more or less write itself, a "report" that aims not at reforming the financial structure but the individual consciousness of those agents within it eludes her.

At least for a while—like the other figures I study in this book, Sedgwick eventually finds her voice after contemplating the crisis. One of her new plans for society had young women sewing, rather than gossiping. (More Susan Aikins, it seems!) But she settles on an even better solution, one that she had begun to develop in *The Poor Rich Man*: a reevaluation of just what it means to fail. And in a contemplative letter from May 1837 to her brother, Charles Sedgwick, she announces a "little article . . . called 'Who and What has not Failed.'" She takes heart, she tells her brother, that the financial "agitations here seem to be pretty much over; at least there is less of it on the surface." "At least" fewer people are talking about the panic—never mind the fact that that is because "men have become accustomed to the new state of things"! So, if the United States is stuck with piles of carcasses—if people become habituated, that is, to the violence of the profit mandate—her article will demonstrate "a great balance in favor even of the real bankrupts."[64]

Produced for editor John O'Sullivan's *Democratic Review* and reprinted in several magazines during the summer of 1837, Sedgwick's article intertwines marriage and business plots. It shows how a recent panic threatens the heroine Helen's marriage to a young lawyer. Helen's father, Mr. J., a man of seemingly incontrovertible financial integrity, like so many other "severe sufferers by these disastrous times," is ruined by the commercial pressure.[65] In light of his own "melancholy tale," Mr. J. believes that "all who had not failed would fail," and he forbids his daughter's marriage, since he (Mr. J.) will no longer be able to supplement his future son-in-law's comparatively meager salary.[66] Rejecting the grounds of her father's decision, Helen exclaims, "not every thing [has failed], my dear father"; "her happiness was secured from failure by *bond and mortgage*."[67] "The moon has not failed," she continues, offering a happy observation that leads the narrator toward "observing who and what has *not failed*."[68] Here, Sedgwick is now quite eager to secure from loss nearly everything that is "independent of this bank-note world!"

Sedgwick's list of "non-failures" would likely have surprised her brother, the political economist, Theodore Sedgwick. In his 1836 *Public and Private Economy*, he catalogs the "principal items of wealth."[69] His sister's heterodox accounting includes moons, books, and so on. But it also includes domestic partnerships that seem more like the Aikins of *The Poor Rich Man* than the couple of Irving's "The Wife." One wife, for instance, avows that "this is no place or time for sentiment," as she adapts the constancy presumed by Irving into work suited for the times.[70] But it is Helen, who terms her eventual wedding to the lawyer a "non-failure," who seems a more interesting character in this context, for she frames her coming nuptials as a "conjugal partnership" forged within the crisis.[71] Helen, indeed, holds "true-love, capacity, industry, and frugality to be sufficient security"—not as transcendent values, but as valuable hedges against the next financial panic.[72]

To end this short story by imagining marriage as akin to a "partnership" that can ride the waves of commercial uncertainty enlists women as agents of the market. But doing so potentially violates Sedgwick's preferred quietist rhetorical stance toward the crises of midcentury capitalist risk-taking. So, she concludes her short piece instead by remembering "a Parisian belle" during a "cholera panic" who "painted over her door, 'no cholera to be spoken of here!'"[73] For Sedgwick, one might "go a little further, and during the panic, not only proscribe the agitating topic."[74] It is good to be prepared for a commercial crisis—husbands and wives can perfect the partnership model that eluded Finley and Aikin's shoe company in *The Poor Rich Man*. But, in the end, it is also advisable to just not talk about the eventuality of further distress.

Coda: "New Way of Paying Old Debts"; or, 1837 Again

A testament to her tenacity in thinking through the problems of widespread business disorder in the antebellum United States, Sedgwick would return once again to the depression era of the late 1830s in a short story entitled "New-Year's Day," which appeared in an 1846 issue of *Columbian Lady's and Gentleman's Magazine* and was reprinted in the annual *The Gem of the Season* for 1849.[75] Perhaps she sensed that her policy of panic ignorance was, finally, ill-suited for life in the midcentury United States. Commercial risk-taking, and its consequences, were too visible to be ignored, and I take the story as evidence of her strengthening belief in middle-class women's active roles in facing this turbulence with their husbands as partners. We saw glimpses of that conviction in *The Poor Rich Man* and "Who, and What, Has Not Failed," and "New-Year's Day" furthers this project with the character Ellen Lyell. Together, Sedgwick's characters from these texts implicitly push back against Irving's "The Wife" and, in doing so, invite nineteenth-century American women to take seriously the psychological protocols of capitalist selfhood.

"New-Year's Day" makes its financial theme explicit in the first sentence. The tale will revisit the depression of the late 1830s when, as the narrator states, "speculation—that black art evasion of the laws God has instituted between labor and property, laws for the protection of human virtue—was at its fever height in the city of New York."[76] Like her 1837 story, the tale focuses on a young woman, Ellen Lyell, and her suitor, Haskett Mercer, and explores how a financial crisis interrupts the marriage plot. Mercer is an impecunious but usually prudent man who, tempted by the "peculiar" "times," accepts Ellen Lyell's father's "urgent" offer to back him in a speculation in "Western lands."[77] (Mercer will join Lyell's brothers in the venture.) The scheme, of course, does not pay out, as Mercer discovers the lots in Illinois to be worthless. Sedgwick borrows from the genre of temperance fiction to illustrate how "the demon of speculation" is followed by "ruin . . . in his train." But her real interest here is the individual response to the "remorse and anxiety" that tallies the psychological toll of this experience. Mercer's initial reaction is not great—to the chagrin of the Lyell men, he remains away from New York and ignores their vituperative letters. But what looks like "scoundrel[ry]" to Mr. Lyell is actually quiet resolve by Mercer to "expiat[e] . . . his faults."[78]

The second half of the story, which picks up five years later, dwells on the Lyells' contrasting responses to their newly straitened existence. Ellen, this "not common character," believes "that it is not our circumstances, but what we make of them, that is our great concern." Her resolve is countered by her father's daily reading "the stock-table" in the newspaper and his consequent "vex[ation]" to "no longer [have] any interest in the prosperous turn the affairs of the city had taken."[79] It would seem appropriate for an anti-finance jeremiad to leave Mr. Lyell to his ineffectual reading—to leave the debts he is owed left unpaid. But the story resolves itself with Mercer's return to New York and his settling up. When he surprises the Lyells at home, we learn that "he has worked hard for five years . . . in China." "He has paid his debt to me, with interest and compound interest—God bless him."[80]

With the resolution of this business plot, Sedgwick shifts her interests from protecting against financial loss as illustrated by Aikin's considerate failure to repaying those losses after the fact. Too often, Mr. Lyell implies, midcentury Americans retreat from excessive debts owed through a process of *"repudiation"*: a "new way of paying old debts," he sarcastically adds, in which one refuses to honor a debt contract.[81] This shift in emphasis from indemnity to repudiation reveals not just Mercer's character, but also Ellen Lyell's. Repudiation, after all, represents to Sedgwick the quickest way to relaunch one's career—the haste to get rich is matched by the haste to avoid repayment. Both Mercer and Lyell, alternately, prefer the slower walk, and they marry as people with shared business values. These two people, it turns out, also share the ability to "read" the market. Like Mercer, Lyell was "was familiar with the stock-table for she read it every evening with her father." She, too, had experienced business fluctuations. If she has internalized the ups and downs of commercial life, though, it has not altered her perseverance: her character "will be the same a hundred years hence," as observed by an unsuccessful suitor. So, as Sedgwick puts it, the story finds in Mercer and Lyell a "true match." It joins a man who has lived through commercial vicissitudes and avoided long-term losses and a woman, "familiar with the stock-table," whose risk tolerance and understanding of the market's legibility matches his own. Perhaps part of a new society that Sedgwick would concoct, these are "real" "non-failures," then, ones defined by the integration of investment returns and an equal partnership, not moonbeams or proscribed topics of conversation.

CHAPTER THREE

Emerson, the Scholar, and the Pace of Enterprise

> The farmer turns his capital once a year. The merchant many times oftener. The scholar cannot. The knowledge which he acquires will not become bread or reputation to him in a year, or two years, or ten. There is no double speeder, no railroad, no mechanical multiplication. He gives himself to the slow and unhonored task of observation.
>
> —RALPH WALDO EMERSON, *Journals*, August 9, 1837

Clearly, financial crises would not disappear (in Sedgwick's words from the previous chapter) as an "all-engrossing topic of the day" in the nineteenth-century United States. Nor would the related problems of capitalist identity. As an editor of *Harper's New Monthly Magazine* understood it in the aftermath of the Panic of 1857, this latter issue was one of pacing. Indeed, the event, which was caused by an excess of speculation in the stock of railroad companies in the western United States, presented go-aheadism with a reckoning of speed. The *Harper's* writer catalogs "the eager and headlong rush" to ruin in 1857 with "every merchant ravenous to be an Astor, every politician a Clay, every clergyman a Channing."[1] From business to politics to religion, the infection of ambition ran throughout US society, and what looked like a "headlong rush" forward was just the opposite: "Our business . . . too often proves to us that 'going ahead too fast' really means going backward."[2] A solution to this pathological feature of capitalist selfhood, from the editor's perspective at least, did not seem forthcoming—"Continually nettled by the failure of our selfish aspirations, we resent as injustice the disappointments of our vanity and greed."[3] Part of that essential trick of life under capitalism—to make one resent the outcome of the game, not its rules—even widespread failure, it appeared, would not displace the grasping individual's sense of self in relation to the downtrodden economy.

Similarly, one year later, in December 1858, the speed of capitalist innovation caught Ralph Waldo Emerson's attention. His lecture in Hartford, Connecticut, which would become the essay "Success" in a late collection, *Society and Solitude* (1870), starts with a seeming paean to the very industry at the heart of the 1857 panic, American railroads. A sign of the United States' "unfolding strength," the "engineries" of industrialism and the "growing valuations" of its firms for Emerson illustrate why "our American people cannot be taxed with slowness in performance."[4] Yet fast "conveniences" like the rail and the telegraph are "local," signs of "coarse superiority," which appeal to a nation made of people who "have less tranquility of mind [and] are less easily contented" (CW, 7:145). Perhaps one might say (in *Harper's* phrase) that "eager and headlong" Americans misread these mechanical inventions as "a lucrative secret" (CW, 7:146). Seeking to circumvent the "tedious" interval between "cause and effect," they asked: "How to leap to the result by short or by false means?" (CW, 7:146). To counter such restlessness, Emerson's "Success" offers the "wide-seeing soul"—that which is "no express-rider" (CW, 7:158).

Emerson's resonance within the capitalist imagination is well documented by literary and cultural scholars. As early as 1940, one intellectual historian could cite a "sharp clash of critical opinion" on Emerson and economics.[5] Is he an apologist for the United States' rugged individualism, in which the merchant figures as a "*speculative* genius [whose] madness" is the "gain of the world" (CW, 6:50; emphasis original)? Or is he, rather, an idealist who disputes the era's crass materialism? Other scholars have either read this dichotomy as a false one or navigated around it by distinguishing between an "early" and "late" phase of Emerson's writing.[6] Thus, Michael T. Gilmore can find in Emerson's earlier work an aversion to market culture—in particular, commodification—while new historians of capitalism like Scott Sandage, Jonathan Levy, Jeffrey Sklansky, and others inevitably see in the later works like "Success" a justification for how deeply that mode of production took control of social life in the nineteenth-century United States.[7]

From my perspective, the meaning of the market economy has been a consistent preoccupation of Emersonian transcendentalism. He writes in the essay "Wealth" that "profligacy consists not in spending years of time or chests of money, — but in spending them off the line of your career" (CW, 6:60). Indeed, self-pacing as a method for managing economic volatility is one "line" of Emerson's "career." Inspired by his oscillating between the structural and individual frames, chapter 3 explores, first, Emerson's attempt at understanding the "symbolical character" of business unrest and, second, his participation in a culture-wide debate over personal identity and its relation to these vicissitudes.[8] Like recent critics, I take for granted his immersion within "market society itself"; his frequent adopting of the language of commercial enterprise in seemingly noncommercial contexts speaks to this point.[9] And whereas Nicholas K. Bromell situates Emerson within the "broad cultural contestation of the meaning of work," I show how he strategically engaged the psychological structures that midcentury capitalism was producing—failure and success.¹⁰ He wanted to redefine these categories in idealist terms, but he always recognized striving, whether for money or not, toward some "work of my own" as essential to realizing an identity (*CW*, 1:150).¹¹

Deliberate striving amid uncertainty, for Emerson, is a given of self-realization. And in works ranging from "The American Scholar" (1837) to *The Conduct of Life* (1860), Emerson sought to reform go-aheadism along an axis of speed. Not unlike Sedgwick in the 1830s and 1840s, capitalism as a mode of production was less a problem for him than how quickly one attained its categories of identity. As he renegotiated business culture, as we see in the epigraph above, he installed the scholar's affect as exemplary for life under the profit imperative. For Emerson, the scholar's "slow and unhonored task of observation" shows the path to success; this even becomes the "remedy" (a term from "The American Scholar") to the problem of market culture's obsessive celerity. He thus licenses a workaholic self-culture in which one construes the world as a "workyard" writ large (*EL*, 2:151). Whereas we might be apt to think of Emerson's writing to nudge us toward a leisurely stroll across the "bare common," he invites us instead, as if we have a choice, to perpetually walk toward some ambitious end.¹²

The "Symbolical Character" of the Panic of 1837

"I am glad it is not my duty to preach, these few Sundays [amid the] screwing panic."¹³ So writes Emerson—who had resigned his pastorate at Boston's Second Church in 1832—on May 14, 1837. Perhaps one of the few men contented to be out of regular work that summer, Emerson's former colleagues in New England were not so privileged. They were left instead to illuminate the Panic of 1837 for their flocks. They did so gamely, attempting to find spiritual meaning in what one pastor termed "the whirl of general disaster," while maintaining a line of separation between their spiritual office and the material one of the imperiled merchant.¹⁴ Wanting to acknowledge that finance had seeped into every aspect of life, but also, in most cases, eager to avoid topics on which they were not experts, Emerson's former colleagues were asked to assess the panic in spiritual terms.¹⁵ Personal identity often provided them with a way forward, as they explored the connections between individual morality and financial failure.¹⁶ What obvious interruptions, they wondered, to the "careful cultivation of . . . virtues in cooperation with a Providential plan" did the commercial chaos expose?¹⁷

If the crisis and its meanings informed public rhetoric like sermons and newspaper columns, it was a lively topic for Emerson's private writing as well.[18] This is true for his journals because, at a fundamental level, he had a personal stake in the antebellum financial markets. The "family banker" since the mid-1820s, Emerson managed his extended family's financial affairs.[19] Although he derived revenue, first, from the ministry and, later, from his lecture series and essays, a significant percentage of his income came from the investment returns of his late wife Ellen Tucker Emerson's estate. "It seems," he remarked in his grief over Ellen, that it "is to continue to benefit her husband whenever hereafter the estate shall be settled."[20] Valued at $11,600, Emerson's settlement, which included dividend-paying bank stocks, allowed him to live comfortably. Similar to Cooper's trouble with the Bridgen suit, "the estate was fully settled" only after protracted litigation, though, and the timing could not have been worse: "Just in time for the Financial Panic of 1837, when interest from the stocks dried up."[21] When his brother William, indebted by a mortgage for property on Staten Island, needed about $2,000 during the spring of 1837, Emerson employed what he termed his "finance faculty" to exhaustion (*L*, 2:137). Dispelling the myth of a disembodied eye soaring above business fluctuations, letters to his brother in 1838 make clear that Emerson could not ignore the financial distress.

Although his correspondence and journals reflect a personal liability in the hard times of spring 1837, they also indicate in Emerson a growing determination to make sense of the outward world and its "stern realities."[22] In an 1844 lecture, "New England Reformers," he would worry, "Am I not too protected a person?," as he questioned the comforting distance he had achieved from the market's dislocations (*CW*, 3:152). In 1837, though, he felt the immediacy of mass failure and, as he wrote to his brother William, would "grieve at the calamitous times" (*L*, 2:64). He seemed to worry over what he perceived as a lack of power to redress that calamity. "I am no very good economist," he tells William on April 3, 1837. But he acknowledges, determinedly, that "economy is a science & must be devoutly studied, if you would know it" (*L*, 2:64).

Emerson here routes his typical idealist intellection from individual experience, first, to "stud[ying]" the macroeconomy. And because of this devotion toward grasping the financial structure, Emerson analyzed that domain from the perspective of a long temporal frame. He would conclude that "the world has failed" (*JMN*, 5:333). The new natural science of geology would help him here, and a month into the commercial disruption, in an extended passage from May 22, 1837, he writes: "What was, ever since my memory, solid continent, now yawns apart and discloses its composition and genesis. I learn geology the morning after an earthquake. I learn fast on the ghastly diagrams of the cloven mountain & upheaved plain and the dry bottom of the Sea. The roots of orchards and the cellars of palaces and the cornerstones of cities are dragged into melancholy sunshine. I see the natural fracture of the stone. I see the tearing of the tree & learn its fibre & its rooting" (JMN, 5:333). Here, he construes what B. L. Packer calls the "revelatory merits of the catastrophe" in spatial terms.[23] (The financial crisis upends the "solid continent.") At the same time, this metaphor of physical upheaval has temporal implications. And naturalizing the clash between the nearly imperceptible rhythms of the crisis' etiology and the suddenness of its devastation, Emerson can start to understand the effects of recklessly striving for capitalist profits.

This naturalist conceit, of course, can look like a turn away from finance. But in his 1837 journals, he recurs to this rhetoric, a fact that suggests how deeply entwined his analysis of society was with business culture. In an earlier account of Emerson and money, Ian F. A. Bell sees an insistent "fiscal metaphor" in his corpus.[24] I would add that, in addition to monetary tropes, Emerson likewise emphasizes the language of commercial enterprise. What the "melancholy sunshine" exposes, indeed, is that "the present generation is bankrupt of principles & hope, as of property" (JMN, 5:332). But this insight does not impel Emerson necessarily to a stance of "antipathy toward trade and commerce."[25] Rather, approaching the commercial volatility as a phenomenon to be read—that is, studying its "symbolical character"—he undertakes to restore individual solvency amid a shaken social foundation (JMN, 5:334). "Let me begin anew," he crows. "Let me ascend above my fate and work down upon my world" (JMN, 5:332). If the earthquake uprooted the previously invisible financial apparatus of society, he would use the opportunity to "enquire if the Ideal might not also be tried. Is it to be taken for granted that it is impracticable?" (JMN, 5:332)

The buildup to and the aftermath of the 1837 panic catalyzed Emerson's critical engagement with finance, and this grappling takes the definitive shape of a narrative of reversal. To describe this trajectory, indeed, Block adopts an Emersonian figure of speech. "Yet in undertaking [a] personal journey of experience and education," he writes, "[agents] achieve through the collapse of the idyll a new self-reliance and understanding of place within post-traditional society."[26] Although Emerson might seem to imagine building a new society from the ruins of the 1837 convulsion, like Hawthorne's Phoebe and Holgrave (see Introduction), he actually returns to "the world" to install what Block (in reference to Emerson) terms "a universal striving" that will govern midcentury life.[27] Hence, by the late fall of 1837, Emerson could pronounce that the "Crisis of Trade . . . always teaches political economy"—"all these instructive slides in our lantern show us something of ethics & something of practicks" (*JMN*, 5:441). Again, he invokes bankruptcy at this time, but certainly not to linger on the severe social dislocations of the era. Rather, he wants to read "the gloomy catastrophe of a bankruptcy" as something promising, first, of legibility and, second, of instruction: "A pod to learn the virtues of a plant" (*JMN*, 5:441). Although this metaphor partakes of a triumphant romanticism, the implication seems clear as the financial rhetoric cedes to a botanical one: in the late 1830s, the path to idealist insight leads through business unrest.

Integrating financial turmoil and idealism, Emerson writes as if the crisis is inevitable—its meaning is "dragged into melancholy sunshine." And this apprehension of commercial ups and downs as compulsory allows him to continue to evolve the idealism he had already articulated in *Nature* (1836) and would refine in "The Poet" (1844). In *Nature*, in the well-known chapter, "Language," he theorized that "words," as "signs of natural facts," symbolize "spirit" (*CW*, 1:17). In seeking to redress the rift between the ideal and the actual that the 1837 panic exposed, he aims, first, to "connect his thought with its proper symbol" (*CW*, 1:20). This crucial initial step zeroed in on "ugl[iness]" as a site of "dislocation and detachment from the life of God" (*CW*, 3:11). As we find years later in "The Poet," this form of idealism strives to "use defects and deformities to a sacred purpose" (*CW*, 3:11). And to illustrate this point, "The Poet" concludes its discussion of reading with comments on money. There, Emerson claims how attention to "the belt of wampum and the commerce of America" can "enhance the great and constant fact of Life" (*CW*, 3:12). Outward phenomena like money, and the financial earthquakes to which they are linked, should lead the eye inward, where the "spiritual fact remains unalterable" (*CW*, 3:12).

So, Emerson tries to fold business vicissitudes into an idealist philosophy, but other problems remained as he vowed to "work down upon the world." How to reform capitalist models of identity, given that "the master of a family learns to translate every article that passes before him as household commodity into a money value" (*JMN*, 5:335)? How to communicate, further, the value of idealism "without loss" (*CW*, 1:20)? Where Catharine Maria Sedgwick undertook a similar project in her didactic fiction (see chapter 2), Emerson would take to the lecture podium. Before delivering "The American Scholar" later that August, he would tackle these vexations in a lesser-known speech, "Address on Education," a June 10, 1837, dedication to the writer, educator, and eventual Confederate sympathizer Hiram Fuller's new coeducational Greene Street School in Providence, Rhode Island. This lecture mines the journal passages devoted to the panic I cite above. Its central claim is that education is a bulwark against the "devotion to the senses," a problem that he explicitly ties to his analysis of the 1837 crisis.[28] He explains to the audience that "in exploring the relations of social man at a period of calamity and alarm, I seem to learn geology the morning after an earthquake" (*EL*, 2:196). Education, Emerson argues, can cure this world that "lies sick." The "high ideal faculties" have suffered "a more than usual torpidity" compared to the alacrity of the era's acquisitive urge, and education can awaken them (*EL*, 2:197).

But even here, Emerson's jeremiad is integrative: it sees the ideal as running through the financial. An ideal education prepares one, as he puts in on May 23, 1837, to "mind your own business" (*JMN*, 5:335); in Providence, he says one will "gain wisdom and virtue from his business" (*EL*, 2:202). He continues, "many years of life in trade" do not disqualify one from self-reliance (*EL*, 2:201). Instead, because commercial enterprise encourages "the higher faculties of the individual be from time to time quickened, he will gain wisdom and virtue from his business" (*EL*, 2:202). Emerson is not advocating that students take a full curriculum of business courses. His argument is, rather, that education in general can prepare one to glean wisdom from one's work by disrupting the "routine" that makes us "only more skillful servants of mammon" — education, he reasons, teaches us how to "translate into general terms" the "symbolical character" of any moneymaking endeavor (*EL*, 2:203). An ideal education, then, prepares an individual immersed within go-ahead culture to manage affective uncertainty through a wider temporal frame. What does "failure" symbolize, he wonders, but a temporary lapse in commerce? With one's vision calibrated so, an educated individual remains "calm in misfortunes and in hard times and sober in success" (*EL*, 2:203).

Calmness, hope, sobriety: these are the personal attributes that will allow one to thrive in times both "hard" and flush. Seeing business fluctuations as unavoidable, Emerson here illustrates (in Block's terms) how "shaping themselves as free agents through their own authority" helped make self-fashioning seem voluntary in the nineteenth-century United States.[29] This process entails the transformation of pursuing freedom from institutions into participating in them, and its conservatism is revealed in a significant revision of the journals for the Providence address. Initially, Emerson had countenanced the severe burdens on the era's laborers; he noted the "sixty thousand laborers, says rumor, to be presently thrown out of work" (*JMN*, 5:304).[30] A month later, he observed further, "Young men have no hope. Adults stand like daylaborers idle in the streets. None calleth us to labor" (*JMN*, 5:331–32). Yet by the summer, he had second thoughts about just who bore the brunt of the catastrophe—in his remarks in Providence, he wrote, "The *educated class* stand idle in the streets. None calleth them to labor" (*EL*, 2:198; emphasis mine).

A generous reading of this emendation might recall that Emerson was speaking at the time to the "educated class," the faculty and students of the Greene School. But in his determination to scrutinize the structural consequences of unemployment and the lived experiences of it, he figures what Joel Pfister terms the "human costs" of capitalism as such in terms of affect, not the hunger, houselessness, drunkenness, and suicide represented by Clay's "The Times" (see Introduction).[31] He thus suppresses the wider social implications of the financial crisis and construes it, more narrowly, as a spur to the era's scholars, rather than its industrial classes. Tapping into the idiom of go-aheadism, he explicitly connects the young pupils to an ideology of patience that, because it vaunts "ambition," invisibilizes capitalist violence. This maneuver wants to guarantee the viability of capitalist institutions as venues for achievement: "Even the thoughtful and prudent, perhaps the best men in society," he continued, "find no employment, no objects of ambition, and waste on trifles a godlike strength" (*EL*, 2:198). For Emerson, the urgent task for schools during the depression of the 1830s is clear: to direct "employment" among the "educated class" toward better "objects." Ambition, understood as compulsory and continually renewed by hope through education, is thus the prerogative of a "godlike" self (*EL*, 2:198).

"A Scholar Doing a Scholar's Office": "The American Scholar"

Emerson's presentation of the scholar as well-suited to a nonnegotiable market turmoil coalesced in "The American Scholar," which he delivered later that summer to the Phi Beta Kappa students of Harvard College on August 31, 1837. In an August 1837 journal passage, he reflects on a recent letter from his friend and former ministerial colleague Nathaniel Langdon Frothingham. That spring, Frothingham had preached on the crisis in a sermon called "Duties of the Times," a jeremiad that urges its audience to "take courage for the future," rather than ramp up "general panic by unreal terrors."[32] Emerson does not refer to this springtime passage in his writing, but the sermon's prescription for a generalized "hope" as the "remedy" to the panic would likely have resonated.[33] And, in his journal, Emerson deems his friend a "Scholar doing a Scholar's office" (*JMN*, 5:358). Preceding this comment, he applauds Frothingham's renown as "fame" that was "bought by many years' steady rejection of all that is popular with our saints & as persevering study of books which none else reads & which he can convert to no temporary purpose" (*JMN*, 5:358). Ambition, here, is recast as a long game, in which one's persistence over time leads, ultimately, to a successful transaction ("bought")—this is the "Scholar's office."[34]

Delivered not long after this meditation, "The American Scholar" attempts to recruit young men to the "persevering study of books" by resisting the commonly accepted meanings of ideas like ambition, success, and failure. Indeed, the scholar's office is a site from which to rebut those "so-called 'practical men' [who] sneer at speculative men, as if, because they speculate . . . they could do nothing" of value (*CW*, 1:59). Such a tack unravels the opposition between those who produce something and others who seem to produce nothing at all, and it works, in part, by co-opting the language of industrial production to demonstrate the value of the scholar's speculations.[35] Such value is easy to miss, of course, since the dogged pursuit of knowledge is neither quick nor efficient. And that is OK. In "The Poet" (1844), as cited above, Emerson would hope to communicate philosophical insight "without loss." Here, in the 1837 text, he concludes, the "process . . . of transmuting life into truth" is never "quite perfect": "As no air-pump can by any means make a perfect vacuum, so neither can any artist entirely exclude the conventional, the local, the perishable from this book, or write a book of pure thought that shall be as efficient, in all respects" (*CW*, 1:55–56).

This polemic about their productivity undermines the "notion that the scholar" is "unfit for any handiwork or public labor, as a penknife for an axe" (*CW*, 1:59). But Emerson's speech reverberates within the financial sector of the antebellum economy too, as he elevates "speculation" as a worthy activity. In the mid-1800s, the value of financial speculation was an open question. In 1839, in the *New-Yorker*, Horace Greeley would acknowledge that the practice had both costs and benefits. He defined it as "the buying of an article, not for personal or immediate business use, but with the hope of selling it again at a profit."[36] Most discussions of speculation, however, maligned it as the "haste to be rich." A group of businessmen's article, "Report of the Committee," a retrospective analysis of the 1837 crisis reprinted in *Niles' Weekly Register*, found that "among the causes of the ruinous results" were "the extensive and rash contracts in the purchase of land, city stocks, and other property, in which men of limited resources, in their zeal 'to make haste to be rich,' have engaged."[37] Emerson's acquaintance, the Victorian travel writer who also authored a series of popular illustrations of political economy, Harriet Martineau, noted the speculators' zeal to "go ahead" as widespread in the United States. Denouncing the speculative ethos, she observed, "Where there is hasty enterprise, there is usually much conceit. The very haste seems to show that the man is thinking more of himself than of the subject on which he is employed."[38] Emerson might counter and pose the question of what other subject warranted such scrutiny as man "himself." The critical problem for Emerson, that is, is not self-examination, but rather the duration—and tempo—that regulates that analytical work.

This temporal critique of speculation, both financial and intellectual, would have important, lasting social implications. In a well-known account, Christopher Newfield sees Emerson to naturalize obedience to the so-called laws of profit accumulation in the context of a rising corporate culture.[39] From my perspective, Emerson's time-based approach ennobles workaholism, as he normalizes the unceasing pursuit of knowledge as a definitive feature of self-culture. In the aftermath of the 1837 panic, Emerson's former colleague, the Unitarian minister Orville Dewey, commented on go-aheadism's "passion for fortune." He lamented that "even literary labor—labor of the mind, the noblest of all labor, has suffered under this disparaging estimate" of work.[40] Emerson does not wring his hands over his culture's low estimation of the scholar's office, but instead installs the scholar as an endlessly plodding worker. To this end, "The American Scholar" again uses another mechanical analogy: "experience" is the "raw material out of which the intellect moulds her splendid products. A strange process too, this, by which experience is converted into thought, as a mulberry leaf is converted into satin. The manufacture goes forward at all hours" (*CW*, 1:59). The language of industrialism here seems tempered by a craft ethos—the factory of the intellect churns out "splendid products." But, crucially, it does so in a "strange process" that is ceaseless, going "forward at all hours." The eminent Emerson scholar Lawrence Buell has written, "Overall [in "The American Scholar"] [Emerson] seems more anxious to warn scholars against acting hastily rather than to exhort them to act."[41] I would add that what looks like a paean to painstaking self-authorization is in fact a call for that self's never-ending enterprise for life under midcentury capitalism.

The imbrications of natural, industrial, and financial registers in "The American Scholar" point to a semantic battle to redefine the scholar as a truly ambitious, uniquely industrious figure. Focused on "the long period," this person is not an iconoclast of the go-ahead age, then, but the realization of this ethos' possibilities. In a passage I quote from at length, he says:

> In the long period of his preparation he must betray often an ignorance and shiftlessness in popular arts, incurring the disdain of the able who shoulder him aside. Long must [the scholar] stammer in his speech; often forgo the living for the dead. Worse yet, he must accept—how often! poverty and solitude. For the ease and pleasure of treading the old road, accepting the fashions, the education, the religion of society, he takes the cross of making his own, and, of course, the self-accusation, the faint heart, the frequent uncertainty and loss of time which are the nettles and tangling vines in the way of the self-relying and self-directed; and the state of virtual hostility in which he seems to stand to society, and especially to educated society. (*CW*, 1:62)

If "The American Scholar" amounts to a recruitment call, this is a curious one. For here, Emerson invites the audience behind the curtain, which typically "hides . . . the processes of composition and revision."[42] The *Harper's* editorial I quote at the outset of this chapter complained that, "continually nettled by the failure of our selfish aspirations," people stew in "resent[ment]." Emerson here makes the struggle through "nettles" a virtue, as the passage contrasts the easy and the hard roads, the quick and the "long" ones. But its most potent rhetorical punch revolves around the implied opposition between a passive "accept[ing]" and an active "making" as a method through which to achieve an identity. Indeed, the scholar is the risk taker who embraces "uncertainty . . . in silence, in steadiness, in severe abstraction." And for the scholar who "will bide his own time," as noted above, "success treads on every right step" (*CW*, 1:63).

But in trumpeting the persistent fight through "tangling vines" as a precursor to "success," Emerson cannot escape the paradox of the go-ahead era and the protocols of capitalist identity. For even the contrast between "accepting" and "making" breaks down in the extended passage above. The scholar, too, is compelled—"he *must* accept." A sleight of hand, Emerson's solution is to transform what Caleb Smith, writing mostly of Henry David Thoreau, would call a "discipline of attention" into a seemingly voluntary activity. For Smith, such disciplines "seek to restore the self's agency and display a kind of ethical virtue."[43] This is a "paradoxical business," though, since the "willingness to attend" is "an act of self-opening that is also an effect of self-mastery. Attending is surrendering—but willfully."[44] Also drawn to the paradox of transcendental freedom, the historian Block, in a passage cited in part above, sees Emerson as a key architect of a "universal striving which throughout the century defined American citizenry."[45] The mandate to attend in "The American Scholar," then, becomes an "effect" of an individual's choice to strive, rather than an external motivation.

This overwriting of a paradoxically compulsory but willed "universal striving" was not just a philosophical matter, though, especially if one must ultimately surrender to seemingly corrupt business institutions. It was also a matter of life and death. "Young men of the fairest promise, who begin life upon our shores, inflated by the mountain winds, shined upon by all the stars of God," Emerson writes, "find the earth below not in unison with these, but are hindered from action by the disgust which the principles on which business is managed inspire, and turn drudges, or die of disgust, some of them suicides" (*CW*, 1: 69). Suicide was an "epidemic" in antebellum US business culture.[46] This is the case, for Emerson, because the striving self struggles to square his ideals with "the principles on which business is managed."[47] With the reference to suicide, he thus indirectly exposes the conjunction *or* in the idiom *sink or swim* as a sly but dark misdirection. This is a menu not with choices but an obligation that was reinforced with dire consequences. The project of "The American Scholar" then, is not just to rewrite capitalist identity categories and institutions in transcendentalist terms. Naturalizing them as potentially self-affirming, he also wants to persuade the audience of his reformed program's viability.

Earlier in 1837, searching for answers to "harder times," Emerson asked, "Is it to be taken for granted that it is impracticable?" In the August address, he asks a related question that repeats a word from Frothingham's panic sermon: "What is the remedy?" (*CW*, 1:69) Although not obviously "practicable," philosophical idealism could repair go-aheadism's riot of the senses that impeded "young men of the fairest promise" from cultivating their characters — or, as seen above, from worse. Emerson believed he discovered a passage through these "barriers." For these young men "did not yet see, and thousands of young men as hopeful now crowding to the barriers for the career, do not yet see, that if the single man plant himself indomitably on his instincts, and there abide, the huge world will come round to him. Patience — patience; — . . . for solace, the perspective of your own infinite life; and for work, the study and the communication of principles, the making those instincts prevalent, the conversion of the world" (*CW*, 1:69). This passage contrasts the self-reliant scholar, "the single man," and the herd of workers "crowding to the barriers for the career." Why seek a career, one measured by "vulgar" "prosperity," and likely to induce one to "sleep-walk" by rote, when one can rely "on his instincts" to effect the "conversion of the world"? We might expect a commencement speaker to ask graduates to use their education to change "the world." All the better for one's "patience— patience," though. For, in a final incitement to action that quietly installs the scholar's ceaseless toil as exemplary, Emerson implies that, like the ideal self, this work is "infinite."

"Enough Time" After the Earthquake

After "The American Scholar," Emerson further honed his perception of this ideal work in which the ambitious striver aims "to communicat[e] . . . principles." In popular public lecture series and essays in the late 1830s, for instance, he addressed how the self could develop—and sustain—protocols to absorb the shocks of capitalism and, thereby, maintain their career.[48] Slower pacing remains a key theme in his thinking about the intersection of the individual and the macroeconomic context. Throughout lectures like "Doctrine of the Hands" (1837), Emerson counters normative go-aheadism by targeting its compressed temporal values. Decrying the "barbarous" times, he laments how we cannot "grant [Honesty] enough time" (EL, 2:242). The age is characterized by impatience, which frustrates an "industrious man"; a person can little "afford to wait so long as the slow growth of a good reputation demands for the returns of his capital" (EL, 2:242). By now, we might recognize this old Emersonian saw—and the fact that the solution to barbarism is *not* a radical overturning of the economic system. Again, it is a self-discipline that will be codified in midcentury conduct literature and holds that "all great, grand, and most durable things are of slow growth."[49]

The passage cited above was published in 1856 by Freeman Hunt, the editor of *Hunt's Merchants' Magazine*, in a piece called "Getting Along Slowly." There, the writer decrees that "gradual development is the great law of nature" and adduces "grand old trees of the forest" as evidence. And, as in nature, so too in commerce: in pursuing a slow growth of profits and reputation, one can avoid "danger." In a new historicist reading of Emerson and economics, Howard Horwitz has shown transcendentalism's surprising overlap with a Whiggish political economy that favored protection of the midcentury domestic market, rather than the free trade policies valued by Democrats. Transcendentalism, from this perspective, sought a secure external structure that could safeguard the individual's self-culture.[50] In observing Emerson and Hunt's shared politics of self-pacing, though, we see how transcendentalism adapted instability to its own ends: unrest provided a context in which to normalize striving as a deliberate activity that spanned beyond a singular event.

For Block, this "message of persevering participation became a cultural drumbeat" in the nineteenth-century United States. And the alternative outcomes of failure and success were presumed to be "given ends [and] laid out [as] self-evident."[51] But Emerson's efforts within this project also entail his continuing struggle to recast business culture in idealist terms—that is, to expose these terms as contingent, disavow them, and then renaturalize them within the vernacular of business itself.[52] "The American Scholar" primes us to recognize this dynamic; such a pattern reveals itself, too, in "Doctrine of the Hands" in a mixed metaphor of natural growth that is replete with market language. There, he imagines a scenario in which one seeks to "raise an estate from the seed." At first, one realizes "one cent; then two; then a dollar; . . . then a shop; then a warehouse." Importantly, this transformation from the natural to the commercial is an outcome of "higher instruction." At least, it can be—if not pursued "on this dangerous balloon of credit." And the antidote to this risk is, perhaps surprisingly, speed. *Hunt's* found in 1856 that "speed [in commerce] either debilitates or insures danger."[53] For Emerson, too, speed has its affordances in insuring against risk. He explains in "Doctrine of the Hands" that "moneystocks depreciate, in the few swift moments which the Yankee suffers any of them to remain in his possession. In skating over thin ice, our safety is in our speed."[54] Indeed, the fact "that our New England trade . . . saves itself [by] tak[ing] banknotes good, bad, clean, ragged" and "speed[ily] pass[ing] them off" is an object lesson for that "higher instruction" (*EL*, 2:243).

The above passages from the late 1830s give us a sense of how Emerson was fine-tuning his vision to accommodate what he understood as the inevitability of capitalist volatility. A mindless obsession with speed, he reasoned, would be undesirable—it would lead to the commodification of social life, as he worries in the "Address on Education," and it would result in the catastrophe of easily obtained credit, as he worries immediately above. But speed could also be prudential. And by 1841, in the address "Man, the Reformer," he weighed the costs and benefits of "a great prospective prudence" in terms of tempo (*CW*, 1:159). A true reformer, Emerson says, "should not be a subject of irregular and interrupted impulses of virtue, but a continent, persisting, immovable person" (*CW*, 1:160). It is correct that Emerson wanted his ideal scholar to embrace uncertainty, but here he adds to that argument to establish "persisting" as an affect for surviving the era's earthquakes. The trick, again, is to develop an internal consistency as a shock absorber for external inconsistency. And, drawn to another industrial metaphor, Emerson hails "men who have in the gravity of their nature a quality which answers to the fly-wheel in a mill, which distributes the motion equably over all the wheels and hinders it from falling unequally and suddenly in destructive shocks" (CW, 1:160).

This preparation for "destructive shocks" in "Man, the Reformer" becomes a "sublime prudence" that is based on a "vast" timescale (CW, 1:160). In orienting the self toward a "vast future—sure of more to come than is yet seen," one, like a shrewd investor, "postpones always the present hour to the whole life" (CW, 1:160). But this self-culture is also one that, paradoxically, rejects the seductions of "routine" (CW, 1:147). In a February 1838 text, "General Views," Emerson charges his audience to not "surrender to routine," which can spell ruin in quickly changing commercial contexts (EL, 2:362). Indeed, it poses potential problems in business because it can invite a lethargy that lets a merchant's affairs "unfold themselves after no law of the mind; but are bubble built on bubble without end" (EL, 2:362–63). In the later writing, because it counters the enlargement of one's perspective necessary for successful enterprise, routine remains troubling. As he warns in his essay "Wealth" from *English Traits* (1856) while discussing the English factory system: "The incessant repetition of the same hand-work dwarfs the man, robs him of his strength." When aggregated at the social level, moreover, "in these crises, all are ruined except such as are proper individuals . . . capable" of self-trust (CW, 5:95). Patterns of busyness, routines can undermine the sustained value production that Emerson lauds. Whereas for the merchant, "in trade, the momentary state of the markets betrays continually the experienced and long-sighted," for Emerson's "persisting" reformer, the "shocks" of the "moment" are but temporary irregularities to be apprehended by the "law of the mind" (EL, 2:362).

Across these post-"American Scholar" writings, Emerson's chief frustration with routine is how it leads to a narrower sense of enterprise and its possibilities over a span of time. And this problem informs perhaps the most canonical of Emerson's essays, "Self-Reliance" (1841). The 1841 text complains about young people's impatience for success. In an extended passage about the enterprises of "young men" and the "young merchant," he writes: "If our young men miscarry in their first enterprises, they lose all heart. If the young merchant fails, men say he is *ruined*. If the finest genius studies at one of our colleges, and is not installed in an office within one year afterwards in the cities or suburbs of Boston or New York, it seems to his friends and to himself that he is right in being disheartened, and in complaining the rest of his life" (*CW*, 2:43; emphasis original). These sentences neatly encapsulate Emerson's participation in a project to refine go-aheadism and to "order individual motion" toward the outcomes of capitalist selfhood.[55] It is at once polemical and prescriptive. Impatient for success, both individual and cultural responses to the initial miscarriage of enterprise violate the mandate to "get along slowly." In treating failure as a decisive event, these people consign themselves to the absolute loss of speed and, hence, miss the work of "successive years," during which one "always, like a cat, falls on his feet" (*CW*, 2:43). To let a singular instance loom in one's psyche—that is the opposite of self-reliance.

What is missing—and what is modeled by the scholar—is thus a wider apperception of failure. The solution to this problem appears consistently from 1837 to the Civil War addresses. In one of the latter, "Perpetual Forces" (1862), Emerson would comment that "what we do and suffer is in moments, but the cause of right for which we labor, never dies, works in long periods, can afford many checks, gains by our defeats, and will know how to compensate our extremest sacrifice."[56] Such an insight resonates with another 1841 essay, "Circles," which approaches failure as but a moment in time.[57] There, what looks like a failure—the obliteration of the self because of "the calamity" or "black events"—is a success. "The great man," that is, "is not convulsible or tormentable," but is able to "draw a new circle." In responding to failure, Emerson concludes, one can exaggerate such "particular events" or one can "draw a new circle" and "triumph" over it by reducing a calamity to "an insignificant result" (*CW*, 2:190). One does "not postpone his life," then, but sees individual failures and successes as part of one's (unending) career.

This response to the inevitability of failure as the precondition of success returns us to "Self-Reliance" and the "sturdy lad" from the country who stands opposed to that new graduate impatient for success in the city (*CW*, 2:43). Like Holgrave in Nathaniel Hawthorne's *The House of the Seven Gables*, Emerson's "lad" tries "all the professions." "He walks abreast with his days," Emerson writes, "and feels no shame in not 'studying a profession,' for he does not postpone his life, but lives already. He has not one chance, but a hundred chances" (*CW*, 2:43). Maurice S. Lee is drawn to this very anecdote in a historicist examination of US canonical literature's relation to the probabilistic revolution of the mid-1800s.[58] It resonates, too, in the context of Emerson's modulation of the rhythms of go-getting. For the plenitude of "chances" makes clear that one must continue to take them *in due time*. No need to unduly worry over the market structure, both "early" and "late" Emerson can agree. Simply act like a scholar and perpetually strive within it.

Coda: Alan Greenspan and the Moral of Tsunamis

From the Panic of 1837 to the Civil War, Emerson's style of observing financial vicissitudes as an opportunity for moral, not structural, reform intensified. So, *The Conduct of Life* (1860) sheds his initial bashfulness to "teach the finite its master" (his determined words from May 1837) and wholly embraces political economy as something that "is as good a book wherein to read the life of man . . . as any Bible which has come down to us" (CW, 6:54). Indeed, in the essay "Wealth" from *The Conduct of Life*, he discusses money's symbolical character as the "representative" vehicle *par excellence*. "Money is representative," he writes, "and follows the nature and fortunes of the owner. The coin is a delicate meter of civil, social and moral changes" (CW, 6:54). Once again drawing attention to the rate of money circulation, he further adds that the "clerk's [dollar] is light and nimble; leaps out of his pocket . . . but still more curious is its susceptibility to metaphysical changes—It is the finest barometer of social storms, and announces revolutions" (CW, 6:54). No longer needing to read market swings belatedly—to understand an earthquake the "morning after"—Emerson came to see the market as tracking, even anticipating, metaphysical changes in real time.

This account of the ups and downs of the market and their relation to an individual situated therein would endure, even if it seems opposed to the financial reading practices that were normalized in the late nineteenth century during the Gilded Age and Progressive Era. And yet Emerson's approach to unrest has been as influential as those postbellum practices Peter Knight historicizes as omnipresent in the current financial and popular media.[59] Whereas most readers today would recognize the genre of the "market report" (one of Knight's key discursive formations from the late nineteenth century) as grounded in technical analysis, Emerson's idealism continues to resonate, as Americans construe crisis not just as inevitable, but as an opportunity patiently to seize success from failure.

The naturalization of sudden macroeconomic swings has been a constitutive—and consistent—feature of this rhetorical tack. Case in point is the former central banker of the United States, Alan Greenspan, who testified to the US House of Representatives Committee on Oversight and Governmental Reform in October 2008 in response to the global financial meltdown of 2007–8. Referring to a historic decline in credit-based assets and sounding rather like Emerson from May 1837, Greenspan declares: "We are in the midst of a once in a century credit tsunami."⁶⁰ It is a tsunami, of course, that does not lead one to reimagine social relations. Rather, the mystifying shift from the economic to the natural register in Greenspan's response is meant to narrativize a return to the profit imperative of capitalist societies after the storm. The tsunami, hence, is a kind of plot device, as it disrupts an ugly routine of basing financial wealth on so-called toxic assets (underwater home mortgages), only to demand, more urgently, that market agents resume normal business operations. In addition to this social effect, though, the figure of the tsunami lets Greenspan communicate how unexpected the 2008 credit crisis was even to *the* reader of the global market—Alan Greenspan. As if he is still shocked by the sudden demise of seemingly rock-solid instruments like mortgage-backed securities, he tells the US House of Representatives Committee on Oversight and Government Reform, the Great Recession left "those of us who have looked to the self-interest of lending institutions to protect shareholders' equity, myself especially . . . in a state of shocked disbelief."⁶¹ Despite *already* knowing geology, Greenspan missed a tsunami!

Part of what "shocked" the central banker was the illegibility of asset prices. Normally, these data would tell a man like Greenspan all he needed to know—like Emerson's coin above, risk would already be accounted for in efficient lists of current prices. What happened that such figures no longer boasted the "representative" value Emerson ascribes to it in "Wealth"? Asset prices were more like the nature Emerson worries about in "Experience" (1844), "scene-painting and counterfeit" and "teach[ing] me nothing, nor carry[ing] me one step into real nature" (*CW*, 3:29). Thus, for Greenspan, "It was the failure to properly price such risky assets that precipitated the crisis." With market values for securities—supposedly backed by pools of sound mortgages—illegible and artificially buoyed by the "rosy ratings" of the "credit agencies," a "period of euphoria" trumped the science of economics.⁶² Dispassionate business realism was no match for the romance of trade. This is "reality . . . with a vengeance," as Greenspan would write in retrospect.⁶³

In the context of 2008, Greenspan had technical ideas about how to move from crisis to prosperity. But what might allow the story of the tsunami to take the generic shape of a comedy, and not a tragedy, was to grasp it as but one event in a series over time. And here, in his memoir *The Age of Turbulence: Adventures in a New World* (2008), is where we see Emerson's needling of the merchant—for mistaking a momentary state for an eternal one—

dovetail with Greenspan's tale of success. For the central banker, the long-term questions were: How to "return to stability"—to a "more sustainable" period of business activity?[64] How to restore the market to legibility? How, in other words, to resume reading the economy's symbolical character so as to enable the drama of capitalist identity? To face down the "calamity," one could not just see what was in front of them, but instead had to draw on the full range of their experiences over time. "Having been in similar situations myself over the past quarter century," he writes, "I know that judging the balance of risks in such complex circumstances with little time for thoughtful analysis or deliberation is a singularly intense experience."[65] This passage suggests that Greenspan had grown accustomed to "tsunamis," as he construes a global meltdown—a mass failure event that surely would have grabbed the attention even of the early American political economist Daniel Raymond (see Introduction)—as just another opportunity to succeed! Speaking to Congress, the Fed Chairman assures the committee, "This crisis will pass, and America will reemerge with a far sounder financial system."[66] Here, Greenspan evinces what Lauren Berlant might call a "technology of patience," which (in this case) asks the majority of Americans to bravely brace for economic immiseration because it will be over soon enough.[67] It is a lesson he might well have learned from Emerson. For like a seed into a warehouse, crisis gives way—slowly, inevitably, naturally—to hope, then ambition, then identity, and then profit.[68]

CHAPTER FOUR

Hawthorne's Soft Ambition, Melville's Bright Future, and Fern's Repeated Failures

> And if it be said, that continual success is a proof that a man wisely knows his powers—it is only to be added that, in that case, he knows them to be small.
>
> —HERMAN MELVILLE, "Hawthorne and His Mosses," 1850

As we have seen in the first three chapters, Cooper, Irving, Sedgwick, and Emerson, respectively, sought in failure the germs of success. For Herman Melville, success could just as easily yield failure.[1] And with the literary model of Washington Irving in mind, in his 1850 review of Nathaniel Hawthorne's *Mosses from an Old Manse* (1846), Melville looks askance at seemingly successful writing that evinces a "studied avoidance of all topics but smooth ones."[2] For Melville, midcentury readers would be wrong to equate Hawthorne and Irving, the latter of whose "continual success" registers as paltry precisely because of its consistency. What seem like Irvingesque "soft ravishments" in Hawthorne's writing are thus misleading—its "great beauty," rather, "is but the product of [his mind's] strength."[3] Essential to grasping Hawthorne's work, here, is the embrace of difficulty, a point that leads Melville to generalize about success and failure. "But it is better to fail in originality" he writes, "than to succeed in imitation. He who has never failed somewhere, that man cannot be great. Failure is the true test of greatness."[4]

Melville cites no explicit commercial context in this paean to failure. For Ellen Weinauer, however, "Hawthorne and His Mosses" is utterly about economy—in particular, "the vexed link between authorial identity and the discourse of property that operated in antebellum culture as a whole."[5] The text, indeed, reveals the extent of Melville's inability to sever ties with a proprietary model of "literary ownership."[6] If he initially wants "to argue against such proprietary models of 'literary individualism,'" he concludes that "the notion of shared genius is as threatening as it is enabling, for it demands a renunciation of boundaries, of the very proprietary impulse upon which the Lockean liberal subject is based."[7] Like Whitman in the late 1800s, then, Melville ennobles failure by sidestepping its link to capitalist structures of subjectivity. But in landing on the importance of invidious comparisons for identifying "true" success, he cannot dispense with a "proprietary impulse" after all.

"Hawthorne and His Mosses" is thus a kind of failure—a familiar one to us by now. Deciding against what we have heard the historian Block term the "renunciation of boundaries" and instead endorsing individual risk-taking as the path to an identity, Melville's essay repeats the era's narratives of reversal. What is reversed, here, is the total aestheticization of the categories of capitalist selves, failure and success, that "Hawthorne and His Mosses" wanted to put forth. (The ideology of achieved identity is tenacious.) For the present chapter, this inability to relinquish go-aheadism indicates, rather than diminishes, Hawthorne and Melville's—and, in a coda, Fanny Fern's—sustained interest in "the secular forms of spirit, subjectivity, and emotional relations" that enable capitalist subjects to reproduce themselves.[8]

These are Joel Pfister's words for what he invokes as the antebellum era's "soft capitalism."[9] And what Melville downplays as Hawthorne's "soft ravishments" in his supposedly quiet (and allegedly neglected) early tales actually critique the dramas of capitalist self-making. If Melville (as well as Hawthorne and Fern) "saw no way out of the dynamics of the market," that fact also invites us to see the extent to which they reflexively approached those dynamics through the lens of capitalist personhood.[10] Whether in texts that are explicitly about enterprise (like Melville's "The Happy Failure" [1854], *The Confidence-Man* [1857], Hawthorne's "Mr. Higginbotham's Catastrophe" [1834], and Fern's *Ruth Hall* [1855]) or not (like Hawthorne's "The Ambitious Guest" [1835]), these writers imagine self-making to imply risk-taking within the unavoidable institutional context of the market. And drawing attention to the "soft" underpinnings of capitalist identities, such texts reveal mid-nineteenth-century writing's preoccupation with market unrest as a premise not just for constituting the self, but for unmaking it as well.[11]

The Ambition of the *Twice-Told Tales*

Hawthorne's *The House of the Seven Gables* (1851), as I argued in the Introduction, is a romance intrigued by capitalist identities. This is true of Holgrave and Phoebe, but does this approach hold for "poor Clifford," a comparatively "inert" character seemingly far removed from go-ahead dictates as well? (*HSG*, 157). Addressing this "poor" man, the narrator apostrophizes, "You are partly crazy and partly imbecile; a ruin, a failure, as almost everybody is—though some in less degree, or less perceptibly, than their fellows" (*HSG*, 157–58). Here, Hawthorne seems to imagine failure as an "almost" universal condition, but he qualifies this statement by placing it on a sliding scale. (One can fail less than someone else!) And yet, importantly, this definitional quandary does not preclude Clifford from having to strive. It might be true, the *Gables* narrator continues, "fate has no happiness in store for" Clifford, but that simply means that he must find something like happiness nevertheless. For "why not?"—"If not the thing itself, it is marvelously like [happiness], and the more so for that ethereal and intangible quality which causes it all to vanish at too close an introspection. Take it, therefore, while you may. Murmur not,—question not,—but make the most of it!" (*HSG*, 158).

The narrator's imperative mood here ("take it, therefore, while you may"; "make the most of it!") illustrates that for Hawthorne personal identity at the midcentury was contingently constructed through apparently voluntary risk-taking that was in fact compulsory. This is the case whether one is situated in an explicit financial context, like Holgrave and Phoebe, or not. In 1821, however, it was something Hawthorne, then a college student, strenuously wanted to avoid. Facing a crisis of vocation, he took momentary solace in a world without necessity. Or, as he put in a letter to his mother, he wanted to "to live without a profession."[12] Here, Hawthorne longs for a release from a market society and its institutions, a yearning that Block documents as the preface to a narrative of return. And, with this insight in mind, the first part of this chapter shows that Hawthorne did not just return from this fantasy of no "profession" in his personal life, but contributed in his writing to this "larger story of the consolidation of a novel society of individuals" enmeshed in commercial relations.[13]

An actual Hawthorne preface from 1851 elucidates the extent of this reversal from the dream of freedom to the reality of an identity linked to enterprise. I am thinking of that year's new edition of *Twice-Told Tales* issued by Ticknor and Fields, which followed the publication of the first volume in 1837 and the second one in 1842. Written by Hawthorne while he finished *The House of the Seven Gables*, this preface, which is replete with direct references to ambition, success, and failure, has received considerable critical attention. His presentation of himself, "the author," as "for a good many years, the obscurest man of letters in America" has been especially noteworthy.[14] Some literary scholars have wanted to read his text "as a candid explanation of the motive for his seclusion, and as an accurate account of his early reception," which was based (in his estimation) on the publication of minor tales in newspapers, magazines, and gift books.[15] These readers take at face value, in other words, the ambition of his preface. As Meredith McGill puts it, "If Hawthorne can succeed in identifying this fiction with the admittedly distended, but suddenly remote period of his minority, this minor fiction can be superseded and redeemed by the success of his later work"—those very romances he produced in a three-year burst of creativity in the early 1850s.[16] With her perceptive account of the field's "tendency . . . to trade on Hawthorne's investment in obscurity," McGill intervenes to consider Hawthorne's relation to the shifting midcentury literary marketplace, which this "fiction of obscurity," well, obscures.[17] As she writes, the preface is "one of the means by which Hawthorne, who is thoroughly, and in many ways successfully embedded in the literary marketplace, *renegotiates* a relation to the reading public."[18]

I, too, turn to *Twice-Told Tales* as a site of cultural renegotiation. Where McGill does so to understand the evolution of the literary marketplace, an "exhilarating and frightening" space "in which it can make forms of literary value both appear and disappear," I consider how Hawthorne textualizes the equal volatility of capitalist selfhood.[19] Tapping into the go-ahead discourse, Hawthorne understands that individual success requires the possibility of failure for legibility. But crucially, he wants to challenge the notion that an individual can predict these outcomes. Acknowledging in his preface the authority of go-aheadism, he gently chides his former self for lacking ambition. In fact, "if the Author had ever been greatly tormented by literary ambition, (which he does not remember or believe to have been the case,) it must have perished beyond resuscitation, in the dearth of nutriment" (*TT*, 4). He doubly denies ambition—he either never felt it or cannot remember feeling it. But what is more interesting for Hawthorne is that even without this grasping affect, the tales could still succeed. Indeed, those earlier volumes won some "success"—"occasionally" and "unexpect[edly]"—within the literary marketplace (*TT*, 6, 5).

In the previous chapter, we saw Emerson approach success as the individual's ability to draw a new circle around a seeming failure. Hawthorne thus recasts the concepts of ambition, failure, and success *not* by removing them from the market, but by wondering to what extent they can be linked reliably to individual exertion therein.[20] A simultaneous acceptance and renunciation of go-aheadism, Hawthorne's work acknowledges the possibility of the "world finding him out and calling him forth."[21] His performative passivity emerges as an alternative form of psychological management within nineteenth-century US commercial culture. In his phrase from the 1851 preface, he seeks to reconcile "the long run" with the reality of constant shock experiences to weaken the market's control over one's identity (*TT*, 3). Because success in the forms of "praise" and "support" can be "unexpected," one must not hope for particular outcomes. *Twice-Told Tales* thus grapples with the conundrum of striving without preconditions.

What I want to call this soft ambition repudiates those "stern and black-browed" Puritan ancestors who would have dismissed Hawthorne in the nineteenth century as "an idler."[22] It does so by pointing out one problem with having an "aim." As Hawthorne writes in "The Custom-House" (1850), the prefatory essay to *The Scarlet Letter* (1850): "No aim, that I have cherished would they recognize as laudable; no success of mine—if my life, beyond its domestic scope, had ever been brightened by success—would they deem otherwise than worthless, if not positively disgraceful. 'What is he?' murmurs one gray shadow of my forefathers to the other. 'A writer of story-books! What kind of a business in life . . . may that be?'"[23] The issue with linking one's identity to such goals for "success" is that they are not guaranteed to be seen as "laudable." What can feel like serious "business" to one person can just as easily be scorned ("deem otherwise than worthless, if not positively disgraceful") by others. If Hawthorne here perceives the ideology of achieved identity as inflexible, he might have seen it to extend from the Puritan errand to his present. And the *New-England Magazine*, a conservative Boston-based newspaper to which Hawthorne frequently contributed stories in the early 1830s, in a piece called "Hints to Young Ambition," describes the "eagerness, with which . . . youths strive to break through the barriers."[24] Likewise employing the term "idle" and meditating on succession—those who *succeed* others—another piece from the magazine takes the capitalist profit imperative and its attendant psychology as givens. They write, "Here, we all work . . . Nearly all must work or want; and they who need not to work, do work, to become richer and leave more for their executors to divide—or, because if they are idle, they can find none to keep them in countenance or in amusement."[25] Surrounded by a system of "*active usefulness*" that is naturalized as nonnegotiable and as transhistorical, Hawthorne wants to reevaluate the very terms that frame the value of an aim.[26]

Such is Hawthorne's interest in weakening the ties between self and market that he even refuses to cite the whirl of business as the sole excuse for the commercial failure of *Twice-Told Tales*. After all, he could have used the 1837 financial crisis to explain away his book's sluggish sales. In a letter to his Bowdoin College classmate, the popular American poet Henry Wadsworth Longfellow, two months after the first volume's publication, he writes, "When I last heard from the publishers [Goodrich] . . . the book was doing pretty well. . . . I suppose, however, these awful times have now stopped the sale" (*TT*, 506). Yet even in discussing the "awful times," Hawthorne denies a strong relation to the market and would write subsequently to Longfellow about his "literary efforts": "They would have been better, I trust, if written under more favorable circumstances. I have had no external excitement—no consciousness that the public would like what I wrote, nor much hope nor a very passionate desire that they should do so" (*TT*, 516). For early analysts of business fluctuations, unbridled enthusiasm—an unchecked "spirit of enterprise and production," as the New England political economist Willard Phillips put it in 1828—could explain market ups and downs.[27] But Hawthorne avoids reducing success or failure to a single "external excitement." If such outcomes cannot be predicted, neither can they be confidently reconstructed. And, given this difficulty, Hawthorne does not instantiate any final relation between success and intention that might or might not be frustrated. Not wanting to strongly correlate outside events like financial panics and interior states ("passionate desire"), he takes subtle pleasure in the fact that paths to success and failure are much more difficult to map than they seem.

This psychological approach manifests in the "twice-told tales." I single out two here for analysis, "The Ambitious Guest" and "Mr. Higginbotham's Catastrophe." Not typical magnets of Hawthorne scholarship, they suggest themselves for my study because they at once define and reveal the limits of this view of capitalist identity.[28] Indeed, "The Ambitious Guest" evinces a primacy of the unexpected in Hawthorne's response to go-aheadism. First appearing in an 1835 issue of the *New-England Magazine* and subsequently included in the 1842 edition of *Twice-Told Tales*, it reworks the true story from 1820 of a deadly avalanche in the White Mountains. Although not explicitly about commerce, the tale quietly weaves the market into its narrative fabric, as it focuses on a family that runs a modest inn, which benefits from its location on a stagecoach route—a "great artery, through which the life-blood of internal commerce is continually throbbing" (*TT*, 325). Nestled in the "romantic pass of the Notch," the family's "cottage" is in constant peril, with the "old Mountain" occasionally hurtling rocks toward it "for fear we should forget him" (*TT*, 326). On the evening of the story's setting, a young man crosses "the very threshold of their romantic and dangerous abode," and we learn that the "secret of the young man's character was, a high and abstracted ambition" (*TT*, 327). Where the setting seems to invite meditations on human frailty amid this natural sublime, the young man assumes total control over his life course. Imagining future success as a necessity, his "yearning desire had been transformed to hope; and hope, long cherished, had become like certainty, that, obscurely as he journeyed now, a glory was to beam on all his path-way" (TT, 328). "I cannot die," he avers, "till I have achieved my destiny" (TT, 328).

Hawthorne uses this character's frank disclosure of ambition to illustrate how contagious it is. In response to the guest's effusions, formerly content to serve the great flow of commerce rather than control it, the inn's sturdy proprietor ponders an alternative lifepath for himself. He narrates his own ambition in which he figures as the owner of a "good farm" who "should want to stand well with my neighbors, and be called Squire, and sent to General Court, for a term or two" (TT, 329). Furtively listening to the guest's discourse, even the children "all seemed to have caught the infection from the fireside circle, and were outvying each other, in wild wishes, and childish projects of what they would do, when they came to be men and women" (TT, 330). And when what the matriarch of the family terms "wishing and planning" seems to come to a halt as the avalanche—"The Slide! The Slide!"—courses down the mountain, it gives rise to more planning yet. "The victims rushed from their cottage," we learn, "and sought refuge in what they deemed a safer spot—where, in contemplation of such an emergency, a sort of barrier had been reared" (TT, 333). But this contingency scheme—the product not of "childish" but deliberate "projects"—goes awry: "Alas! they had quitted their security, and fled right into the pathway of destruction" (TT, 333). In a "cataract of ruin," the torrent of snow "annihilated everything in its dreadful course" (TT, 333).

This ending makes it tempting to read "The Ambitious Guest" as a parable about the dangers of market ambition. It perhaps illustrates how the "pathway[s]" that a character like Cooper's Harvey Birch creates facilitate traffic not just in goods and services, but also the (highly contagious) affects sustaining the protocols of capitalist selfhood. Or perhaps the point is that these conventions, which through the vector of the hopeful young man are reproduced in old men, women, and children, are but laughable in the face of nature's indifference. But what seems equally possible is that "The Ambitious Guest" presents a powerful fantasy about *not* achieving a self via go-aheadism. The locals were able to recover and commemorate the stricken family, but the young man's "death and his existence" are uncertain. An obverse of Holgrave in *The House of the Seven Gables*, indeed, the "stranger-youth" is "utterly unknown; his history, his way of life, his plans, a mystery never to be solved" (TT, 333). Even his death amid this "catastrophe" is "equally a doubt!" (TT, 333) From this perspective, then, the avalanche liberates the young man from the strictures of capitalist personhood by preventing him from cashing his ambition in for an identity—in death, he neither succeeds nor fails, his identity deferred. The "ambitious guest" remains, forever, just that.

If "The Ambitious Guest" delays the outcome of success or failure—if it prolongs, indefinitely, a life without market compulsion—"Mr. Higginbotham's Catastrophe," also a tale first told in the *New-England Magazine*, complicates this outlook by exploring a near catastrophe that ends in a normative (business) success. The tale's plot follows Dominicus Pike, "a young fellow, a tobacco-peddler by trade" (*TT*, 106). Like Birch in *The Spy*, Pike traffics in information, just as much in wares. "Inquisitive, and something of a tattler, always itching to hear the news and anxious to tell it again," Pike learns of the murder of "Old Mr. Higginbotham," a well-propertied but stingy merchant, "whom he had known in the way of trade" (*TT*, 106, 108). A major theme of the story is how this gossip defies efforts to authenticate it. And whether true or false, the story of Mr. Higginbotham's supposed death grows to meet the demands of the crowds Pike encounters. When, to his chagrin and near ruin, this gossip is twice debunked, Pike decides to settle the matter once and for all. He heads to Kimballton and finally meets Higginbotham just as the merchant is about to be murdered. Pike thereby solves "the riddle"— the "simple machinery by which this 'coming event' was made to 'cast its shadow before'": "Three men had plotted the robbery and murder of Mr. Higginbotham; two of them, successively lost courage and fled, each delaying the crime one night by their disappearance; the third was in the act of perpetration, when a champion, blindly obeying the call of fate, like the heroes of old romance, appeared in the person of Dominicus Pike" (*TT*, 119–20). Taken in "high favor" by the wealthy Higginbotham for his valor, Pike becomes "like the hero of old romance" and, in "blind" adherence to "fate," stands to inherit Higginbotham's wealth. No longer having to sell cigars, he will now own the means of production; as we learn from the narrator in the end, Pike "established a large tobacco manufactory in my native village" (*TT*, 120).

This overview of "Mr. Higginbotham's Catastrophe" points to multiple anxiety-inducing contexts that impinge on the story, including the evolving distinctions between decentralized and centralized markets, old and new media, gossip and literature.[29] But if, as Michael C. Cohen has argued, "Mr. Higginbotham's Catastrophe" is a "primer on antebellum anxieties," it questions, more specifically, the point of anxiety in a commercial society in the first place.[30] For the tale is obsessed with the ceaseless agitation that is a presumed affect of people on the make. It is not just that Pike is "always itching to hear the news, and anxious to tell it again" while traveling from town to town, but also that stories "ran through the town like fire" and the citizens of Parker's Falls "rush into the street" (*TT*, 112). Anxiety, expressed by the townspeople in a "terrible loquacity," is omnipresent to the point of being overwhelming (*TT*, 113).

Mr. Higginbotham, to the contrary, is a New England industrialist whose "character and habits of life" are regular and not "rushed." They might not be morally estimable habits, as the story implies that his business ethics are akin to those of a greedy miser ("he was a crusty fellow, as close as a vice" [*TT*, 109]). But they have enriched him. The problem is that these habits cut two ways—if they have allowed him to thrive materially, they also seem to subject him to mortal danger. We hear, for example, "from a former clerk of his [who] testified that the old gentleman was accustomed to return home through the orchard, about night-fall, with the money and valuable papers of the store in his pocket" (*TT*, 108). We see the same scenario repeated at the societal level, since Higginbotham's successes are also those of the village. He employs his capital in the region, thereby helping sustain "the shopkeepers, the millmen, and the factory girls" (*TT*, 114). The "willful falsehood" of his death, as his lawyer puts it, thus threatens "Mr. Higginbotham's credit," an instance that "has excited this singular uproar" (*TT*, 113). If his business acuity has contributed to the larger economy, it also subjects the townspeople, enmeshed in Higginbotham's web of credits and debts, to economic hardship too.

The extent of anxiety in this story thus might make it attractive to economically inflected Americanist criticism (see Introduction). The fact that nearly everyone in the story experiences anxiety on his behalf makes it even more significant that Higginbotham is himself exempt from such concern. To save him, Pike "rushed forward" to Kimballton, "blindly obeying the call of fate" (*TT*, 119–20). But we never see Higginbotham sweat. Nor, in fact, do we hear him utter a single word. By story's end, his "credit" remains intact, his property in place, his factory clear of any troubling fluctuations in supply and demand. Absolutely unbothered by anxiety, in other words, he is "allow[ed]" to reproduce the status quo for the next generation. Accordingly, he "settled his whole property on [Pike and his niece's] children, allowing themselves the interest" (*TT*, 120).

That Hawthorne sees no need to sacrifice the capitalist Higginbotham in the prime of his life, as he would do in the later romance with Jaffrey Pyncheon, suggests the strength of the return narrative for Hawthorne even in the mid-1830s. Saved from a would-be death, Higginbotham's legacy is still more secure by story's end, whether he itched for success—or not. But it is

Pike's own ending in which Hawthorne ultimately questions the ability to liberate oneself from market affects. In his preferred itinerance at the beginning of the story, Pike strengthens the ties that bind together developing markets through commerce and, it seems, the exchange of anxieties. This lack of satisfaction brought some pleasure—his "always itching" after the next piece of gossip propelled him forward. But this ceaseless feeling is itself stalled, and, in the final sentence of the story already cited above, we learn that Pike "established a large tobacco manufactory in my native village" (*TT*, 120). Perhaps it is the case that he will sell his own cigars now on the road, but, really, he is positioned to become the next Mr. Higginbotham—treading the same path between work and home, carrying money and receipts, annoying his clerks, and subjecting the self, and the town's economy, to a catastrophe that ends up not so catastrophically. If Hawthorne's *Twice-Told Tales* thus explains how the fantasy of a vocationless life succumbs to the compulsion of the market, it also shows how the market can interrupt one's aimless but pleasurable avocation. Sometimes college graduates must get a job; sometimes free-ranging tattlers end up predictable business executives. In a word from "Mr. Higginbotham's Catastrophe," this, alas, is "fate."

China Aster's Bright Future

Skepticism over the identity protocols of midcentury capitalism deepens in the fiction of Hawthorne's one-time friend, Herman Melville. The latter's well-known "Bartleby, the Scrivener: A Tale of Wall Street" (1853) seems equally aware of the business elite's comparative lack of anxiety over security. Indeed, with the tale's narrator, Melville shows the ease with which such a figure could presume to deny commercial fluctuations. A proprietor of a Wall Street law firm, the narrator strolls the easy path in life and, at the story's outset, recalls being awarded the enviable position of "Master in Chancery." The "good old office" was useful, after all, since "it was not very arduous . . . but pleasantly remunerative."[31] Because this self-identified "unambitious lawyer" had mistaken the contingent rewards of this office as necessary, he warms at the memory of "the sudden and violent abrogation of the office of Master in Chancery, by the new Constitution"; he deems it "a [damned] premature act, inasmuch as I had counted upon a life lease of the profits whereas I only received those of a few short years!"[32] Becoming uncharacteristically "rash," the narrator deplores the unseating of his expectation for unceasing prosperity.[33] Although Hawthorne's narrator in "The

Ambitious Guest" cultivated an orientation toward the unexpected before the slide, Melville's representative of the managerial class can muster no such equipoise. For the Wall Street lawyer, the unexpected is something that happens to others, not to people like him who (he likes to imagine) control their financial fate.

This scene in "Bartleby" evinces Melville's critique of go-aheadism as reproducing the status quo of midcentury US commercial culture. According to its social dicta, one should seek to scratch the itch of ambition as a spur to success, rather than complain about the loss of passive income. I will say more about "Bartleby" in this book's Epilogue; for now, I will note that the story's interest in laws that are applied unevenly across classes of people in the United States also appears in comparatively lesser studied texts, including the diptychs "Poor Man's Pudding and Rich Man's Crumbs" (1854) and "The Paradise of Bachelors and the Tartarus of Maids" (1855), which further explore economic themes of income inequality, industrialization, and globalization. Written anonymously for magazines, these pieces helped Melville earn an income even as his value suffered in the literary marketplace after the failure of his novel *Pierre* in 1852. But a comparatively infrequently studied text, "The Happy Failure: A Story of the River Hudson," published in *Harper's New Monthly Magazine* in 1854, also critiques go-aheadism, but from the perspective of individual identity, rather than systemic class oppression. Flagging a key term of the go-ahead United States, failure, the tale further registers the biting criticisms of the psychological underpinnings of the antebellum economy.

Melville's narrator of this short tale is the nephew of a local "projector" in upstate New York. Through his outlook, we learn of a new invention, the "Great Hydraulic-Hydrostatic Apparatus," to be used "for draining swamps and marshes, and converting them, at the rate of one acre the hour, into fields more fertile than those of the Genesee."[34] The uncle's attitude toward his invention recalls the outlook of Hawthorne's ambitious guest, as the inventor anticipates "far future days" when his machine will resonate with "your children, and your children's children."[35] His nephew stokes this fire by avowing "if you do but succeed (as I know you will), you will earn the glory denied to a Roman emperor."[36] The narrator thus agrees with his uncle's rosy outlook and casts an individual economic innovation as a world historical event. His point is to activate the era's ideology of achieved identity through this if-then statement—he makes clear, thereby, that the uncle will have "earn[ed]" an exalted success by his own efforts.

As its plot evolves, the tale's chief interest, though, is to probe how capitalist selfhood can withstand actual failure considering this projected success. Sounding rather like Emerson in his contemplation of the scholar's office (see chapter 3), the inventor claims, "*this* is the hour which for ten long years has, in the prospect, sustained me through all my pains-taking obscurity."[37] But what to do when such little regarded efforts amount to nothing? What happens, in other words, when the invention fails? The answer, it seems, is to be thankful for failure. "It was horrible at first," the projector declares, "but I'm glad I've failed. Praise be to God for the failure!"[38] As we saw in chapter 2, Block describes the era's secularization of personal discipline in the service of bolstering the compulsory search for capitalist profits. Here, Melville's narrator nearly deifies the thwarting of those protocols, thankful for the "peace" that will ensue.[39] Failure is indeed a quasi-religious experience that leaves the inventor's "face kindled with a strange, rapt earnestness."[40] As the narrator undergoes this conversion, the story thus invites us to read the failure of the invention as liberation from the identity imperatives of the market. This leaves the narrator "content" and "peaceful" for the rest of his days, and on his deathbed, he clings to this mantra of seeing failure as a blessing from God.[41]

This moment seems to resonate with "The Ambitious Guest" and its complete annihilation of the striving subject as an imaginary solution to the ideology of achieved identity. But, like "Mr. Higginbotham's Catastrophe," Melville's tale charts its own narrative of reversal, and it concludes that there is no escaping the business protocols of a capitalized self. For in response to the uncle's charge to "invent" happiness and renounce ambition, the nephew stands mute: "I said nothing."[42] Either unwilling or unable to speak, the narrator decides against decoupling a projection of the future with individual aspiration. What is more telling about the mandate to strive is how the narrator resolves that failure can even be rerouted toward success. Where the narrator praises the failed machine as God's intervention, the nephew sees it as scrap material to be exchanged for "tobacco-money."[43] Perhaps weighed down by the thought of posterity ("children's children," we heard the inventor say), the nephew cannot forsake future success. He cannot imagine a future, in other words, in which the compulsion toward ambition does not exist, in which it does not move him to want something else at some later time. The title "The Happy Failure" almost implies the diptych form Melville employed in his other midcentury tales. As we have seen in his review essay "Hawthorne and His Mosses," indeed, he had no trouble imagining something like a "sad success." Whether a happy failure or a sad success, though, the point would remain the same: liberation from the profit imperative and its personality practices was unlikely.

Melville might have especially felt this way in the 1850s. Privately indebted to a friend and over-mortgaged on his Massachusetts farm, Arrowhead, he had reason to question the utility of ambition as many Americans pushed upward and onward during a prosperous era in the US economy.[44] "The period from 1850 to 1856," one twentieth-century economic historian explains in a passage I quote in part in the Introduction, "was one of unbroken prosperity. Almost any set of statistics shows the remarkable growth of the United States and supports the high hopes of 1850."[45] But what goes up must come down, and more and more Americans could sympathize with Melville's vexed finances in fall 1857 when the Ohio Life Insurance & Trust Company, a firm specializing in financing western infrastructure, land development, and agriculture, suspended payments at its New York City branch, triggering the Panic of 1857. The crisis, in the contemporary J. S. Gibbons's phrase, "struck on the public mind like a cannon shot."[46] As one writer in *Hunt's Merchants' Magazine* observed in January 1858, this seemingly isolated event eventually shook the entire financial system, as conditions evolved from "panic, senseless and causeless," to a "pressure"; "at length," it assumed "the dignity and importance of a crisis."[47] Like Hawthorne's "Slide" in "The Ambitious Guest," as Gibbons recalled, the indiscriminate panic ripped through financial markets as an "avalanche of discredit," sweeping "down merchants, bankers, moneyed corporations, and manufacturing companies, without distinction."[48]

"Without distinction," the event also led Americans to a widespread loss of confidence. As one correspondent put it pithily, "No money, no confidence, no value to anything."[49] From the perspective of Melville's final novel, *The Confidence-Man* (1857), this outcome, which awed the populace, hardly surprised. A scathing critique of the protocols that compelled people to grasp at financial success, the novel portrays a single day aboard a Mississippi River passenger steamer, the *Fidèle*, heading south from St. Louis to New Orleans. People come and go from the ship, with much of the novel focusing on a confidence-man in various guises seeking to win some token of trust from a revolving cast of passengers. For the scholar Gale Temple, "the plot of *The Confidence-Man* . . . is driven by the quest for a sense of integrated selfhood" across this chaotic social backdrop. In undertaking such a "quest," though, the novel also reveals that the labels of that selfhood rest on a speculative projection of that self into the future as a necessarily successful one.[50] As we have seen in the previous chapter, Emerson turns a forward-looking hopefulness into a virtue. But *The Confidence-Man* exposes it as a midcentury business strategy that seizes on the paradox of capitalist identity—that constant unsettlement leads to an "integrated self"—to feed, and maintain, the era's profit imperative.[51]

Working to this end, the novel makes explicit the relation between business turbulence (whether imaginary or not) and what Jeffrey Sklansky terms "a new democracy of the psyche," in which the expansion of commerce promises to "liberat[e] the self from its proprietary confines."[52] Indeed, in one early series of confidence games—first, with Henry Roberts, a "forwarding merchant, of Wheeling, Pennsylvania," and, second, with a "collegian" as his marks—the confidence-man invents business "fluctuations" (his term) to exploit them as opportunities for financial profit.[53] With Roberts, the confidence-man *cum* John Ringman uses a sinister but fictional corporate plot to secure his listener's investment. Previously, Roberts had offered charity to Ringman and, to repay his generosity, Ringman offers this "rare chance" at a quick, righteous profit. The scheme arises from a complicated scenario in which a beleaguered firm, the Black Rapids Coal Company, thwarts an internal "panic contrived by artful alarmists." Whereas the event led "some credulous stock-holders" to sell out at a loss, Black Rapids Coal Company:

> managed . . . to get into its own hands those sacrificed shares [and] resolved that, since a spurious panic must be, the panic-makers should be no gainers by it. The Company, I hear, is now ready, but not anxious, to redispose of those shares; and having obtained them at their depressed value, will now sell them at par, though, prior to the panic, they were held at a handsome figure above. . . . For, the panic subsiding more and more every day, it will be daily be seen how it originated; confidence will be more than restored; there will be a reaction; from the stock's descent its rise will be higher than from no fall, the holders trusting themselves to fear no second fate. (*CM*, 30)

As one popular insider account of Wall Street put it in 1840, a panic has "existence without entity."[54] Here, the author of *A Week in Wall Street, by One Who Knows*, Frederick Jackson, illustrates a conventional view of panics as purely psychological phenomena, which possess "the power of motion and flight exceeding that of all cognoscible beings."[55] Panics can be contrived by scoundrels, Jackson admits, but once ignited, in an analogy that might recall Sedgwick's response to the Great Fire of 1835, "the whole nation cannot extinguish" them. It "cannot" be "[bound]," and if "it is a very good servant . . . [it] sometimes consumes those who kindle it."[56]

Soft Ambition, Bright Future, and Repeated Failures 95

But Melville's confidence-man brushes against the grain of Jackson's text. Instead, Ringman peddles a fantasy of control over this ungovernable "entity." Indeed, the fictional firm in question enjoys a perspective with neither anxiety ("but not anxious") nor "fear." It has, it seems, this particular panic in a bind. With this tale of (imagined) comeuppance, the confidence-man thus leans on the listener's desire to actuate the self through controlled dealings within the potentially bewildering financial structure. This desire leads the merchant Roberts to "forget" himself by dreaming of a new one remade through financial investment (CM, 31). As an engaged merchant, he deludes himself that "he had heard of the company, and heard well of it, but was ignorant that there had latterly been fluctuations" (CM, 30). The uncritical acceptance of business turbulence as the premise of self-making seals his fate—it allows, ironically, the careful businessman on the make to become an easy mark. "He added that he was no speculator," we learn, "but in the present case he really felt something like being tempted" (CM, 31).

As Roberts is "tempted" to recast his business acuity as an eye for a sure thing, we see how the strictures of a capitalist identity are as likely to dissolve the self as they are to integrate it. A later episode involving the "collegian" and the confidence-man in his guise as the "transfer agent" of the Black Rapids Coal Company drives this point home further. It does so by illustrating how badly individuals want to believe that liberation from commerce is coextensive with mastery over it (CM, 55). I single out this scene, too, because it implicitly talks back to the Emersonian program of education for business turbulence I discuss in the previous chapter. Given that most of its loosely connected episodes emphasize optimism, confidence, and hope, other scholars have seen in *The Confidence-Man* a critique of transcendentalism, including the notion that this idealist philosophy "might redeem the developing market."[57] The confidence-man Mark Winsome, a New England philosopher in the image of Emerson, and his practical disciple Egbert, à la Thoreau, support such a reading. Less obviously, the collegian, initially taken with the pessimism of the ancient Roman scholar Tacitus, seems integral to Melville's transcendentalist exposé as well. After all, the young man mistakes philosophizing with business investing—and pays dearly for it.

The chapter in question is entitled "Two Business Men Transact a Little Business," and, like Roberts, the collegian seeks not to speculate but to "invest" (his term).[58] The young man, we learn, had overheard Ringman's tale to Roberts of the controlled panic. And the confidence-man exploits his new listener's philosophical bent to equate "the growling . . . bears" of finance who manufactured a "depression" with pessimist historians—indeed, the former are recast by the confidence-man as "gloomy philosophers of the stock market," rather than Roman history (*CM*, 56). When the collegian is presented with a chance to accrue money without risk, it turns him from a pessimist to an optimist. This paradigm shift enables him (in the confidence-man's sardonic phrase) to imagine himself "a business-man" (*CM*, 55). The newly optimistic philosopher even thinks himself equipped to comprehend a balance sheet of the Black Rapids Coal Company—a contrived report that "tells a very fine story"—which warrants his idea that an investment in the firm is a guaranteed success (*CM*, 56).

We could read this scene today as a parody of the "transferable skills" ideology that reigns in twenty-first-century higher education. The downtrodden humanities student, here, repurposes the love of the arcane into financial profit! But, for my purposes, it throws into relief Melville's apprehension of the era's financialization of the self and that self's relation to the world.[59] In fact, it is enticing to wonder if, in between his studies of Tacitus, the young student had read the New York City investor William Armstrong's *Stocks and Stock-Jobbing in Wall Street* (1848), a text that inaugurated in the United States the genre of investment advice.[60] There, Armstrong walks the reader through technical business terms such as "fluctuation," "time operations" (futures contracts), and "interest," and seeks to help readers imagine "routes to market success."[61] Whether or not this advice works, as a group of scholars working in the Economic Humanities has recently surmised, what books like Armstrong's "actually deliver are means of conjuring alternative and expanded forms of selfhood: opportunities for readers to conceive of themselves as resourceful, decisive risk-takers or possessors of privileged insights into the true nature of the forces shaping the markets."[62] Like *Stocks and Stock-Jobbing*, then, the confidence-man offers the collegian the opportunity to see himself otherwise—as one with a "privileged insight" less into the mysteries of ancient philosophy than the recondite operations of a single firm.

Melville's point is that what the confidence-man offers is the fundamental paradox of capitalist identity I have mentioned throughout this study, which Armstrong wants to naturalize—to achieve stability, the self must perpetually be in crisis.[63] We see Melville (tacitly) approach this idea in "Hawthorne and His Mosses" in the critique of "continual success." But his most potent assessment of the capitalist self as a figure that looms ever beyond one's grasp in *The Confidence-Man* is "The Story of China Aster," a parable that ruthlessly mocks this unstable model of stable selfhood earned over time. The chapter revolves around a hypothetical story told by the character Egbert (the novel's Thoreau-like "practical" disciple of Mark Winsome) to the confidence-man in the guise of the cosmopolitan; it targets a widespread willingness to "take the bright view of life" in the context of self-making (*CM*, 211). A character named Orchis, a cobbler in the frontier town of Marietta, Ohio, advocates the "bright view" of financial decision-making. Previously known as "Doleful Dumps," Orchis wins the lottery. This manifestation of the financialization of everyday life allows Orchis to frame a sudden personal transformation: "All at once," the narrator tells us, "by a capital prize in a lottery, this useful shoemaker was raised from a bench to a sofa" (*CM*, 212). The surprise of the lottery also allows Melville to show that although such "prosperity" here is contingent, Orchis equates the accident of his winning with necessary success. He henceforward endorses the view, as he argues to his friend, the chandler China Aster, that "for every one, good luck is in store" (*CM*, 209–10).

The misapprehension of winning a lottery as part and parcel of an ideology of achieved identity further propels Orchis toward financial markets. So, he encourages Aster to take $1,000 from his winnings as a loan for capital improvements to the chandlery. In doing so, Aster will turn this sum into "ten thousand, as you soon enough will" (*CM*, 209). Orchis's infelicitous capitalist induction, that his random success means that Aster's own effort will yield it too via improving his business, is a clear target for critique. But what does he do to convince the otherwise conservative China Aster to accept the loan, which eventually ushers in widespread "ruination" (*CM*, 212)? As it turns out, not much. "As destiny would have it," the same night on which Aster tried unsuccessfully to refuse the loan, he

> had a dream in which a being in the guise of a smiling angel, and holding a kind of cornucopia in her hand, hovered over him, pouring down showers of small gold dollars, thick as kernels of corn. "I am Bright Future, friend China Aster," said the angel, "and if you do what friend Orchis would have you do, just see what will come of it." With which Bright Future, with another swing of her cornucopia, poured such another shower of small gold dollars upon him, that it seemed to bank him up all round, and he waded about in it like a maltster in malt. (*CM*, 212)

China Aster's previous refusal of the loan was bolstered by his friends Old Plain Talk and Old Honesty. But the dream is too seductive of a portent and overrides these quaint voices of moderation; he "lay[s] out the money the very same day in buying a good lot of spermaceti [rather than tallow] to make candles, by which operation he counted upon turning a better penny than he ever had before in his life; in fact, this he believed would prove the foundation of that famous fortune which the angel had promised him" (CM, 213).[64] As a site of capitalist identity formation, even one's dreamscape naturalizes a financialized model, in which the striving self is consolidated through the supposed surety of commercial investment. Finally, the dream's vision of natural plenty, in which (to riff off Whitman) the self "need never be bankrupt," leads Aster to accept the loan.

We have seen versions of this outcome throughout my study, but in this case, an actual dream of escaping risk while still gleaning profits proves illusory. And Melville makes this point darkly—for Aster's decision to take on this debt is one that initiates a waterfall of more debt that ultimately destroys him. Like Roberts and the collegian, Aster misunderstands midcentury business culture's invitation to "just see what will come of it" to guarantee an outcome. For what comes of a bad debt, Aster finds out, is more bad debt that is undertaken not to nudge the self toward success, but, in desperation, to safeguard it from the snares of failure. Indeed, "he considered what he should do towards reestablishing himself" (CM, 215). Taking on additional loans from acquaintances other than Orchis, Aster walked a well-worn path in the antebellum United States. According to Edward J. Balleisen, the era's bankrupts often sought "postfailure success" in financial help offered through their personal networks.[65] That could spell trouble, though, since "even in the absence of financial pressures that arose from the interlinked obligations of personal business circles, discharged bankrupts who received substantial financial aid sometimes failed again, especially if they lacked commercial skills or embraced risky enterprises."[66] Aster belongs to this latter group. If in his imagination he had already come "in fact" to possess a fortune, by the episode's end, he is embittered, destitute—and dead (CM, 219).

To use a key term from Sedgwick's "Romance in Real Life" (see chapter 2), there appears to be no indemnity in the tale's conclusion. "Orchis never got a penny for his loan," and Aster's widow, who had used her inheritance from a wealthy uncle as security for yet another loan, is also "left penniless" (CM, 218). As a belated compensation, Aster's conservative friends try to erase the perpetual unease that led Aster to try to align his reality with his interpretation of his recurring Bright Future dream. Indeed, at the story's end, when Old Plain Talk and Old Prudence erect a tombstone on Aster's behalf, they discover in his otherwise empty purse "an epitaph, written, probably, in one of those disconsolate hours, attended with more or less mental aberration, perhaps, so frequent with him for some months prior to his end" (CM, 219–20). It reads: "FOR HE WAS RUINED BY ALLOWING HIMSELF TO BE PERSUADED,

AGAINST HIS BETTER SENSE . . . INTO AN ARDENTLY BRIGHT VIEW OF LIFE" (CM, 220). But even this final summation is a sleight of hand, as it begs the question: Persuaded by whom? Is China Aster persuaded by Orchis? By the negative example of his father, who died a failure on the western frontier? By the angel Bright Future?

Such questions are left unsettled, an indication of how Melville's novel troubles any individualist ideology of success and failure. The point is, rather, that what Aster takes as persuasion, which implies the choice (say) to accept a loan or not, is in fact a compulsion. He dreamt of liberation from the market. But that dream throws him, repeatedly, back into a vicious cycle of capitalist identity: seeking to return to a stable self that had, previously, launched itself into the market, Aster enters the market to achieve a (future) stable self.[67] That the epitaph offends the town "capitalist—one of a very cheerful turn—who had secured his loan to China Aster by the mortgage," and thus was the only one made whole, further reveals that this paradox is fundamental to the profit imperative (CM, 220). The epitaph, then, glosses over the fact that, even in midcentury Ohio, to have a "career" is impossible without commercial risk (CM, 220). This is a revealing omission, which instantiates the fact that in establishing a self worthy of a "story" (the title of chapter 40 is the only one in The Confidence-Man to contain the word), catastrophic failures are always a safe bet. That Melville here implicitly agrees with, of all writers and texts, Irving's 1840 financial history—that financial ruin yields the stuff of good stories—is just to add one more failure to The Confidence-Man's list.

THERE WOULD BE one more failure yet. In the mid-twentieth century, F. O. Matthiessen saw a discrete end in The Confidence-Man: "If not a dead-end, [it] marked at least the completion of a cycle. It added the final proof . . . that Melville's books had no market."[68] With this final full-length novel, Melville acknowledged "the completion of a cycle," and, at last, relinquished control of his ruined art. And the history of The Confidence-Man's ill-fated publication itself during the Panic of 1857 seems to take his refusal of the "ardently bright view of life" as a nourishing context for the capitalist self to its logical conclusion. Published by Dix, Edwards, and Co., a firm that dissolved on April 27, 1857, Melville's novel was purchased, along with the residue of Dix, Edwards, and Co.'s assets, by Miller and Co. When Miller and Co. in turn failed, and Melville's literary property was auctioned amid the 1857 panic, "on 19 September the plates of [The Confidence-Man and The Piazza Tales] were offered and then withdrawn (the only ones [auctioned by the firm] to receive this treatment)."⁶⁹ In fact, while "some plates went at phenomenally low prices . . . no one would risk a dollar on Melville."⁷⁰ No one indeed: not even Melville himself. Although he had a contractual right "to purchase the plates at 25 per cent of their first cost," he refused.⁷¹

So, Melville declined to believe in a necessarily prosperous future for his art. In a letter to his editor George William Curtis, he clarifies this decision: "It strikes me . . . that under the circumstances . . . [the plates] can bring but little at the Trade Sale, or any other sale. Whereas, if held on to for a while, they might be transferred to me to the common advantage of all concerned. But I do not wish to suggest anything in the way of a prompt settling up of the affairs of the late firm. Do with the plates whatever is thought best."⁷² Here, Melville brushes up against a normative market prudence, as he ponders what "might" happen were the plates "held on to for a while." But not wishing "to suggest anything in the way of a prompt settling up," he washes his hands of this "affair." Clearly conflicted, as he nevertheless communicates to Curtis two weeks later, "I will try and do something about the plates as soon as I can. Meantime if they bother you, sell them without remorse. To pot with them, & melt them down."⁷³ The words etched on *The Confidence-Man*'s plates implicated the self's constant struggle to stay afloat in the expectation of endless prosperity or, perhaps, a return to a state of prefailure. When his art seemed secure in its failure, though, Melville released it, consigning his plates to the smith's fire—to a place of no future, let alone a bright one.

Coda: *Ruth Hall*; or, The Devil's Stock

Around the time Melville renounced success through prose fiction, in Liverpool, England, the US Consul, Nathaniel Hawthorne, continued his meditation on that affect in 1855, the very year that Fanny Fern's *Ruth Hall* embraced women's go-ahead aspirations in the literary marketplace. As is well known, from the office of the consulate, Hawthorne worried to his publisher and friend William Ticknor about the "damned mob of scribbling women." What stands out to me in this familiar missive, though, is how it is shot through with the language that preoccupied his preface to *Twice-Told Tales* in 1851. Discussing financial affairs with Ticknor, including his growing comfort with "risk," Hawthorne considers the advantages of his position, which allowed him time to cultivate "the germ of a new Romance in my mind, which will be all the better for ripening slowly."⁷⁴ "Besides," he continues, "America is now wholly given over to a d—d mob of scribbling women, and

I should have no chance of success while the public is occupied with their trash—and should be ashamed of myself if I did succeed."[75] Here, Hawthorne fears his own works being squeezed out by the "100,000" copies of Maria Susanna Cummins's *Lamplighter* (1854). To this spatial language, the letter adds a temporal concern as well. His ethic of "ripening slowly" makes this point, but he also reasons that the market cannot *always* be this crowded with "trash"—something like real success will be worth the wait. The letter thus argues that the pursuit of such nobler accolades belonged to serious writers—that is, to men—over time.

In a follow-up letter to Ticknor, Hawthorne makes one exception to his prior "vituperation of female authors"—Fern's *Ruth Hall*, precisely a story of a woman who actively pursued success in response to masculine financial ruin.[76] In Hawthorne's estimation, Fern "writes as if the devil was in her"; in the terms I have proposed throughout this study, we might say she writes not just with but about ambition.[77] Indeed, although scholars of the novel have emphasized women's relation to the material conditions of literary production, the text also stresses the character Ruth Hall's embrace of go-aheadism in response to financial necessity. Hall's ascent to fame through her own exertions expresses her comfort with risk-taking in a post-failure context ushered in by her husband's demise, rather than her turn away from the vertiginous affects of capitalism. A feminine critique of the era's strictures of success that Hawthorne and Melville ironized but could not escape, *Ruth Hall* exposes any distance from the ideology of achieved identity that these and other (white) men gained as a privilege.

In some sense, *Ruth Hall*'s plot rehearses a common one for women writers in the nineteenth century who turned to the literary marketplace in response to what one historian terms "unwelcome financial exigencies in their personal lives."[78] Part of what makes this popular novel stand out for scholars is the degree to which it unapologetically embraces professional authorship as a response to such exigencies.[79] It is an anti-"The Wife." With the death of Hall's husband, Harry, *Ruth Hall* acknowledges the shock of financial ruin *within* the home instead of positing it as an unchanging bulwark against financial unrest. Finance even penetrates Harry's deathbed scene, that sacrosanct textual space of the sentimental novel. For there, the failing husband imagines "the city's whirl of business" and worries that "he had stocks to negotiate; he had notes to pay; he had dividends due."[80] And as Harry stresses over a future that he will not experience, he knows that such business concerns do not expire with his body—instead, they become Ruth Hall's problem to solve. Against the model of Irving's titular wife, poverty alters her as she becomes enmeshed in her late husband's "whirl." So, Harry Hall's death occasions a "shocking" financial crisis as the "failure of parties for whom [Harry] had become responsible" leaves "little or nothing for the widow and her children, when his affairs are settled" (RH, 67).

The man's ruin spurs Ruth Hall's achievement of an identity. And as it undercuts the tendency to disassociate women and risk-taking, Fern's novel formally emphasizes this process of identity formation, whereby Ruth Hall moves from modest to more ambitious enterprises. Initially, she "resolved" to pursue "an opportunity" (RH, 119); the narrative discourse, however, builds on this resolution, all of a sudden incorporating language about investment "capital" and, in Hall's direct discourse, queries about the "probability of success" (RH, 120).[81] The reader also finds her in new masculine settings such as "counting-room[s]"—the hostile domain of her hateful cousin, Mr. Millet (RH, 124). The repeated experience of failure in these spaces is ultimately instructive for Ruth, who learns to become a persevering businessperson. "Poor Ruth! And this was human nature," the narrator opines, "which for so many sunny years of prosperity, had turned to her only its *bright* side!" Crucially, "She was not to be discouraged" (RH, 125). Applying for a teaching position that she does not "stand as good a chance" to get, she remains resolute. Numerous studies have convincingly shown that Hall doubles down on the era's individualist ethos.[82] From my perspective, this amounts to a more stringent grasping at an identity—Hall wants to transmute "repeated failures" into constant successes (RH, 155). Aiming at a capitalist self, Hall seeks stability through constant flux.

This anticipatory ethos culminating in a "business-like" approach to the literary marketplace is literalized in the form of a specific financial investment (RH, 210). Indeed, *Ruth Hall*'s conclusion offers a striking image of the heroine's transformation into a "bank-stock holder" of the Seton Bank (RH, 269) (see fig. 4.1). Tellingly, although prompted by her mentor, John Walter, to comment on her change in circumstances from her "dismal attic one year ago" to the owner of $10,000 in securities, Hall remains silent, her "talkative" daughter Nettie instead jumping in to say, "We are proud of her." Nettie yearns to make this pride public; she wants to "tell that 'Floy' [Ruth Hall's nom de plume] is our mother" (RH, 270). Yet "mamma won't let us tell," she definitively reports, to which Mr. Walter replies: "When your mamma says *No*, there is an end to all argument" (RH, 270). The novel proliferates the discourses of (strict) motherhood and childish pride only to deepen Ruth Hall's silence toward her success. Feminist literary historians recognize this kind of non-utterance to bear out the tensions arising from the culture's

> **THE SETON BANK.**
>
> IN THE CITY OF ―――.
>
> SHARES, $100 EACH.
>
> Be it known that Mrs. Ruth Hall, of ―――, is entitled to one hundred shares of the Capital Stock of the Seton Bank, and holds the same, subject to the conditions and stipulations contained in the Articles of Association of such Institution; which shares are transferable on the Books of the Association by the said Mrs. Ruth Hall or her Attorney, on surrender of this Certificate.
>
> In witness whereof, &c., &c.
>
> CAPITAL STOCK, $2,000,000.

FIGURE 4.1 Fanny Fern's 1855 novel, *Ruth Hall*, includes an image of the (fictional) Seton Bank stock earned by the eponymous character Ruth Hall. Courtesy of Google Books.

demand that women writers separate public and private selves.[83] For Hall, though, this silence is a deferral; it is equally part of a business strategy—her writing will project her financial success into the future through "constant [self]*fashioning*" in the marketplace so as to increase her store of stock.[84]

Thus, the salient point about the novel's intervention into the gender dynamics of go-aheadism has less to do with women's ability to withstand financial instability that threatens the home. It has more to do, rather, with reinforcing a narrative of crisis, in which a commercial disturbance exists as an opportunity to remake—or, more accurately, capitalize—the self. Women can participate in economic institutions, the novel argues, insofar as they can enact the psychological habits of boom-bust capitalism that midcentury society wanted to deny them. And driving this notion home in the mid-1850s, *Ruth Hall* insists that Ruth's authorship is an act that aims to secure her future indefinitely. As Mr. Walter says in the novel's final line, "Life has much of harmony *yet* in store for you" (*RH*, 272; emphasis added). First naively drawn to the "bright view of life" and then turned toward the hard knocks of business culture, Fern is no China Aster—it is as if the brightness, emanating from her own achieved self, is here to stay.

CHAPTER FIVE
Early African American Literature and the Freedom to Fail

In *Ruth Hall*, Fanny Fern embraced a project to transform the feminine self into an agent of the market. Midcentury Black American writers, too, were drawn to the capitalist psychological model of striving for success. In doing so, though, they modified the individualist drive displayed in Fern's novel. In a recent study of early Black American print culture, Derrick R. Spires holds that many writers "reject[ed] definitions of 'citizen' based on who a person is, a preordained or predefined subject or subjectivity, in favor of definitions grounded in the active engagement in the process of creating and maintaining collectivity, whether defined as state, community, or other affiliative structure."[1] As Spires makes clear, such practices yoked individual and collective successes, but they coalesced within one "affiliative structure" in particular—the market. If this development reveals how "citizenship practices and economics were inextricably linked," it also resulted in "the kinds of fluid subjectivities best suited to navigate [uncertain economic] terrain."[2]

As we have seen throughout my study, these "fluid" forms of selfhood were presumed as necessary for pursuing success and risking failure in the antebellum United States. Further, as is well known because of the narratives of formerly enslaved people like Olaudah Equiano, Frederick Douglass, William Wells Brown, Harriet Jacobs, and others, the opportunity for African Americans to enact these protocols of the self were severely limited. From Manning Marable's perspective, though, this historical exclusion of Black people from US commercial culture is in fact a radical "integrat[ion] [of Africans Americans] . . . into the system."[3] "The system exists," he states, "not to develop but to *underdevelop Black people*."[4] For the twenty-first-century journalist, Ta-Nehisi Coates, the financial sector of the economy remains an egregious site of underdevelopment for African Americans; he deems it a key arena of "Black plunder." In the conclusion to his 2014 *Atlantic* essay, "The Case for Reparations," which looks as far back as the 1619 importations of enslaved Africans to colonial Virginia, Coates singles out the bank Wells Fargo's shepherding Black clients into "predatory loans regardless of their creditworthiness" in 2005.[5] When, in 2009, amid the subprime mortgage crisis that so astounded Federal Reserve Chairman Alan Greenspan (see chapter 3), "half the properties in Baltimore whose owners had been granted loans by Wells Fargo . . . were vacant[,] 71 percent of those properties were in predominantly Black neighborhoods."[6] Whether in post-contact North America or the neoliberal mid-Atlantic, market capitalism (in Equiano's apt phrasing from the 1700s) has "taken advantage of . . . a negro man."[7]

As this quick citation of Equiano's *Narrative* (1789) suggests, critical responses among Black American writers to racial capitalism predate what Spires calls "the market revolutions of the 1820s and 1830s."[8] Such reactions, further, were far from uniform, and tensions existed between those writers who advocated for uplift through wage labor of any kind and those who worried about the degradations of that very work. When in 1848, at the National Convention of Colored Freemen, Douglass sought to accommodate both viewpoints, he positioned his past experiences as a day laborer as "central to [his] present success."[9] In this chapter, I pursue a related but different textual phenomenon—not the recasting of the midcentury Black writer's past as "central" in the present, but the projecting of that self's future secured in advance by risk-taking: the capitalization of the Black self. Writing in the early 1840s, the French observer of US culture, Alexis de Tocqueville, noted the universality of ambition across the social ranks, but insofar as racial capitalism acknowledged Black peoples' ambition, it did so in narrow ways. As Abraham Lincoln would put it, emancipation meant "all [would] have equal privileges in the race of life, with all its desirable human aspirations."[10] All would "have an open field . . . and a fair chance for your industry, enterprise, and intelligence."[11] The shelf life of Lincoln's vision, as W. E. B. Du Bois recognized in *Black Reconstruction in America* (1935), was to be short. But that does not erase how midcentury writers identified, critiqued, and sought to alter this trajectory of underdevelopment by representing—and speculating on—Black peoples' achievements within a market bound by structures of racism.

Formerly enslaved writers accomplished this work by integrating themes of economic fluctuations, risk-taking, and business to insist on commercial activity as coextensive with (in Spires's term) "economic citizenship." So too did newspaper contributors, as I show in the case of the *Colored American*. In doing so, as we see at the outset of this chapter, writers implicitly worked against white nineteenth-century political economists like George Fitzhugh and others who refused to impute economic agency to African Americans. The rest of this chapter considers Frank J. Webb's novel, *The Garies and Their Friends* (1857). This text, published in the panic year of 1857, confronts striving in the market as essential for Black identity, while also recognizing the limits to that approach. Its ambivalence, I argue, on the one hand, targets the egregiousness of "Black plunder" in the antebellum United States; on the other, it dwells in the possibilities of struggling to achieve an identity within an economy subtended by racial violence. Webb's is a novel torn between the reality of racism and Irving's "romance of trade"—to be an agent of market culture and seek an identity through the United States' economic institutions, it concludes, is fraught but inevitable. *Garies* thus offers a powerful accounting of go-aheadism, simultaneously chronicling the violence to Black bodies, properties, and relations that upholds the profit imperative, as well as the trials and tribulations of those who strive, as Webb puts it, "at any rate."[12]

"Periodical Revulsions" and Wild Cat Banks

The renewed study of business fluctuations in the antebellum United States has prompted some historians to bring "the story of enslavement back into the center of" US financial history.[13] This ongoing scholarly project acknowledges the midcentury impulse to "talk over and over about the deep links between the Southern slave economy and the national economy."[14] Within the era's periodical culture, the discussions of such linkages were uneven. Indeed, even though the (white) antebellum business press "had little difficulty grasping slavery's capitalism," editors selectively framed enslavement's relation to events like the Panic of 1857.[15] For example, an article entitled "Lessons of the Panic," originally published in the antislavery newspaper *New York Evangelist* and reprinted by William Lloyd Garrison in the October 23, 1857 issue of the *Liberator*, lamented that "to-day is all panic and fear" and that efforts "to restore confidence" would be the "slow work of time." As a solution, the author said little about the traffic in humans, but offered instead bromides about seeking "true riches."[16]

When the abolitionist press wanted explicitly to couple slavery and market swings, it focused less on how the economy affected enslaved people than the perdurability of US institutions. Such work assumed the shapes of both gradualist and immediatist abolition. In the former case, seeking a "substantial transformation of [American] habitudes," *The National Era*, which had serialized Harriet Beecher Stowe's *Uncle Tom's Cabin* (1851), imagined US economic prosperity to eventually culminate in abolition.[17] Its writer asserts a faith in capitalist "competition" among enslavers as teleology: "In a prosperous state of things, competition obliges every owner to enhance the value of his slaves to the utmost; in doing so, he is but lifting them toward the point at which he can no longer hold them."[18] Other writers in 1857, though, would take a stronger (that is, immediatist) approach. An original column in the *Liberator* signed by a writer named Radical Abolitionist explicitly connected "The Panic and Abolitionism" and thereby acknowledged that the "money pressure and financial panic supply the all-engrossing topic of the day."[19] The author argued that, just as it was during the Panic of 1837, slavery will be "found to lie at the bottom of our financial difficulties."[20] Unlike *The National Era*'s yoking abolition to an optimistic market telos, Radical Abolitionist presumes, alternately, failures in the cotton market to be inevitable because that commodity's value relies on the "hatred of labor."[21] Adapting the jeremiad form, the writer finds that "a nation thus poisoned by contempt and hatred of labor, with a corresponding love of idleness, gambling, [and] speculation . . . *such* a nation . . . are always subject to periodical revulsions, as inevitable as they are remediless, without repentance and reformation."[22] Adding an abolitionist edge to Emerson's question in 1837, "What is the remedy?" (see chapter 3), the writer uncovers the catastrophic reality for the United States of the simultaneous practice of enslavement and the financialization of the economy.

This politico-economic debate within the abolitionist press over the relation between financial markets and slavery elides the enslaved person as a striver, a fact that is especially evident when Northern commentators framed the commercial unrest as a Southern problem.[23] From the perspective of *The National Era*'s column cited above, the Black man's ambition was a nonstarter, at least in the short run. Rather, tapping into the era's ideology of achieved identity, the writer exhorts *Southern white men* to "go ahead" to solve the problem of enslavement: "To the South," the editorialist writes, "we say . . . Go ahead; take good care of yourselves; get rich the quickest and best way you can invent." "Catch the spirit of civilized progress," he continues, and "raise yours as fast as you can to the level of Christendom's work," clearly assuming capitalist selfhood to be the sine qua non of the nation's identity protocols in spite of different specializations among regional economies.[24] In short, "principles can wait" for this civilizing work "till practice is orderly."[25] Until "another equal period" of time passes, the mandate to grasp after riches so as to abolish enslavement in the antebellum United States was the moral prerogative of white people.[26]

Southern apologists would counter this argument, which yoked financial and industrial progress to a reformed capitalist psychology, and dismiss it as mere rhetoric. Indeed, the Panic of 1857 further emboldened outlets like the New Orleans-based *DeBow's Review* to declare the solution to such convulsions to be "Southern commercial independence," rather than market-driven abolition.[27] The South did not lack ambition, this viewpoint held, but rather economic freedom from the North. "Certain it is," the editor James De Bow argued, "that at the South [the "existing pressure"] has not been felt, except through her commercial relations with the North."[28] If the South would be left *"alone,"* De Bow reasoned, "the recuperative energies of a free and industrious people, in a time of general peace, will soon begin to manifest themselves, and prosperity will resume again its empire in every section of the land."[29]

DeBow's Review was a regular venue for George Fitzhugh, the well-known Virginia planter and lawyer who outraged Northern abolitionists with his vociferous defense of chattel slavery as a superior moral institution in texts like *Sociology of the South; Or, the Failure of Free Society* (1854) and *Cannibals All!* (1857).[30] In *DeBow's*, he supplemented the speculative arguments over the South's economic future cited above with writing that used commercial volatility to adduce the weakness of Black people's economic capacity. His 1859 article "Trade and Panics" illustrates this approach. A piece that describes passengers floating "down the Mississippi" who "never were so melancholy in our life," the text blames this mood on Northern capitalist striving.[31] The barrenness of the landscape as seen from the boat results from the fact that "trade sweeps off in its current whatever the river has spared, and conveys with all the force and speed of steam, the wealth . . . of the valley"; "it is a poverty-stricken region."[32] In other words, the reader is to behold the visual evidence of the ravages born of the "worship" and "practice" of trade.[33] Go-aheadism here, branded as Northern, was simply a project of Southern impoverishment.

Fitzhugh's imagined trip down the Mississippi repeats the setting of Melville's *The Confidence-Man* (see chapter 4). But his sketch looks outward from the boat to the landscape in order to wage its argument against free trade, rather than inward to the selves — and fantasies of the self — that the market economy has wrought. In doing so, it takes refuge in one fact of the vista, which alone seems to resist the sweep of Northern commerce: "Rows of comfortable negro-cabins."[34] For Fitzhugh, these structures — and by extension those who inhabit them — are untouched by the go-ahead psychology of Northern capitalism "that makes all mankind restless, insecure, and unhappy."[35] If such values are allowed to reign, "there can be . . . no stability in men's fortunes, faith, or opinions; and hence no stability in government, nor in governmental, religious, or other institutions."[36] A society dominated by trade is thus "like the Mississippi valley": "Change rules everything, and is the only thing that never changes."[37] Whereas the "negro-cabins" represent stolidity—the endurance of Southern habits and institutions—"outbursts of trade" represent the opposite. Not stability but "panics, revulsions, and universal bankruptcies" rule the day.[38]

Fitzhugh's point about the South's superior institutions, probably willfully, misses that, as US society evolved, individual "restless[ness]" and "insecur[ity]" were constitutive features of its institutions. From the perspective of go-aheadism, to rid society of "panics, revulsions, and universal bankruptcies" would be to rid it of the very selves, Black *and* white, who comprise it. This, then, is part of the polemicizing against Northern commerce doubly by racializing capitalism. Just as much as the abolitionist discourses cited above, this typical screed against Northern trade erases Black economic agency in its meditation on the era's financial unrest. It does so, of course, by eliding African Americans' labor as a source of value, but it also links commercial volatility explicitly to "Anglo-Saxons, a restless, speculating, roving, filibustering, rapacious race."[39] Capitalist agitation is a racial but regional problem that must be solved, lest the South be ruined by it.

As Spires notes, Black American writers distanced themselves from this (racialized) "rapacious[ness]" as well.[40] But Fitzhugh's aversion to risk-based capitalism turned away from the ideology of achieved identity that African American writers and editors would view as necessary. And if they insisted on their race's economic capacity, they put forth in their own terms the idea that people had the wherewithal to participate in a market society defined by uncertainty. To this end, Samuel Cornish's *Colored American* (1837–42) illustrated the reality of Black striving within market capitalism. Founded in New York City during the panic year of 1837, the paper typically stressed more traditionally republican habits, often modeling how their readers could positively relate to commerce.[41] Previously the editor of *Freedom's Journal*, the first Black newspaper in the antebellum North, Cornish and his co-editor, John Brown Russwurm, saw a "uniform propriety of conduct" as a means to demonstrate "that we are worthy of esteem and patronage."[42] Published days before New York City banks suspended specie payments because of the Panic of 1837, the May 6, 1837 issue of the *Colored American* cautioned that in order to "assure success," African Americans must "change long-standing habits, and throw off useless practices." The "useless, vulgar, and sinful habits"—that is, the deleterious "effects of slavery"—"must be broken off." Rather, the race must adopt not only "untiring habits of industry," but also "rigidness of economy."[43]

Such republican discourse drew together important figures like Frederick Douglass and Martin R. Delany. The latter's exhortation in his book *The*

Condition, Elevation, Emigration, and Destiny of the Colored People of the United States (1852) for African Americans "to understand the political economy and domestic policy of nations" speaks to this point.⁴⁴ Such a broad conversation within print culture, as Erica L. Ball has established, would show aspiring Black readers "how to acquire and maintain the precise manners, moral habits, and restrained, virtuous character that would help them to rise in status."⁴⁵ As such, it included typical middle-class paeans to what the New England abolitionist Hosea Easton would term in 1837 a "most rigid economy."⁴⁶ These writings expanded bourgeois individualism, linking one's adaptations of habits to racial politics so as to "endow the individual behaviors, habits, and social graces associated with the Northeastern middle class with extraordinary political significance."⁴⁷ As the *Colored American* advised in 1837, "on our conduct and exertions, much, very much depend. It is our part, by virtue, prudence, and industry to uphold the hands of our devoted and sacrificing friends."⁴⁸ Rather than purvey a comprehensive economic reformism, then, these jeremiads of Black print culture — "all eyes are upon us," as one Winthropesque writer in the *Colored American* put it in the month prior to the Panic of 1837 — saw normative business behavior as one key to racial uplift.⁴⁹

I might proliferate textual examples from Black print culture that contributed to the formations of an economic citizenship. But my point is to emphasize how this prescriptive literature works, in Ball's words, to "enable [African Americans] to safeguard the virtue and moral integrity necessary to navigate the vicissitudes of a dangerous, often dishonest new market-oriented culture."⁵⁰ This discourse, that is, sought to produce selves that could fully participate in the institutions of a US agency culture — accordingly, it turned toward the market as a locus of identity. To be sure, the *Colored American* tempered its enthusiasm for finance as one such site, as its writers targeted for critique the causes behind "such fluctuations" as the Panic of 1837, and blamed the distress not only on the busted banking system, but also on "spirit of the age."⁵¹ Indeed, the periodical largely avoided the technical banking issues that manifested in the era's "deranged" currency. Instead, it routed its investment advice through the field of real estate, as articles from late 1837 continually referred to the panic's devastation of land values in particular.⁵² According to Cornish, his rival editors were complicit in fomenting the plummeting of real estate prices, as they conspired with speculators in "chicanery and puffing" of "houses and lands." In doing so, he reasons, other newspapers were guilty of directing readers' attention away from the "domestic habits" that ought to lead to racial elevation through property ownership.[53] Of more consequence yet, in stimulating this craze for finance, these bad-faith editors distorted the specific meaning of real estate ownership, which the *Colored American* saw as an emblem of elevated habits. So, in a column entitled "The Cause of the Hard Times," one article suggests that readers become land proprietors and seek a financial asset the value of which could moderate one's ambition and curb the undue devotion to the comparably "boundless" avenues to wealth that directed attention "not to immediate emancipation but immediate opulence."[54]

As part of its program to create a monied class through real estate investment, the *Colored American* here constellated pace, affect, and commercial acuity. In doing so, by insisting on African American property ownership, the periodical achieved a level of specificity rare in its writings on banking. A piece, "Our Banking System," for instance, calls for a national currency, but does so because decentralized banking tends to "fatten the rich."[55] This call to reform the institutions of finance capitalism reflected the paper's hope to steer African Americans toward farming, thereby limiting readers' exposure to debt, speculation, and thus the fluctuations of capital markets. Even still, the author recognized a trend toward urbanization among readers and offered advice on how to invest prudently. In the teeth of the contraction, July 1837, the paper advised that in the likely event that one is looking to remove money from the bank, given the "deranged state of the currency," he must invest it in real estate. If a reader must buy city rather than country lots, the author encouraged them to procure tracts "near to the harbor, or to some growing business section, or on or near important Avenues, or public squares."[56] He offered five tips on maximizing this investment, recommending a keen knowledge, for example, of local ordinances, the quality of roads to avoid costly tax assessments in the future, and so on.

The *Colored American*, in short, advises how to safely steer one's portfolio amid a financial panic. Its advice for navigating a turbulent market, that is, ceded its staid republicanism and embraced shrewd investment. The starkest example of the paper's financial turn here is a third column for the *Colored American*, which concludes the paper's series on "Purchases of Real Estate." And in this piece, the recent panic figures as a call to action, since "reduced prices" represent opportunities for investment. We have seen in previous chapters similar efforts to bolster the self through investing during market swings. But, for the *Colored American*'s conflation of personal and racial success, the shock experience of crisis now, and even more urgently, enjoins individuals to property ownership, an obligation that "increases with the pressure of the times, and the growth of the speculating spirit." Even as the author advocates "caution" in light of the "deception" of "swindlers," he finds that "in the midst of such fluctuations," there is "no good reason . . . why honest men may not deal in Real Estate, as well as in other articles of trade."[57] Whereas Fitzhugh would seek to exempt Southern asset values from capitalist turbulence, the *Colored American*, to the contrary, sees debased land values as a premise for individual Black achievement and collective economic development.

In contemplating the 1837 crisis, then, the editors of the *Colored American* arrived at (to borrow Houston A. Baker's pithy phrase from a different context) a "fully commercial view" of life under capitalism.[58] In doing so, they theorized a path for African Americans to contribute to what the historian Block assesses as the United States' market or agency civilization. As formerly enslaved writers like Douglass, Harriet Jacobs, Charles Ball, and Henry Bibb well knew, though, this sense of the world as rife with possibilities for the capitalized self was not without complications, given the risk-taking required for them, in some cases, to win their literal liberation. William Wells Brown's autobiographical narrative stands out in this context. Indeed, Brown takes the *Colored American*'s recognition of the potential for risk-taking to achieve an identity one step further. And in comic but scathing irony about the financial logic of (in Coates's term) "Black plunder" in the antebellum United States, Brown's narrative immerses itself precisely in the flood of paper money in the western states that contributed to the Panic of 1837.[59] Black Americans could thrive in capitalist institutions, no doubt, Brown avers — but would they be allowed access? And, if so, would they even want to participate therein?

The nineteenth-century writer Caroline Kirkland, in *A New Home—Who'll Follow?* (1839), which dramatizes the white settlement of Michigan, draws attention to "some thirty banks or more [that] were the fungous growth of the new political hot-bed": the "wild cat" banks for "cunning and stealthy bloodsuckers."[60] In his *Narrative of the Life and Escape of William Wells Brown* (1853), in an episode likewise set in frontier Michigan, Brown comically eschews the republican critique of such financiering and presents instead his own foray into the free-banking system. Legislative freedom led to the expansion of what would become (as Kirkland's novel attests) known as "wildcat banks" on the western frontier during the manic prosperity phase of the economy in the early 1830s. Wildcat banks, or "institutions founded by unscrupulous financiers in remote areas for the express purpose of making it difficult, if not impossible, for the notes to be exchanged for gold or silver,"[61] were named as such because a customer would have to seek for the bank's typically nonexistent hard currency reserves "among the retreats of the wild cats."[62] In a striking episode of his narrative, Brown's operation of one such establishment illustrates the financial machinations that fuel business successes—and failures. In performing the risky strategies of this fledgling industry, Brown and his narrative press the limits of "free" banking. Mimicking the financial logic of capitalism, he exposes its corruption in racial terms.

First, with its banking anecdote, though, Brown's *Narrative* shows his facility with financial capitalism. Working as a competitive barber in Michigan, still then a US territory, he issues "Shinplasters," small promissory notes "made payable on demand."[63] After "a good deal of exertion on my part," his bills circulate, and he uses the deposits as capital to improve his shop. He enjoys success until "a party of young men . . . determined to give [the bank] 'a run.'" Confused by how to handle multiple demands for payment, he at first panics, "escap[ing] by the back door."[64] But he is saved by sage advice, which relies on the forward-looking logic of monetary exchange. "When your notes are brought to you," his friend counsels, "you must redeem them, and then send them out and get other money for them; and with the latter, you can keep cashing your own Shinplasters." When he "immediately commenced" this plan, "my efforts were crowned with such success that . . . my Shinplasters were again in circulation, and my bank once more on a sound basis."[65]

Melville's *The Confidence-Man* exposes the antebellum economy as a house of cards framed by confidence in money's (and selves') future exchangeability. Critiquing the relation between an uncritical "circulation" and the "sound"-ness of currency as a tool of whiteness, Brown evinces this logic to instead link it to "Black plunder." Indeed, the *Narrative* reveals Brown's immersion in this speculative economy—not just as a banker, but also as an enforced assistant to a slave trader in New Orleans, James Walker.[66] This widened perspective makes clear the extent to which market risk-taking—its affects, its tempos—is interlinked with Black underdevelopment. After purchasing "another cargo of human flesh," an enslaver Walker "order[s] Brown to prepare the men, women, and children 'for market.'" Here, the narrator demonstrates a republican work ethic, performing "the office of the barber tolerably"—but, in doing so, he works toward a barbarous end: a system of ever-forward-looking exchange in which Walker can sell a woman's child "for the small sum of *one dollar*."[67]

In a reading of Brown's banking anecdote, Michael Germana finds Brown to expose the "parallel between the socially constructed values of racial difference and paper money."⁶⁸ I would add that in that scene and in the one above, Brown's *Narrative* does more than expose the intersection of the abstractions of finance and the embodiment of chattel enslavement. Brown reveals, further, how the capitalist profit mandate racializes the distribution of risk, which he understands as necessary to capitalist profit, in the mid-century United States. He later continues this meditation on the relation between risk-taking and the circulation of (abstract and embodied) values in *Memoir of the Author*, the preface to his book, *The Black Man: His Antecedents, His Genius, and His Achievements* (1863). Revisiting this experience with Walker, there he recites a familiar tale in abolitionist literature of the cruelty wrought by slaveholders' imprudent investing. His enslaver, Dr. Young, had "by speculation and mismanagement, lost much of his property," necessitating that Young "let [him] out" to a "slave-trader named Walker."⁶⁹ Serving alongside "this heartless, cruel, ungodly man," Brown "had opportunities, far greater than most slaves, of acquiring knowledge of the different phases of slave life.'"⁷⁰ But, as he later recalls in his *Memoir*, his best occasion to observe the enslaved person as financial asset comes when "hired out as an under steward on the steamer Patriot, running to New Orleans."⁷¹ Observing a game of chance among enslavers, commonplace events that "completely ruined" the gamblers, he recalls a Mr. Jones who finds himself "broke, all but my boy . . . he is worth a thousand dollars, and I will bet the half of him." Losing "half the [enslaved man]," he exchanges the bill of sale for five hundred dollars. In response to this transaction, normalized among the enslavers/gamblers, Brown flatly concludes, "Such is the uncertainty of a slave's life."⁷²

Uncertainty is a constant in all "phases" of enslavement for Brown, but he distinguishes between risk exposure faced by white capitalists and African Americans. Near the end of her *Incidents in the Life of a Slave Girl* (1861), Harriet Jacobs, too, engages this theme, in this case differentiating between an enslaver's financial risks and a speculator's. Luke, a friend of Linda Brent's, says, "De risk ain't so bad for me, as 'tis fur you. 'Cause I runned away from de speculator, and you runned away from de massa. Dem speculators vont spen dar money to come here fur a runaway, if dey ain't sartin sure to put dar hans right on him."⁷³ Jacobs's Luke thus recognizes, precisely as he impugns it, the financial logics of (slave) speculation and reveals how levels of risk correspond to the "sartin[ty]" of putting "dar hands right" on human chattel. The point is that for writers like Brown, and here Jacobs, Black Americans critiqued racial capitalism in the very terms of go-aheadism. These writers certainly imply that white capitalists were agents of Block's historical

Early African American Literature and the Freedom to Fail 115

market civilization—they confronted risks in the market and at the card table that impeded their ability to achieve, and sustain, a "successful" self. But for African Americans, these texts make equally clear, to achieve a fully commercial point of view via an exposure to "uncertainty" was starkly different than pursuing what we heard Washington Irving laud as the "romance of trade."

Mary E. Webb, Frank J. Webb, and the "Right to Compete"

The tension between pursuing an identity through commerce and critiquing this pathway trod by the risk-taking self as obstructed by racism frames Frank J. Webb's novel *The Garies and Their Friends* (1857). Appearing in London in 1857, this second published novel authored by an African American writer, on the one hand, asserts Black peoples' aspiration in the market, and on the other one, cautions against racist barriers that impede individual economic striving. In doing so, the text anticipates in narrative form recent scholarship that shows how "antebellum African Americans navigated an age of 'expectant capitalism.'"[74] Juliet E. K. Walker uses this term, "expectant capitalism," in her two-volume history, *The History of Black Business in America*. Such a term might seem redundant, as it is difficult to imagine non-expectant capitalist forms of production and subjectivities. Yet in the context of African American business history, it emphasizes how the affects of capitalism inform how African Americans strived for success in business in post-contact North America. Webb's work fictionalizes this struggle. Even though it presumes go-ahead striving as inevitable, the novel shows how the ability to realize a self was far from a given for African Americans in the antebellum United States because these social, psychological, and economic habits of capitalist subjectivity deliberately took shape under the constant threat of racism.[75]

Detailed information about Webb's life remains elusive, but scholars attest to his engagement with the business and popular culture of the nineteenth-century United States. In her preface to *Garies*, Harriet Beecher Stowe states that Webb lived as a free "coloured young man, born and reared in the city of Philadelphia" (*GaTF*, 41). His profession was not authorship—rather, Eric Gardner places Webb "in the clothing business," likely a self-employed tailor in midcentury Philadelphia.[76] In addition, Webb's wife, Mary, won fame as an elocutionist who debuted her public readings in April 1855 in Philadelphia. She successfully performed Stowe's *The Christian Slave* (1855), a dramatized version of *Uncle Tom's Cabin* (1852), which was written, as that text's subtitle reads, "express for the readings of Mrs. Mary E. Webb." A firsthand observer of his spouse's success, Webb accompanied her on tours of *The Christian Slave* across the United States and Great Britain from 1855 to 1856.[77]

Whereas these biographical traces reveal Webb's active participation in the Philadelphia economy and beyond, his "Biographical Sketch," which prefaced Stowe's *The Christian Slave*, indicates his rhetorical approach to the relation between business activity and identity. There, Webb describes failure as a necessary precursor to success. "At the age of seventeen," Webb writes of Mary Webb, "she was united to Mr. Webb, who was engaged in business in Philadelphia."[78] The grief Mary Webb suffered from the "sudden death" of her mother, the result of "anxiety produced by the passing of the infamous Fugitive Slave Law," was further compounded by economic anxiety, which Webb plainly attributes to "Mr. Webb's failure in business."[79] And in response to such losses, the Webbs "reflect[ed]," rather than panicked: her husband's failure "led Mrs. Webb to reflect upon the possibility of turning her marked elocutionary powers to some practical account."[80] "Turning" toward economic prospects—that is to "possibility"—the Webbs enacted the flexible protocols of go-ahead capitalist psychology.[81]

In valorizing his wife's response to loss, anxiety, and failure in these terms, he endues her with the ability to integrate the self's performance into the economy. He endues her, that is, with economic agency. As Webb, explains, Mary earns success by overcoming "appalling difficulties, which she must encounter in her undertaking."[82] If Webb's point is to level the economic field for women, he is equally drawn to the project of doing so for African Americans as a race. Indeed, his use of the word *appalling* here raises the specter of racism—its root word, the Old French *apalir*, means "to wax pale"—a specter that Webb goes on to single out in the context of achievement ("merit").[83] "[Mary Webb] had not only to surmount the barriers which beset the path of every aspirant for public distinction, but above all—and most discouraging was the fact—that she must storm the ramparts of prejudice, and wring from the unwilling lips of the despisers of her race a confession of her merit. The vastness of this undertaking can only be properly estimated by those who know and appreciate the strength of complexional distinctions in the United States."[84] Here, Webb praises his wife's aspirations to "surmount the barriers" and, therefore, lauds her struggle for an identity won through her own exertion. But if he sees the competitive marketplace as an ideal arena in which to act, he also recognizes this vision as not yet aligned with reality. For the African American "aspirant" must "wring [praise] from the unwilling lips of the despisers." Drawn to the possibility of a meritocracy, he acknowledges that this "undertaking" requires more than talent. To achieve an identity amid US institutions requires, in his martial metaphor, a full-blown attack.

Webb's romantic discourse of his wife's conquest through market exertion is thus anticipatory, even as it recalls the past. And just as the authors of conduct literature in venues such as the *Colored American* connected the personal and the racial, so too did Webb link this individual genius to "my devoted people," as he imagines public venues in which to earn an identity in the future.[85] "Mrs. Webb's success in this country," he writes, "will . . . serve a noble end."[86] And this noble end is routed through competitive striving. Her activity, indeed, "will prove . . . that our claim for the right to compete with [white people] in the world of art for the prizes it offers, is not made without strong foundation for its support."[87] "Genius," he concludes, "will be no longer something considered as the exclusive attribute of one race or another."[88] Individual genius, grounded in both talent and "training," can assume political importance and earn African Americans "the right to compete"—the right to succeed or fail on their own.

"Set Up in Business Again": *The Garies and Their Friends*

Webb would take up this battle over the achievement of African Americans in *The Garies and Their Friends*. It is a text that engages the conflict between the reality of racism and the ideal of formerly enslaved and free Black Americans achieving economic selves through commercial activity. To introduce an idealistic view of an earned economic success, the novel begins with a conversation between the white Southern planter, Mr. Garie, and George Winston, a formerly enslaved relation of Garie's (African American) wife. The men debate how Southern print culture reinforces racist assumptions about the "impossibility" of Black Americans' achievement and, with this premise in place, advocates in bad faith for colonization. Garie and Winston dismiss a local planter's "pamphlet[s]," which submit that Black Americans "ought to be all sent to Africa, unless they are willing to become the property of some good master" (*GaTF*, 46). Garie counters this discourse from within the Southern plantation. And in refuting the racist social science of men like Fitzhugh, Garie maintains that such a view defies "the real facts" of the lives of a group of people who "can and do prosper" amid "such tremendous difficulties" (*GaTF*, 46–47).

With this early scene, the novel asserts the "real facts" of Black prosperity as tenuous. In doing so, the novelistic discourse emphasizes not the question of whether people are "capable," in Stowe's term from the preface to Webb's novel, but instead the "tremendous difficulties" that impede Black Americans' economic achievement and determine their underdevelopment. Influenced by Manning Marable, Carla L. Peterson has assessed Webb's novel as one of several midcentury documents that illustrate "the systematic exploitation and underdevelopment of Black America."[89] That the novel initially responds to this reality through the example of Winston is telling. For Winston represents the commercial potential of newly liberated people, as he had become a self-possessed businessman. Now a "fine-looking gentleman," the narrator explains, Winston "had been fifteen years before sold on the auction-block" in Savannah where his mother was also sent, but to "separate owners" (GaTF, 49–50). Purchased by a "cotton broker from New Orleans," Winston "began to exhibit great signs of intelligence," eventually going "through all the grades from errand-boy up to chief clerk."

He, in other words, realizes a tale of uplift that resembles what the scholar Thomas Augst chronicles as "the clerk's tale." Assembling a literary counterhistory through an archive of mercantile clerks' diaries, Augst "suggests how mass literacy helped to both democratize and standardize ethical practices that for centuries had belonged largely to aristocratic elites."[90] For Winston, good business habits have an even more dramatic effect, and his enslaver, so pleased with his bondsman's enterprise, decides to "make you a present of— . . . of yourself" (GaTF, 53). Winston initially calls this "good fortune," but, as the novel emphasizes, his story entails more than luck (GaTF, 53). Free but determined to continue in the New Orleans cotton market, Winston eventually inherits from his former enslaver "a sufficient legacy to enable him to commence business on his account" (GaTF, 54). This legacy might enable a white clerk to align the expectations for and the reality of success; for Winston, however, racism mars this opportunity. And after touring Northern society, he "therefore decided on leaving the United States, and on going to some country where, if he must struggle for success in life, he might do it without the additional embarrassments that would be thrown in his way in his native land, solely because he belonged to an oppressed race" (GaTF, 54). Structures of underdevelopment, Winston surmises, are potent, impervious social realities, be it in the North or South.

Winston's course of action to leave the United States suggests Webb's skepticism toward the meritocratic pretensions of the ideology of achieved identity. But the novel persists in exploring its potential for Black identity through the Philadelphia-based character of Charlie Ellis. Younger than Winston, Ellis more aptly represents Webb's interest in the "expectant" affect of the era's would-be successes. Even so, this young man's striving proves difficult to accommodate. First of all, it is a source of debate between the Ellises, who are tradespeople, and the novel's representative of the Black merchant elite, Mr. Walters. Indeed, at first made nervous by Charlie's ambition, the Ellises contain the reach of their "bright-faced pretty boy, clever at his lessons," enlisting him as a servant for a wealthy woman in the city (*GaTF*, 56). Meanwhile, Walters, a prominent landowner, disagrees with this decision because he fears that "the habit of working for a stipend" as a boy will lead him to "depend" on others for a living. For Walters, the Ellises ought to "do as white [parents] do":

> Do you ever find them sending their boys out as servants? No; they rather give them a stock of matches, blacking, newspapers, or apples, and start them out to sell them. What is the result? The boy that learns to sell matches soon learns to sell other things; he learns to make bargains; he becomes a small trader, then a merchant, then a millionaire. Did you ever hear of any one who had made a fortune at service? Where would I or Ellis [Charlie's father] have been, had we been hired out all our lives at so much a month? It begets a feeling of dependence to place a boy in such a situation; and, rely upon it, if he stays there long, it will spoil him for anything better all his days. (*GaTF*, 94)

Just as Emerson thinks of the "strange process" whereby the mulberry leaf becomes satin over time, so too Walters imagines a future progression from "trader" to "millionaire." The crucial question for Walters is how to ensure that something "better" comes to fruition.

Formerly "young and poor," but now "blessed . . . with abundance," Walters is modeled on men like Robert Purvis (*GaTF*, 242). A wealthy Philadelphian who inherited a fortune from his white father in South Carolina, Purvis identified as African American. Although he inherited, he nevertheless adopted the terms of Black conduct discourse that Webb uses to frame Walters's fictional behavior. In his *Appeal of Forty Thousand Citizens* (1838), a polemic against the repeal of Black male suffrage in Philadelphia, Purvis challenges "the charge of idleness" in particular: "We fling it back indignantly," he affirms.[91] Exuding confidence in Black economic development, Purvis's words resonate across Webb's novel as well, for this "indignant" denial of "idleness" gives life to Walters's further fantasy of Charlie's movement from bootblack to millionaire.

Inherent in the novel's projected rags-to-riches story is the notion of Charlie's increasing facility with risk calculus. *Garies* makes its interest in his affecto-commercial development along these lines most explicit in the chapter "Charlie Seeks Employment." There, the model of an achieved identity shimmers with possibility. It does so in response to race-targeted trauma that befalls the Ellises—the ruinous injury of the family patriarch during a riot that destroys his career as a carpenter. With the loss of his father's income from trade because of violence, Charlie will have to earn for the family through wage labor. Small jobs, however, do not match his ambition, and he vents frustration over ministering to his father and "collecting rents and looking up small accounts for Mr. Walters . . . not occupying half his time" (*GaTF*, 280). "I wish I could find some regular and profitable employment," he explains to his sister Esther. Indeed, Charlie prefers anything, even domestic service, to "being idle," which makes him "feel very uncomfortable" (*GaTF*, 280). Although feeling sidelined, he recognizes racism as a barrier to realizing his ambition—"the majority of white folks imagine that we are only fit for servants," he says—but he determines to "hazard the experiment at any rate" (*GaTF*, 280).

This "at any rate" mindset intrigues Webb, as it reflects the fact that for Charlie to go ahead is compulsory. Set on taking risks ("hazard") that can affirm his identity, Charlie responds by post to an ad for a "youth who writes a good hand, and is willing to make himself useful in an office" (*GaTF*, 282). This moment of self-determination is privileged in the narrative discourse, as the narrator romanticizes Charlie's foray into the market "by post." Contrary to Melville's "Bartleby," which ends with a bleak vision of Bartleby's seemingly aimless toil in the Dead Letter Office, Webb appears to celebrate the potential for change represented by the "ever-distended and insatiable brass throat" of the mailbox (*GaTF*, 282). Though the narrator's romantic paean to the mailbox encompasses both success and "ruin," "hope and despair," after dropping his application "down the abyss below," Charlie cannot but help envision a prosperous future (*GaTF*, 282). And, like the fledgling writer Ruth Hall, in doing so, his walking pace matches that of his go-getting: As he "sauntered homeward," he did so "building by the way houses of fabulous dimensions with the income he anticipated from the situation as if he succeeded in procuring it" (*GaTF*, 282). The pace quickens the next day, which he spends "in a state of feverish anxiety and expectation" (*GaTF*, 282). Aware of racism as a barrier, Charlie nevertheless adopts the mindset of "as if" that—combined with a ceaseless ambition "at any rate,"—propels life under capitalism.

But this upbeat outlook leads to more disappointment. Because of racism, Charlie's would-be clerk's tale fails—his expectation deemed but another dead letter. The narrative discourse, though, uses this supposed individual failure to show how (white) commercial agents conspire to reinforce the racist structure. Invited to interview with the firm Messrs. Twining, Western, and Twining based on his written application, Charlie enters the office just as the narrative perspective reveals the principals praising his application (as per a lisping Mr. Western) as "well witten" (*GaTF*, 284). Western says further, "I hope he will make as favouwable an impression as his writing has done" (*GaTF*, 284). This hope for a meritocracy even seems to survive the interview, in which the white principals quiz the African American aspirant, who must defend his letter as "my own writing and composing" (*GaTF*, 284). As Western concludes to one of his partners: "Don't you think we had better engage him?" (*GaTF*, 285) For Twining, however, "the thing's absurd; engage a coloured boy as under clerk! I never heard of such a thing" (*GaTF*, 285). Perhaps in New Orleans, he adds, but "such a thing never occurred in Philadelphia" (*GaTF*, 285). Deeming his "complexion" a "*fatal* objection," the men decline to "cweate a pwecedent" lest the rest of the firm's clerks "all feel dreadfully insulted by our placing [Charlie] on an equality with them" (*GaTF*, 285–86; emphasis original).

If Webb's fictional firm's worries about a "pwecedent" reveal the boundaries of Lincoln's "open field," as quoted above, the novel contrasts this restriction with the abiding tenacity of Charlie's compulsion to strive. Awaiting the firm's decision, with a "hopeful countenance," Charlie tells his sister Esther, "I feel *sure* they are going to take me" (*GaTF*, 286). It turns out that this sureness is (in one of the firm's partner's terms) "impossible" (*GaTF*, 285). And yet Charlie Ellis responds "determinedly" by vowing to "keep on trying" for employment (*GaTF*, 286). As Jeffory A. Clymer notes, previous scholars of *The Garies and Their Friends* "chafed at what they regarded as Webb's unproblematic celebration of capitalism."[92] For one such critic, James Kinney, "Webb's work is a Black version of the American dream of material success."[93] Although the novel closely explores capitalism's emotional logic with Charlie, it does so, from my perspective, to emphasize the double bind that Black Americans face in achieving the "American dream." For Webb, they must adopt capitalist habits of mind to sink or swim, while doing so in a society that negates the very premise of Black economic agency. A more sophisticated response to capitalism than previous critics have allowed, Webb lingers with Charlie's capitalist psychology to reveal it as simultaneously unavoidable and "impossible."

Drawn to this conflict, the narrator remains interested in (if suspicious about) whether Charlie can align his expectations and reality in free

Philadelphia. To this end, Webb follows his aspiring clerk through yet *another* job search that places Charlie directly within midcentury monetary politics—he applies as an apprentice to a bank-note engraver, Thomas Blatchford, who is known as an abolitionist. Here, at the intersection of money and finance and abolitionism, Charlie seems to thrive; he receives glowing feedback after showing Blatchford his portfolio sketches: "These are excellently done," the printer says, inviting Charlie to his home that evening to finalize the terms of a formal agreement (*GaTF*, 287). Once more on the path to success, "Charlie seemed to tread on air as he walked home" (*GaTF*, 288). Such transcendence, which repeats his prior certainty in gaining a position as a clerk, however, is again illusory; the following day, Blatchford's shop unites against "—apprentices!" "Let him be a barber or shoe-black," one of the men yells: "If he comes, we go" (*GaTF*, 290). For Charlie to "go" ahead in this shop means that white laborers will flee.

The white working people see Charlie's presence as threatening their access to capitalism's identity-sustaining protocols. Webb's novel portrays, then, the enforced denial of access to African Americans to the ideology of achieved identity as a tool that allows white business owners to secure their financial capital from risk. He does so not to question the primacy of the market, but to expose hypocrisy in white business practices therein. Black business leaders, of course, had long pled for equal access to refute this "racio-economic hierarchy," in which white people deemed Black people fit only for the positions of laborers or service providers ("a barber or shoe-black").[94] And in portraying a worthy Charlie Ellis's multiple failures, Webb emphasizes the extent to which white people refuse to take risks that would promote racial equality. To this end, the novel privileges for the reader Western and Twining's private conversation, in which they muse about the likely racist reaction among their clerks to Charlie's presence in the office. Thus the discourse privileges, too, the engraver Blatchford's (again, private) dilemma that, because "he had just received larger orders from some new banks which were commencing operations," "to accede to his workmen's demands he must do violence to his own conscience; but he dared not sacrifice his business and bring ruin on himself and family, even though he was right" (*GaTF*, 291). To make clear that the expanding money supply in the 1830s that led William Wells Brown to wildcat banking does not interpellate African Americans, one of Blatchford's advisers states, "there is no question as to what you must do. You mustn't ruin yourself for the sake of your principles" (*GaTF*, 291). The market here is posited as amoral. Yet, as Webb suggests, if that is the case, this reality stems from choices that white individuals enact behind closed doors when they choose to withdraw their capital from the risks of racial integration. As the novel shows, then, the white man's right to strive after identities and capital profits is thus guaranteed by the Black man's exclusion from doing so, rather than his incapacity.

Given this situation, Webb asks: How can white merchants be made to refuse indemnity for themselves in the face of racist blowback? How can they "dare" to give talented Black prospects access to moving forward? Against the examples of the Twinings and Blatchford, the novel imagines the conditions for liberal reform in Charlie's third interaction with a white capitalist, George Burrell. The solution, it turns out, is rather like the one proposed in *Uncle Tom's Cabin* to counteract racism in federal politics. For just as Stowe's Mrs. Bird employs sentimental rhetoric to secure her husband Senator Bird's help for the fugitive Eliza Harris, so too does Mrs. Burrell urge her husband to secure a position for Charlie. Burrell, a printer like Blatchford, had in fact advised Blatchford *against* hiring Charlie. But, in phrasing that combines the words, *indignant*, which we have seen from Webb above, and *risk*, Burrell's wife "exclaimed . . . indignantly," "I wouldn't allow myself to be dictated to in that manner. . . . Had I been [Blatchford], I should have stuck to my principles at any risk" (*GaTF*, 293). Adapting the language of risk-taking to her own ends, she further encourages Burrell to hire Charlie by turning the language of necessity against him. Whereas her husband claims he does not "want an apprentice," she says, "Yes, but you must *make* a want" (*GaTF*, 294; emphasis original). And flouting the "stern necessity" of racism, Burrell, at his wife's urging, relents — he offers Charlie an office berth (*GaTF*, 297). Derided by early critics of the novel, this sentimentality serves the political-economic end of exposing how markets are upheld by private decisions that (white) people make — or not. Through Charlie Ellis's long, winding clerk's tale, the novel posits that (white, powerful) individuals can make different decisions — they can stick to their principles "at any risk" to enable access to identity-achieving opportunities for all.

The novel's preoccupation with Charlie's clerk's tale naturalizes the case for Black economic agency through his dogged attempts to find a position that will yield him independence. Webb takes for granted that Black Americans' economic achievement is possible when considered from the perspective of the individual's desire to strive in the future. It balances the arduousness of this vexed clerk's tale, though, with the character Mr. Walters, Charlie's eventual brother-in-law. Walters has *already* earned an identity, and here Webb tests if such achievement and such an identity, which animates Charlie's life course, is sustainable in the supposedly free North. Earlier in the novel, Charlie's father, Mr. Ellis, introduces Walters as "a dealer in real estate," which prompts this default response from George Winston: "Oh, then he is a white man?" (*GaTF*, 84) Enjoying this misalignment between the expectation of whiteness and the reality of Walters being "as Black as a man can conveniently be," Mr. Ellis goes on to enumerate the extent of Walters's enterprise: "He is very wealthy; some say that he is worth half a million of dollars. He owns, to my certain knowledge, one hundred brick houses. . . . [H]e owns ten thousand dollars' worth of stock, in a railroad extending from this to a neighbouring city" (*GaTF*, 84). Owning more tangible assets than Charlie Ellis's castles in the clouds and investing in both real estate and financial instruments (railroad stock), Walters is "certain[ly]" in the market.

Walters most powerfully represents Black economic power by purchasing a hotel from which he is denied service because of his race.[95] As narrated by the novel's archvillain, the white speculator and distant relation of Garie, "Slippery" George Stevens:

> There's not a better man of business in the whole of Philadelphia than that same Walters . . . ; and no one offends him without paying dear for it in some way or other. I'll tell you something he did last week. He went up to Trenton on business, and at the hotel they refused to give him dinner because of his colour. . . . What did he do but buy the house over the landlord's head. The lease had just expired, and the landlord was eager to negotiate another; he was also making some arrangements with his creditors, which could not be effected unless he was able to renew the lease of the premises he occupied. (*GaTF*, 145–46)

What Stevens observes here is Walters's unqualified savvy—"there's not a better man of business in the whole" city. Walters's shrewdness thus seems to result in a clear identity—success—through his own exertion, as Stevens's begrudging admiration attests.

By "accumulating property," the literary critic Elizabeth Stockton writes of Walters's investments, "African American men can enact racial justice outside of the biased and racist legal system."[96] This power to "enact racial justice" in the extralegal arena of the financial market means he can make or break "rather ticklish" business dealings brokered by white men like Stevens (*GaTF*, 147). Indeed, Walters denies a business proposal from Stevens "with some not very complimentary remarks upon my assurance in offering him such securities" (*GaTF*, 147). And yet Walters's security in this identity is always tenuous, a reality that is not explained away merely by the nature of competition over scarce profits. It is, rather, that men like Stevens find any financial power imbalance that favors a Black man "almost unendurable"—a wrong to be righted by any means necessary (*GaTF*, 147).

Although Mr. Ellis's introductory anecdote (cited above) establishes Walters's self-reliance, it also reveals the limits of his (racialized) capital. "I met him the other day," Ellis continues, "in a towering rage" (*GaTF*, 84). Although Walters owns a large stake in the railroad, the railroad treats him unequally. "Having occasion to travel in it for some little distance," Ellis explains: "He got into the first-class cars; the conductor, seeing him there, ordered him out—he refused to go, and stated that he was a shareholder. The conductor replied, that he did not care how much stock he owned, he was a n—, and that no n— should ride in those cars; so he called help, and after a great deal of trouble they succeeded in ejecting him. 'And he a stockholder! It was outrageous,' exclaimed Winston. 'And was there no redress?'" (*GaTF*, 84).

No redress, indeed, since markets—be it the labor market for clerks or the capital market for railroads—exist behind race-based barriers that are "impossible" to overcome. Although he "would have been obliged to institute a suit against the [railroad]," it "would be impossible for him to obtain a verdict in his favour" (*GaTF*, 85). Invested (in Coates's modern term) in Black plunder, white institutions remain unwavering in their commitment to limiting African Americans' affecto-economic development. They police the racial boundaries of just who gets to feel, and act, like a capitalist.

In fact, to highlight further the tenuousness of identity achievement among midcentury Black Americans, the novel insists that Walters's economic power makes him a target of white speculators like Stevens and his associate Mr. Morton. The men plot a nightmarish inversion of the *Colored American*'s real estate investing guide. As "Slippery George" observes, "You are probably aware that a large amount of property in the lower part of the city is owned by n——" (*GaTF*, 181). From Stevens's perspective, race-based terrorism can solve this problem. And to allow white speculators to acquire these buildings at depressed prices, Stevens proposes to "create a mob" to drive African Americans out of the neighborhood in fear for their "security and protection" (*GaTF*, 181). The point is to "render the district so unsafe, that property will be greatly lessened in value—the houses will rent poorly and many proprietors will be happy to sell at very reduced prices" (*GaTF*, 181). With no attempt to hide its theft, Stevens's "little scheme . . . conceived for getting into our hands a larger portion of property in one of the lower districts, at a very low figure" (*GaTF*, 181).

As we have seen in chapter 4, Melville's *The Confidence-Man* imagines how stock manipulators fraudulently manufacture financial crises to pit bulls against bears. In his critique of racial capitalism—that is, how capitalist profits presume the capture of Black-produced value by white people—Webb goes further and reveals how such engineered unrest is part of a structure of theft that undermines the achievement of Black people by foreclosing on a future secured by ongoing financial returns ("rent"). *Garies* thus best illustrates this theft by fictionalizing the race riots in Philadelphia that occurred in the 1830s. The novel exposes, indeed, what one historian terms the "importance of the economic factor in the Philadelphia riot."[97] This "factor" is deeply structural, as shown in the fact that city officials ignore Mr. Walters's entreaties for protection against Stevens's goons: "Although the authorities of the district had received the most positive information of the nefarious schemes of the rioters, they had not made the slightest efforts to protect the poor creatures threatened in their persons and property, but let the tide of lawlessness flow on unchecked" (*GaTF*, 212). Property-based rioting in *Garies*, condoned by the state and coordinated by the white competitors of Black capitalists, is a mechanism to ensure underdevelopment for African Americans and financial supremacy for white businesspeople.

In the face of this structural reality, however, Webb will not shake a commitment to indexing market rewards to Black economic acuity. In the end, the value of real estate abides. And unlike Charles W. Chesnutt's *The Marrow of Tradition* (1901), a turn-of-the-century realist novel of Reconstruction and the Wilmington, North Carolina race riots, Webb's fictional account of Philadelphia in the 1830s imagines an alternative horizon of history: in what amounts to a wish-fulfillment plot, real estate owned by Black investors in the *Garies* maintains its value despite white violence. The solution to the problem of economic racism reveals itself in the plot of Charlie Ellis's friend, a young man named Kinch, and his tale of sudden—and, seemingly, unearned—success. As the novel scans the social world for the possibility and sustainability of Black success, it settles on Kinch, who finds that his father owned real estate that had one day became valuable. For Kinch, "The fates had conspired to make [his father] rich"—"He owned a number of lots on the outskirts of the city, on which he had been paying taxes a number of years, and he awoke one fine morning to find them worth a large sum of money. The city council having determined to cut a street just beside them, and the property all around being in the hands of wealthy and fashionable people, his own proved to be exceedingly valuable" (*GaTF*, 327). This sudden transformation of "lots on the outskirts of the city" into a "fashionable" suburb seems like the realization of the dream of men like Melville's China Aster. It is, in short, good luck. But even good luck can be routed through an ideology of Black achievement, after all. If *Garies* imagines Black development as an outgrowth of civic engagement (taxpaying), it still retains ties to Black economic savvy. For the *Colored American* series "Purchases of Real Estate" might see Kinch's good luck instead as the outcome of his father's business acuity. From this perspective, the Black investor (and his family) can be rewarded for alertly buying depressed real estate that might one day benefit from such municipal decisions as "cut[ting] a street just beside them." What looks like unearned wealth is in fact the product of prudent capitalization.

This intervention of the "fates" thus represents a compromise between the difficulties that Charlie Ellis faces in achieving an identity and that Walters faces in maintaining one. As such, it is not without cost. As it is for Hawthorne's Dominicus Pike, such success can have ambiguous unintended consequences, for Kinch's sudden wealth signals the end of business exertion too. As the narrator of *Garies* explains, "It was a sad day for the [newly enriched] old man, as Kinch and his mother insisted that he should give up business, which he did most reluctantly, and Kinch had to be incessantly on the watch thereafter, to prevent him from hiring cellars, and sequestering their old clothes to set up in business again" (*GaTF*, 327). (Mr. Kinch had maintained his life by selling recycled clothing.) And, as the novel realizes in the end, the lure of "set[ting] up in business again" would confront barriers for African Americans, no doubt, but such a compulsion is a tough—perhaps "impossible"—habit to break in the midcentury United States.

Coda: Let Him Fail!

With the wish-fulfillment scenario depicted with the Kinches and their suddenly valuable suburban lots, like other texts examined throughout this book, *Garies* plots a narrative of reversal. The novel clearly assesses the economic field as a limited one, but it is drawn to it, still, as a source of identity. Of course, from the perspectives of scholars like Spires, Peterson, Marable, and Ball, such maneuvering is not atypical among midcentury Black American writers. To conclude this chapter, I would like to turn to one of the most well-known contributors to the debate over financial achievement, Frederick Douglass. I do so to highlight his concern over individual exertion and identity—a drama of self-making that, crucially and inevitably, unfolds in a capitalist institutional context.

For Douglass, this theme expresses itself as a freedom not just to succeed, but to fail.[98] Indeed, one of Douglass's most popular addresses from the era,

"Self-Made Men" (1859), makes this very point. "Crafted before the war and . . . in frequent demand after the conflict," in this text Douglass mapped failure in enterprise as a sign of freedom for African Americans as the US economy stabilized after the Panic of 1857.[99] His text includes a republican paean to labor in a series of increasingly emphatic declarations: "We may explain success mainly by one word and that word is WORK! WORK!! WORK!!! WORK!!!!" He says that "not transient and fitful effort, but patient, enduring, honest, unremitting, and indefatigable work into which the whole heart is put, and which, in both temporal and spiritual affairs, is the true miracle worker."[100] But he qualifies this enthusiasm with the caveat: "Give the negro fair play and let him alone. If he lives, well. If he dies, equally well. If he cannot stand up, let him call down."[101] Extending his call for the immediate abolition of enslavement, he further urges that reparations for the injustices of the past mean "justice in the present."[102] In doing so, he imagines "fair" access to the institutions of life under capitalism: "Throw open to him the doors of the schools, the factories, the workshops, and of all mechanical industries. For his own welfare, give him a chance to do whatever he can do well."[103] What Douglass imagines here is not just equal access to capitalist sites, but to capitalist affects too. Thinking of his African American brethren, he states, "If he fails then, let him fail!"[104]

This problem of access to the identity matrix of the market continued to manifest at the intersection of individual freedom and institutional restraint. It would provide fodder for Douglass, who would resume this theme in his speech "What the Black Man Wants" (1865) as well. He first delivered this oration in April 1865 when a Union victory seemed imminent, as he parroted the question, "What shall we do with the Negro?" The answer, he maintained, was not much. There was "but one answer" to this question—the same one he "ha[s] had . . . from the beginning": "Do nothing with us!"[105] He continues this seeming *laissez-faire* argument with natural imagery and likens the life cycle of an apple to one's ability to thrive. "If the apples will not remain on the tree of their own strength," he avers, "if they are wormeaten at the core, if they are early ripe and disposed to fall, let them fall! I am not for tying or fastening them on the tree in any way, except by nature's plan, and if they will not stay there, let them fall. And if the Negro cannot stand on his own legs, let him fall also. All I ask is, give him a chance to stand on his own legs! Let him alone!"[106]

With this appeal to natural law, "What the Black Man Wants" seems to espouse a classical liberal individualism "insofar," Nicholas Buccola has argued, as "it draws on the philosophy of self-reliance."[107] But this is an incomplete interpretation, Buccola concludes, that "fundamentally misunderstands [Douglass's] message."[108] For what appears to be an unadulterated *laissez-faire* approach hews closer to what Buccola terms the reform liberal position that complicates his individualism, as Douglass insists "that both state and nonstate actors refrain from preventing African Americans from exercising their legitimate rights."[109] For Douglass, if it is vital that African Americans have access to opportunities to fail or succeed through business, it is necessary that institutions do not deny these opportunities as well. In an argument meant for the likes of Charlie Ellis's educators, would-be employers, and others who hold keys to US institutions, Douglass avers: "If you see him on his way to school, let him alone, don't disturb him! If you see him going to the dinner table at a hotel, let him go! If you see him going to the ballot-box, let him alone, don't disturb him! If you see him going into a work-shop, just let him alone, —your interference is doing him a positive injury."[110] The capitalist marketplace, and other institutions of midcentury-US life, are unavoidable, this passage makes clear. If that is the case, they must enable Black Americans' pursuit of individual achievement—they must provide walkable paths on and through which to strive. And in a paradoxical elision of the institutional context here that constitutes the narratives of return we have seen throughout that this book, if that is the case, further, the Black man will "stand" or "fall" on his own.

EPILOGUE
War and Institutions
Striving in the Transbellum Office

The US Civil War (1861-65)—what the historian of failure Scott Sandage terms "the war for ambition"—entrenched identity more as "a matter of new risks than new rights."[1] For Sandage, this victory of "entrepreneurial individualism" signaled the transformation of capitalist personality protocols, as well as the institutions that helped structure them.[2] Just as much as traditional US literary historiography, then, business history has framed the Civil War as a site of transition—in the latter case, as an "ideological shift" in achieved identity.[3] From this perspective, after 1865 one would strive in the United States on behalf of the "large, corporate business structures in exchange for consumer independence in the late nineteenth and early twentieth centuries."[4]

In the domain of US literary studies, scholars like Christopher Hager and Cody Marrs have scrutinized this notion of the Civil War as a "terminus."[5] Melville has figured centrally in the attempt to destabilize the war as zoning off "major" (or prose) and "minor" (or poetic) eras of his work. Here, Elizabeth Renker, in her study of Melville as a "realist poet," sees this divide to distort his contribution to the realist aesthetics traditionally associated with the prose works of postbellum writers like Charles W. Chesnutt, William Dean Howells, Henry James, Mark Twain, and Edith Wharton. As Renker argues, "the focus in literary scholarship on Melville the antebellum writer of fiction has elided the phenomenon of Melville the postbellum poet."[6] In this Epilogue, though, I believe the war as "terminus" may also elide a related phenomenon in Melville's work relevant to the supposed transition from "entrepreneurial individualism" to its bureaucratically managed instantiation across the late nineteenth century. Collectively, with their emphasis on market agency—that is, the presumption of striving as a social compulsion amid economic uncertainty within the putatively free domain of the market—the texts I have studied throughout my book can be read to suggest that the "managerial revolution in American business" in the postbellum era was an evolution in the existing cultural meaning of ambition, rather than a complete rupture.[7] And briefly focusing on Melville, first his poetry and then his prose, we can see how his midcentury work reveals mandatory striving—on behalf of something or someone external to the self—truly as a "transbellum" concern.⁸

Viewing the Civil War through the lens of financial history helps us see the seemingly altered, bureaucratically motivated notion of go-getting to connect across the Civil War. In spring 1865, as a Union victory looked increasingly sure, a "brief but crucial financial panic . . . played a key, nearly forgotten role in speeding the discharge of soldiers."⁹ And, facing up to this crisis, federal office workers would help save the Union. The historian Mark R. Wilson has shown that the military bureaucracy was put under enormous stress when "the project of Civil War mobilization that started in April 1861 quickly overwhelmed the existing capacities of American government."¹⁰ Focusing especially on the Union Quartermasters Office, he reveals the "surprising" agility that this office displayed in managing "the North's massive, four-year procurement project."¹¹ But the financial crisis in 1865 threatened this machine's efficiency, as the urgency of an immediate muster of the troops became clear. In short, institutional endurance butted up against the haste to shed the Union Army's payroll that spring. The war bonds that funded the campaign "tied the government's borrowing to the price of gold."¹² Gold's value relative to the ubiquitous "greenback dollars" (Union paper money) fell as a likely Northern victory lessened the attraction of lending to the government in exchange for interest payments in gold (see fig. E.1).¹³ Although a complicated scheme by financiers (including Jay Cooke) and federal officials (such as Secretary of Treasury Hugh McCulloch) "saved the Union," the panic revealed the government's tenuous ability to pay its bills.¹⁴ What was the solution to this slackened flow of incoming funds? "The payroll of the army," in one journalist's words to Cooke, "should be instantly subjected to unsparing scrutiny and unsparing hewing + chopping."¹⁵ Clerks in federal offices would do to the budget something akin to what General William Tecumseh Sherman had unleashed on the South. Not slash and burn—but muster out!

For Gregory P. Downs, a historian of Reconstruction, this fiscal discipline among Washington officials stabilized the Union through the financial turmoil. And from the perspective of Lincoln's final treasury secretary, McCulloch, such recognition by today's historians of the era's managerial competence is long overdue. In his memoir, *Men and Measures of a Half Century* (1888), McCulloch demonstrated the extent to which financialization—in addition to its attendant forms of subjectivity—had become normative after the Civil War: "Of the two evils—excessive circulation of paper money, and excessive use of personal credit—the former is the lesser, but

FIGURE E.1 A lithograph published by Currier & Ives in 1864—the text criticizes President Lincoln's handling of the Civil War, including his administration's fiscal policy. Courtesy of the Library of Congress.

both lead in the same direction—to dangerous enterprise; to efforts to make money rapidly, and not by persistent industry; to speculation; to panics."[16] We have seen such concerns by writers throughout my study over the volume of currency and the pace of its accumulation. But what stands out here is that McCulloch also vents his frustration that the public, typically training their eyes to the financial sublime, had not fully appreciated the maneuverings of the federal bureaucracy during the war: "The movements of the armies, the great battles that were fought with varying success on both sides, so absorbed the public attention that comparative little interest was felt in the measures that were adopted to provide the means to meet the enormous and daily increasing demands upon the treasury. It was the successful general who was the recipient of public honors, not the man by whose agency the sinews of war were supplied; and yet but for the successful administration of the Treasury Department during the war, the Union would have been riven asunder."[17] As cultural historian Brian P. Luskey writes, "the Civil War offered clerks the chance to prove they were men by answering the call of their country," presumably on the battlefield.[18] McCulloch might protest this view. In his memoir, he thus wages a belated attack—one over the very meaning of courage, winning and losing, and succeeding and failing. Not soldiers distinguishing themselves during "great battles," but rather office workers sending supplies across the country and shifting soldiers on and off payrolls—these are the administrators to whom the identity category "success" ought to apply. These efficient office workers are the Union heroes for whom the poets ought to sing.

In 1866, a then little-read book of poems by Melville, *Battle-Pieces*, seemingly struggled to accept a society organized by an office filled with clerks toiling in the service of an external motivation. The "successful administration of the Treasury Department," that is, is not too far afield from that book's concerns. Through its chronological arrangement, the volume tracks a shift in worries over a "final disaster to our institutions" (Melville's phrase from a footnote to the poem "The Conflict of Convictions") to an acknowledgement of their endurance from the ante- to the postbellum eras.[19] Given one recent theorist's association of "containers" with institutions, perhaps it is unsurprising that Melville's ambivalence—that is, his apparent anti-modernism about the continuity of US institutions—appears most vividly in his book's naval poems.[20] "In the Turret," a riveting tribute to the commander of the ironclad warship *Monitor*, laments the technological displacement of oaken vessels by iron ones. This poem yields to "The Temeraire," an encomium to the timber-hewn English battleship of the Napoleonic Wars immortalized by J. M. W. Turner's *The Fighting Temeraire* (1838). "O, the navies old and oaken," the speaker intones, "O, the Temeraire no more!"[21] In a footnote to the poem, thinking of Turner's "well-known painting," Melville praises the ship as "the poetic ideal of those great historic wooden warships, whose gradual displacement is lamented by none more than by regularly educated navy officers, and of all nations."[22] Even as "war shall yet be," he ironically adds in the following poem, "A Utilitarian View of the Monitor's Flight," that "fleets heroic" are now but "pivot, and screw," and "warriors are now but operatives."[23]

With its portrayal of the "gradual" transformations of war into industry and the navy's officers into "operatives" who are ignorant of maritime history, *Battle-Pieces* melancholically anticipates modernity and its "managerial revolution." Except that the volume must acknowledge those office structures that held the Union together in the first place. No poem from *Battle-Pieces* better evinces this recognition of bureaucratic managerialism than "The Muster." Although some of the book's poems treat individuals (and boats) in the singular, the volume's dedication treats people in the aggregate and links this mass to the endurance ("maintenance") of the state: "The Battle-Pieces in This Volume are Dedicated to the Memory of the THREE HUNDRED THOUSAND who died in the war for the maintenance of the Union."[24] "The Muster: Suggested by the Two Days' Review at Washington (May 1865)" furthers this interest in an aggregate of "squadrons" and likens the "quotas of the Nation" returning to Washington, DC, to "streams," "torrent[s]," and "rapids" flowing to "the Abrahamic River," the Potomac.[25] In a footnote to the poem, Melville turns explicitly to the management of this process by the War Department. In doing so, he undercuts his own natural imagery — the "torrent" of men is controlled, not natural. Further, he may even evoke the Union's urgent, cost-cutting response to the Panic of 1865. "According to a report of the Secretary of War," he writes, "there were on the first day of March, 1865, 965,000 men on the army pay-rolls. Of these, some 200,000 . . . marched by the President. The total number of Union troops enlisted during the war was 2,668,000."[26]

Here, in what is footnote *q* in the first print edition of *Battle-Pieces*, the romanticism of the individual ship or single battle yields to the political economy of the mass of men, whose movement is orchestrated by some government office. These men are "on the army-payrolls," not the battlefield, their identity lost in the rhythm of a march that was arranged by the toil of faceless clerks. This motion, and this erasure of the soldier's individualism, thus implies a tale of *clerks* — not just the singular clerk's tale that Webb's Charlie Ellis chases or the dream of independence that motivates Irving in the late 1810s and that Sedgwick's Harry Aikin moderates twenty years after. It is these clerks' anonymous but necessary work that has allowed state institutions to endure a panic and mobilize others past "the President" and then off the payrolls. How many of the soldiers marching so, we might wonder in turn, would walk straight from Washington, DC, into a postbellum office owned and operated by someone else? Additionally, then, the poem might let us imagine an army of yet more clerks in the future going ahead, not on their own terms, but on ones set by someone else.

But rather than let *Battle-Pieces* quietly stand in as evidence of an "ideological shift" in the psychology of nineteenth-century US capitalism, I want to consider how it actually connects to a prior Melville story before the Civil War, "Bartleby, the Scrivener: A Tale of Wall Street." It is perhaps inevitable that a study of midcentury literature and capitalist identity would turn in earnest to this tale; in the contexts I have invoked, it seems an irresistible text, which David Anthony perceptively reads to critique the lawyer-narrator's "modes of desire."[27] If Hawthorne's Holgrave and Phoebe pursue identities within the market, Bartleby does not—his is a model that radically refuses integration. What interests me about "Bartleby," though, is what compels Bartleby's co-workers in the Wall Street office to stay, rather than to protest from within its confines. Indeed, in their articulation of the concept, "cruel optimism," which is defined as "a relation to compromised conditions of possibility," Lauren Berlant cites the character Bartleby as the exception, not the rule. "Cruel optimism about imminence," they write, "thus grows from a perception about the reasons people are not Bartleby, do not prefer to interfere with varieties of immiseration, but choose to ride the wave of the system of attachment that they are used to."[28] Berlant is interested in how institutionalized violence is perpetuated through an enduring attachment to a fantasy of the good life routed through ideologies of work. If Bartleby chooses not "to ride the wave of" that attachment, everyone else in the Wall Street office feels as if he must.

Ginger Nut, the "promising lad" who serves "as an office-boy," certainly cannot opt out of the go-ahead mandate.[29] This minor character in such a well-known text has received scant critical attention, but he stands out here for his explicit proximity to go-aheadism. Marked as such within the narrator's discourse, this relation is one degree removed, though. "A lad of some twelve years old," he is apprenticed to the firm by "his father, a carman, ambitious of seeing his son on the bench instead of a cart."[30] If Sedgwick's carman, Aikin, depicts for midcentury readers how to modify an attachment to the capitalist institutions of wealth and prestige, Melville's "ambitious" one shows just how tough that attachment will be to break.[31] To this end, he sends his son on his own errand, working for a man (in Anthony's phrase regarding the narrator and proprietor of the Wall Street law firm) who is "the very embodiment of this new [paper-based, financialized] capitalism."[32]

Perhaps Melville's story invokes go-aheadism in this ambitious father and his obedient son to highlight Bartleby's renunciation of it. No doubt, the famous preference not to—Bartleby's great "motionless"-ness in the face of the office's urgent activity—contrasts with the avid, energetic affect expected by the firm's proprietor and admired by the boy's working-class father.[33] But Ginger Nut's presence also makes clear the power of capitalist psychology, in which the so-called self-directed individual strives on behalf of something or someone outside of that self. In Block's heuristic, this practice of agency informs the narrator's office, just as much as it does the Civil War treasury secretary McCulloch's. From Emerson's scholar to Charlie Ellis to Ginger Nut to McCulloch, an office, naturalized as a site of individual ambition, is thus an institution of the paradox of capitalist selfhood: the self, always externally compelled to do so, chooses to strive within the market.

Reading back from Melville's Civil War in the 1860s to Wall Street in the 1850s, then, suggests that the revolution in aspiration that we tend to associate with the Gilded Age signals an evolution in social life, rather than a stark turnabout. For if this revolution, in which one trades the allure of self-reliance for the quiet risk aversion of a becoming a "company" agent, relies on the war as a line of demarcation, "Bartleby" and *Battle-Pieces* cannot quite agree. They are, finally, transbellum texts that emphasize continuity in the protocols of capitalist identity, rather than difference. In the United States, economic self-making—grounded in the supposedly voluntary, supposedly independent search for success within capitalist institutions—was and is a risk that must be taken.

Notes

Introduction

1. Whitman, "Song of Myself," 77.
2. Whitman, preface to *Leaves of Grass*, 617.
3. Sobel, *Panic on Wall Street*, 80.
4. In *Democratic Vistas*, in addition to this criticism, Whitman "would alarm and caution . . . against the prevailing delusion" of the "fruitage of success" (10).
5. Whitman, "To Those Who've Fail'd," 426.
6. Parrington, *Main Currents*, 3:xix; Sandage, *Born Losers*, 22.
7. *Oxford English Dictionary*, "sink (v.), sense P.1.a," March 2025, https://doi.org/10.1093/OED/2624631438.
8. Whitman, "Song of Myself," 73.
9. Many scholars associate the term *financialization* specifically with the integration of financial markets into everyday life since the 1970s. Throughout my study, I follow cultural materialists like Walter Benjamin and Victorianists like Mary Poovey who use the term because it acknowledges how nineteenth-century "institutions, protocols, and epistemologies comprising 'the financial system'" grew apace with accelerating "flows of capital" that were unleashed in ever urgent quests for financial profit (Kornbluh, *Realizing Capital*, 159n1). See also Benjamin, *Arcades Project*, J62a, 2, and Nguyen, "Capitalism and Primal." For Epstein, the term means "the increasing role of financial motives, financial markets, financial actors and financial institutions in the operation of the domestic and international economies" (Epstein, *Financialization*, 3; quoted in Davis and Kim, "Financialization of the Economy," 204). See also Krippner, *Capitalizing on Crisis*, 4, 27–28. In their synthesis of sociological research, Davis and Kim argue that "how finance is intermediated in an economy . . . shapes social institutions in fundamental ways" (204). Although not the object of their work, they do acknowledge that "ideology and historical circumstance" helped normalize this creep (204).
10. Lepler, "Pictures of Panic." See also Lepler, *Many Panics*, 251. For Sandage, Clay's image resonates beyond even the event of panic and is "the era's best-known engraving" (Sandage, *Born Losers*, 57).
11. Library of Congress, Prints and Photographs Online Catalog, *The Times*, n.d., www.loc.gov/pictures/item/2008661304/.
12. Galbraith, *Money*, 4.
13. *Oxford English Dictionary*, "business (n.), sense II.14.a," March 2025, https://doi.org/10.1093/OED/4971039115.
14. Marx and Engels, *Manifesto*, 476.
15. Balleisen, *Navigating Failure*, 101.

16. Sandage, *Born Losers*, 4. See also Rezneck, *Business Depressions*, 3; Wilentz, *Rise of American Democracy*, 216, 202; and Block, *Nation of Agents*, 312–13.

17. Balleisen, *Navigating Failure*, 65. On the cultural evidence I mention, one literary index of this growth is the development of the business magazine for a general audience in 1839: Freeman Hunt's *Merchants' Magazine*. See Hewitt, "Romances." More in the notes that follow on the tension between the industrial and the financial frames for cultural analyses of the history of capitalism in the United States.

18. Balleisen, *Navigating Failure*, 65.

19. The era's writers preferred the term "business fluctuations" to what economists today frame as the "business cycle." The latter would not receive regular usage until the early twentieth century. Further, as a technical concept, the latter refers to a single macroeconomic cycle from expansion to recession. The writers I study do not always adhere to this strict formalism as they contend, directly or indirectly, with market flux. For social and intellectual histories of the "business cycle" in US political economy, see Rezneck, *Business Depressions*, and Miller, *Banking Theories*.

20. "Political Economy," *Niles' Weekly Register*, January 13, 1821. As antebellum financial markets spiraled downward, textual ones steadily rose. The twentieth-century historian Collman estimates that "millions upon millions of words" constitute historical panic discourse (*Mysterious Panics*, 40–41, quoted in Fabian, "Speculation," 127).

21. Rezneck, *Business Depressions*, 7. For Rezneck, hard times produced "two principal kinds" of economic writing "consisting first of occasional and temporal writings dealing with the specific conditions and causes of particular depressions." Second, there were "more general treatises concerned with the theory and genetics of the business cycle" (5–6). Both kinds of writing emphasized "the social and psychological aspects of depression" (9). As the English economist John Mills put it: "The malady of the commercial crisis is not, in essence, a matter of purse, but of the mind" (quoted in Rezneck, 9). See also Miller, *Banking Theories*, 193, and Kornbluh, *Realizing Capital*, 22.

22. Justiza [pseud.], "Hard Times," *Philadelphia Register and National Recorder*, March 6, 1819.

23. Martineau, *Society in America*, 238.

24. "Conventions of Business Men," *Niles' Weekly Register*, August 12, 1837. This phrase would enter into popular literary culture too; see Arthur, *Making Haste to Be Rich*.

25. Strong, *Diary*, 2:358. This impulse to connect one panic to the next was widespread and reveals a kind of temporal crisis over financial writing's inability to prevent unrest in the future. See *'37 and '57: A Brief Popular Account*.

26. "Afterword," in Zakim and Kornblith, *Capitalism Takes Command*, 279.

27. All quotations are to Raymond, *Political Economy*, 63. Here, Raymond riffs on Smith's *Wealth of Nations* (1776); for a discussion of the relevant passage in Smith, see Henderson, *Romantic Identities*, 43.

28. Anthony, *Paper Money Men*, 3.

29. Greene, *Perils of Pearl Street*, 5.

30. Briggs, *Harry Franco*, 2:212. For a reading of *Harry Franco* that emphasizes Briggs's commercial didacticism, see Sánchez, *Reforming the World*, 71–73.

31. Briggs, *Harry Franco*, 2:216.

32. Raymond, *Political Economy*, 63.

33. Briggs, *Harry Franco*, 2:216. On the spiritual but speculative self, see Sandage, *Born Losers*, 27.

34. Alger, *Ragged Dick*, 97.

35. Agnew, *Worlds Apart*, 4. More recently, cultural historians have illuminated this connection with the diaries of midcentury clerks. See Augst, *Clerk's Tale*; Sandage, *Born Losers*; and Luskey, *On the Make*.

36. In their focus on nervous professionals, such vernacular fictions, to appropriate the words of the historian Seth Rockman from a different context, tend to "float above the messiness of class conflict" (Rockman, "Capitalism Newsworthy?," 463). The humble modalities of the financial revolution in the antebellum United States, which are internalized and reproduced by go-ahead selves, rather than the "blood" of the industrial one, preoccupies these texts, a fact that is likewise true for nearly every writer I examine in this book (Rockman, "Capitalism Newsworthy?," 463). Rockman's article discusses the tendency among the new historians of capitalism to emphasize the financial (and the individualist) over the industrial (and the collective). It is as if these writers—and their subjects—often did not feel "immediately imperiled by industrial capitalism's structures," but rather felt empowered by them (Luskey, *On the Make*, 16). On the tension between industrial and financial frames for historiography, see also Balleisen, *Navigating Failure*, 247n42.

37. Zakim and Kornblith, *Capitalism Takes Command*, 7, 1. The "new history of capitalism" has garnered attention from the mainstream press—see Jennifer Schuessler, "In History Departments, It's Up with Capitalism," *New York Times*, April 6, 2013. And among the many scholarly metareflections on this subfield, see Beckert et al., "Interchange"; Beckert, "History of American Capitalism"; and Clegg, "Capitalism and Slavery." On the allied field of the history of political economy, see Huston, "Economic Landscapes." For a call for the "Economic Humanities" (more on that follows) and the "new history of capitalism" to integrate, see Crosthwaite, Knight, and Marsh, "Economic Humanities," 664.

38. Zakim and Kornblith, *Capitalism Takes Command*, 4.

39. Sklansky, "Elusive Sovereign," 234.

40. Sandage, *Born Losers*, 18. On the mystification of market activity as "intrinsically voluntarist and self-subscribed," see Block, *Nation of Agents*, 314. There is much more on Block throughout my study.

41. Bartlett, *Dictionary*, 147. For Sandage, the phrase "go ahead" was part of a cultural semantic field that included "fast," "ambition," and "individuality." The term *individualism* is for Sandage "a grandiloquent name for the go-ahead creed" (*Born Losers*, 94).

42. Sandage, *Born Losers*, 97.

43. Rockman, "Capitalism Newsworthy?," 463.

44. Winthrop, "Model of Christian Charity," 168.

45. Baker, *Securing the Commonwealth*, 114.

46. In *Capital*, Marx explains the virtualization of the self in dramaturgical terms: "The characters who appear on the economic stage," he writes, "are merely personifications of economic relations" (179). This process manifests in the credit-rating industry that, beginning in 1841, led agencies "to assess, authenticate, index, abstract, and archive people, places, and things" (Sandage, *Born Losers*, 124), in addition to the

securitization of enslaved people in the antebellum United State (Baptist, "Toxic Debt"). McClanahan sees twenty-first century culture as complicating the relationship between the virtualization of the self and credit-rating—see *Dead Pledges*, 55–95.

47. Studies that situate literature in relation to market epistemology include Poovey, *Credit Economy*; Knight, *Reading the Market*; Sánchez, *Reforming the World*; and Hewitt, *Speculative Fictions*. See also Lee, *Uncertain Chances*. For a genealogy of the New Economic Criticism "as an object that is difficult to pin down," see O'Brien, *Literature Incorporated*, 6. See also Seybold and Chihara, *Routledge Companion*. The project of New Economic Criticism is most often approached as a poststructuralist one in which one "read[s] literary and economic texts through their political and social contexts while also considering that those contexts were themselves primarily signifying structures—that socioeconomic systems were ultimately systems of writing" (Crosthwaite, Knight, and Marsh, "Economic Humanities," 662–63). So, Germana begins his study of monetary and racial discourses with the premise that "the meaning of words, the value of money, and the significance of race all fluctuate within economies of difference" (*Standards of Value*, 1). Throughout my book, I endorse the new materialist bent of the Economic Humanities, as I acknowledge that the culture of the market "involves a complex interweaving of conceptual paradigms and material processes" (Crosthwaite, Knight, and Marsh, "Economic Humanities," 664). But I also recognize previous work in the New Economic Criticism was "both more varied . . . than is usually assumed and still evolves productively in the present" (Crosthwaite, Knight, and Marsh, "Economic Humanities," 664).

48. Studies of the British novel and the financial imagination include Baucom, *Specters*; Gallagher, *Body Economic*; Lynch, *Economy of Character*; Brantlinger, *Fictions of State*; and Thompson, *Models of Value*. I have elsewhere brought this scholarship to bear on the early American novel—see Kopec, "Fiction, Finance."

49. Luck, *Body of Property*, 12. For examples of the anxiety thesis, see Anthony, *Paper Money Men*, 2; Templin, *Panic Fiction*, 19; Weyler, *Intricate Relations*, 2.

50. See, respectively, Anthony, *Paper Money Men*; Weyler, *Intricate Relations*; Luck, *Body of Property*; and Wertheimer, *Underwriting*.

51. Anthony, *Paper Money Men*, 28, 2.

52. Leverenz, *Manhood*, 4. On "the figure of the 'unmanned' bankrupt," see Balleisen, *Navigating Failure*, 77–78.

53. Briggs, *Bankrupt Stories*, 5.

54. "Introduction," in Zakim and Kornblith, *Capitalism Takes Command*, 2; Luck, *Body of Property*, 13.

55. Anthony, *Paper Money Men*, 28. See also Denning, *Mechanic Accent*.

56. In this same vein, see Baker, *Securing the Commonwealth*; McGill, *Culture of Reprinting*, 19; Fichtelberg, *Critical Fictions*, 5; Luck, *Body of Property*, 14. As these studies make clear, the problem is a kind of repressive hypothesis that results in criticism that either ignores major writers' consideration of market flux or "perhaps overstates the resistant, or even reactionary, posture of antebellum writers" (Luck, *Body of Property*, 14). Sánchez's *Reforming the World* represents this former position (30), and it has prompted this critique from Gavin Jones: "But to assume that canonized literary figures did not write about the Panic of 1837 . . . is to miss the deeper ways that writers could

respond to questions of finance and failure—at the level of form and affect rather than subject matter and theme" (*Failure*, 17). I share Jones's outlook, but I depart from his work in both periodization and the sense of failure as, foremost, a stylistic problem.

For a Foucauldian critique of "anxiety" in the nineteenth century from the perspective of the "nervous system," see Murison, *Politics of Anxiety*, 8. Although emphasizing a medical humanities approach, rather than an economic one, Murison is rightly skeptical of a repressive hypothesis as it relates to *anxiety*.

57. Crosthwaite, Knight, and Marsh, "Economic Humanities," 665.

58. Anthony, *Paper Money Men*, 10 (emphasis original).

59. Joseph Hopkinson, "Lecture on Commercial Integrity," *Hunt's Merchants' Magazine* 1, 1839, 372 (emphasis original).

60. McGill, *Culture of Reprinting*, 266.

61. Hawthorne, *House of the Seven Gables*, 2:2. Subsequent citations, abbreviated *HSG* and cited parenthetically, are to this edition.

62. Pratt, *Archives of American Time*, 64. Rifkin uses "entropy" in the identical context (*Settler Common Sense*, 44).

63. Pratt, *Archives of American Time*, 71. See also Brown, *Domestic Individualism*; Anthony, *Paper Money Men*; Rifkin, *Settler Common Sense*; Michaels, *Gold Standard*.

64. Gilmore, *American Romanticism*; McGill, *Culture of Reprinting*, 220. More on McGill's scholarship on Hawthorne in chapter 4.

65. Anthony, *Paper Money Men*, 166; Rifkin, *Settler Common Sense*, 45. For these scholars, the romance's investment in self-making is racialized (I address this theme, although not in Hawthorne, in chapter 5). Where Anthony develops this argument from the perspective of paper money, in which whiteness is a hedge against financial instability, Rifkin does so from a Lockean one, in which the erasure of Indigeneity permits the Pyncheons-Maules to continue to assert their land proprietorship. What is important for my purposes now is that both arguments see racialization as nervous reactions to uncertainty in the financial market.

66. Michaels, *Gold Standard*, 101.

67. Anthony and Rifkin have generated insightful readings of characters like Clifford and Uncle Venner as a "a figure . . . incapable of achieving the . . . 'go-ahead' attitude of the early 1850s" (Anthony, *Paper Money Men*, 169; see also Rifkin, *Settler Common Sense*, 42–43). What I want to argue is that emphasizing the romance's deviations from the rigors of capitalist identity can obscure *House's* ultimate investment in it.

68. Luck addresses a similar pattern of embodied frustration with the judge (*Body of Property*, 99). Where Luck focuses on how the novel corporealizes Judge Pyncheon's excessive appetites, I focus on how it financializes them. In doing so, I am observing a diametrically opposite treatment of the corpse in Hawthorne from what Anthony finds in his reading of Zenobia's dead body in *The Blithedale Romance* (1852) and (Anthony, *Paper Money Men*, 155).

69. Michaels, *Gold Standard*, 98.

70. Michaels, *Gold Standard*, 97. There, Michaels discusses Doherty's research on the many nineteenth-century transients who "failed to gain even minimal material success" in urban centers like Salem (Doherty, *Society and Power*, 49; quoted in Michaels, *Gold Standard*, 97).

71. Okker, *Our Sister Editors*, 2.
72. Rifkin, *Settler Common Sense*, 41, 57.
73. Hawthorne uses this performative language at the outset of *House* in a well-known passage about the "fluctuating waves of social life," in which "somebody is always at the drowning point" (*HSG*, 38). This passage warrants Michaels's account of the novel's conservatism—Hawthorne, he argues, turns away from this "tragedy" of fluctuation (*HSG*, 38). I am suggesting, however, that the novel integrates these fluxional dynamics into its economic imagination.
74. Levy, "Capital as Process," 500.
75. Levy, "Capital as Process," 487.
76. Levy, "Capital as Process," 500.
77. Crosthwaite, Knight, and Marsh, "Economic Humanities," 665.
78. Block, *Nation of Agents*, 23.
79. Block, *Nation of Agents*, 316.
80. Block, *Nation of Agents*, 316.
81. Block, *Nation of Agents*, 23.
82. Block, *Nation of Agents*, 316.
83. Block, *Nation of Agents*, 317.
84. Block, *Nation of Agents*, 339.
85. Brown, *Domestic Individualism*, 92–94.
86. Hopkinson, "Lecture on Commercial Integrity," 372.
87. Hopkinson, "Lecture on Commercial Integrity," 372.
88. Miss Sedgwick to Miss K. M. Sedgwick, April 24, 1837, in Dewey, *Life and Letters*, 265.
89. McClanahan, *Dead Pledges*. See also Shonkwiler, *Financial Imagination*; Smith, *Affect and American Literature*; Huehls, *After Critique*; and La Berge, *Scandals and Abstraction*.
90. Bauman, *Liquid Times*, 1.
91. Bauman, *Liquid Times*, 1, 24.
92. Crosthwaite, Knight, and Marsh, "Economic Humanities," 667.
93. This is Shonkwiler's term for twenty-first-century novels that "expand and thicken . . . finance's imaginary" (*Financial Imagination*, 121).
94. See Kornbluh, *Realizing Capital*, 22.
95. Hawthorne, "Custom-House," 6.
96. Zimmerman begins his own monograph on American literature and financial crises, *Panic!*, by situating his study within the turbulence of the 1890s, in which "Americans literally read their fates in panics" (1).
97. The exception here is Crosthwaite, Knight, and Marsh, "Economic Humanities," which I discuss below. Shonkwiler is typical here in seeing the conflicts of the Gilded Age as "set[ting] the stage" for later writers (*Financial Imagination*, xxxi). See also Knight, *Reading the Market*, 192.
98. Shonkwiler, *Financial Imagination*, xxxi.
99. Foucault, *Birth of Biopolitics*; Brown, *Undoing the Demos*.
100. Jackson, *Business of Letters*. See also Sawaya, *Difficult Art of Giving*.
101. Hartigan-O'Connor, "Political Economy," 339.

102. Templin, *Panic Fiction*, 64.
103. Bosco and Myerson, *Emerson Brothers*, 316.
104. Rockman, "Capitalism Newsworthy?," 444.

Chapter One

1. Balleisen, *Navigating Failure*, 21. The phrase "ruined business owners" can be misleading—as Balleisen succinctly states at the outset of his study: "No sector of the antebellum economy was immune from bankruptcy" (2).
2. Balleisen, *Navigating Failure*, 21.
3. Balleisen, *Navigating Failure*, 20.
4. Balleisen, *Navigating Failure*, 21.
5. "Thoughts on The Times," *Virginia Evangelical and Literary Magazine*, October 1819.
6. "Thoughts on The Times."
7. Channing, "Reflections on the Literary Delinquency of America," *The North-American Review and Miscellaneous Journal* 2, no. 4 (1815): 33.
8. For its association with bankruptcy, see definition 2 of "delinquent" (n. and adj.) in the *OED*.
9. Channing, "Literary Delinquency," 35.
10. Channing, "Literary Delinquency," 35. The editor Sarah J. Hale, as Okker demonstrates, makes a similar argument for women's potential to take up this call for producing an original literature in the early United States (Okker, *Our Sister Editors*, 87).
11. Channing, "Literary Delinquency," 38.
12. Charvat, *Profession of Authorship*, 29.
13. Jackson's *Business of Letters* offers the most potent critique of Charvat's materialist model, as it argues strenuously against market consolidation as a lived reality for nineteenth-century literary writers. For Jackson, nineteenth-century writers wrote not just for money, but for "other desirables, such as knowledge, honor, prestige, and legitimacy" (31–32). My point in this chapter, however, is that such affects were beginning to be routed through an ideology of achieved identity that would become the recognizable features of a capitalist self. See also Sawaya, *Difficult Art of Giving*.
14. Bell, *Sacrifice of Relation*, 6. On the "Machiavellian Moment," see Pocock, *Machiavellian Moment*, 235, and Anthony, *Paper Money Men*, 42.
15. Sandage, *Born Losers*, 18.
16. Franklin, *James Fenimore Cooper*, 306.
17. Bridgen, quoted in Franklin, *James Fenimore Cooper*, 314.
18. Spiller, *Fenimore Cooper*, 72–73.
19. Charvat, *Profession of Authorship*, 71. Charvat is summarizing this view, not endorsing it.
20. The "literary enterprise" (Channing's term) was just one among other ventures for Cooper. He also waited for returns from a whaling venture, the *Union*, and he held equity in a country supply store in Dekalb, New York. See Franklin, *James Fenimore Cooper*.
21. According to Franklin, the "evidence of Cooper's authorship" of this and other review essays from 1821 "is firm" (*James Fenimore Cooper*, 290).

22. The unsigned tract is "now attributed to a close associate of Cooper, tammany congressman and free trade advocate Churchill Caldom Cambreleng" (Franklin, *James Fenimore Cooper*, 291).

23. For an account of the early American novel as it relates to the regional inflections of this trade policy debate, see Shapiro, *Culture and Commerce*.

24. Conkin, *Prophets of Prosperity*, 171.

25. Cooper, *Early Critical Essays*, 25.

26. Cooper, *Early Critical Essays*, 25. Modern historiography confirms Cooper's assessment—see Balleisen, *Navigating Failure*, 27.

27. Cooper, *Early Critical Essays*, 25.

28. Balleisen, *Navigating Failure*, 27.

29. Cooper, *Early Critical Essays*, 39.

30. Franklin, *James Fenimore Cooper*, 294.

31. Cooper, *Early Critical Essays*, 40.

32. Cooper, *Early Critical Essays*, 40.

33. Franklin, *James Fenimore Cooper*, 275.

34. See Lukács, *Historical Novel* and McTiernan, "Neutral Ground."

35. McTiernan, "Neutral Ground," 3.

36. McTiernan, "Neutral Ground," 3.

37. Cooper, *Early Critical Essays*, 39. As Franklin documents, Cooper's early arrangements with printers and agents were complicated. It seems that he shouldered the production costs. Even though they did stand to gain financially on the sale and distribution of *The Spy*, his new agents, Charles Wiley and Oliver Halsted, did not have "their own funds directly at risk" (Franklin, *James Fenimore Cooper*, 271). See also Charvat, *Profession of Authorship*, 77, and Okker, *Our Sister Editors*, 86.

38. "Introduction," in Zakim and Kornblith, *Capitalism Takes Command*, 2.

39. W. H. Gardiner, "Review of *The Spy*," *North American Review* 15, no. 36 (July 1822): 266.

40. Levy, *Freaks of Fortune*.

41. Wood, *American Republic*, 68.

42. Larson, *Market Revolution*, 8.

43. Susan Fenimore Cooper, "A Glance Backward," *Atlantic Monthly* 59, no. 352 (1887): 205.

44. Block, *Nation of Agents*, 333.

45. Higham, *Boundlessness*, 14, as quoted in Block, *Nation of Agents*, 333.

46. Block, *Nation of Agents*, 23.

47. Cooper lauds Alexander Hamilton in his 1821 review (*Early Critical Essays*, 31).

48. "Art. IX," *North American Review*, July 1826, 150.

49. Ryan, *Moral Economies*, 34, 25.

50. Ryan, *Moral Economies*, 25.

51. Burstein, *Original Knickerbocker*, 73. Another Irving biographer, Williams, adds that the brothers looked for him to "spawn masterpieces," which might help him earn a reputation—and a living (*Life of Washington Irving*, 1:124).

52. Rubin-Dorsky, *Adrift*, 36.

53. Rubin-Dorsky, *Adrift*, 36.

54. Rubin-Dorsky, *Adrift*, 32.
55. Rubin-Dorsky, *Adrift*, 41, 34.
56. Anthony, *Paper Money Men*, 42.
57. Anthony, *Paper Money Men*, 42.
58. Sandage, *Born Losers*, 5.
59. Sandage, *Born Losers*, 5.
60. Irving, *Geoffrey Crayon*, 8:32. All subsequent references, cited parenthetically in the text, are to this edition and abbreviated *SB*.
61. Burstein, *Original Knickerbocker*, 73.
62. Burstein, *Original Knickerbocker*, 92.
63. Williams, *Life of Washington Irving*, 1:126.
64. Burstein, *Original Knickerbocker*, 109.
65. Irving to Brevoort, October 1815, Irving, *Complete Works of Washington Irving*, 23:425–26. Unless otherwise noted, subsequent references to Irving's correspondence, abbreviated *L* and cited parenthetically, are to this volume.
66. Williams, *Life of Washington Irving*, 1:150.
67. Williams, *Life of Washington Irving*, 1:149.
68. Matson, "Ambiguities of Risk," 598.
69. Matson, "Ambiguities of Risk," 598.
70. Rubin-Dorsky, *Adrift*, 36.
71. Anthony, *Paper Money Men*, 42.
72. Irving, quoted in Williams, *Life of Washington Irving*, 1:152.
73. Williams, *Life of Washington Irving*, 1:152–53.
74. Having succeeded as a fur trader, Brevoort facilitated interchanges between the export and import sides of the Irving business. In a letter dated December 9, 1816, Irving thanks Brevoort for fronting cash to his brothers in New York needed to "weather the storm" (*L*, 23:462). On letter writing between male merchants, see Ditz, "Shipwrecked."
75. Bell, *Sacrifice of Relation*, 32.
76. Balliesen, *Navigating Bankruptcy*, 167.
77. Baucom, *Specters*, 22.
78. For two important studies of copyright and US literature, see McGill, *Culture of Reprinting* and Homestead, *American Women Authors*.
79. Levy, "Capital as Process," 487.
80. Baker, *Securing the Commonwealth*, 162.
81. *Niles' Weekly Register*, November 3, 1821, 145.
82. *Niles' Weekly Register*, May 22, 1819, 209.
83. Hedges, *Washington Irving*, 115.
84. Whale, "City of Culture," 93.
85. Welter, "True Womanhood," 152.
86. Brevoort, "Sketch Book, No. 1," 46.
87. "On the Fluctuations of Property, and the Increase of Speculation," *Panoplist, and Missionary Herald*, October 1820, 453.
88. As Leverenz has shown, "class dynamics become subsumed in gender ideologies," as white men in 1820 began to "measure their worth primarily through their work" (*Manhood*, 72–73). For Leverenz, transformations in gender protocols and in the

mode of production were mutually reinforcing. The problems of manhood "came to be felt with special intensity in the antebellum Northeast as industrialization separated the home from the workplace, where entrepreneurial values placed far more emphasis on risk and competition" (*Manhood*, 73). Rotundo confirms many of Leverenz's insights, arguing that "in the early 1800s, self-made manhood became the dominant cultural form" (*American Manhood*, 7).

89. Templin, *Panic Fiction*, 14.
90. Horwitz, "Rip Van Winkle."
91. Horwitz, "Rip Van Winkle."
92. Horwitz, "Rip Van Winkle."
93. Baker, *Securing the Commonwealth*, 162.
94. Horwitz, "Rip Van Winkle."
95. Horwitz, "Rip Van Winkle."
96. Block, *Nation of Agents*, 336.
97. Parrington, *Main Currents*, 2:207.
98. Irving, *Life and Letters*, 3:148.
99. Mackay, *Extraordinary Popular Delusions*, 1:3; Irving, "Unexampled Prosperity," in *Complete Works of Washington Irving*, 27:303. Subsequent citations are to this edition.
100. The latter term is Irving's ("Unexampled Prosperity," 27:304). On Irving's shift from fiction to fact as an act of risk avoidance, see Bell, *Sacrifice of Relation*. See also Baker, *Securing the Commonwealth*, 165–66.
101. Irving, "Unexampled Prosperity," 27:304.
102. Irving, "Unexampled Prosperity," 27:304.
103. Irving, "Unexampled Prosperity," 27:304.
104. Irving, "Unexampled Prosperity," 27:305.
105. Knight, *Reading the Market*, 195.
106. Raymond, *Political Economy*, 63.
107. Irving, "Unexampled Prosperity," 27:324.
108. Irving, "Unexampled Prosperity," 27:324.
109. Irving, "Unexampled Prosperity," 27:323.
110. Irving, "Unexampled Prosperity," 27:315, 27:313.
111. Irving, "Unexampled Prosperity," 27:323.
112. Irving, "Unexampled Prosperity," 27:323.
113. Irving, "Unexampled Prosperity," 27:323.
114. Irving, "Unexampled Prosperity," 27:303–4.
115. Irving, "Unexampled Prosperity," 27:305.

Chapter Two

1. "Art. II.—Morals of Trade," *Hunt's Merchants' Magazine* 6, 1842, 24–26.
2. "Morals of Trade," 24–26.
3. James Hoban, Jr., "The Character of Woman," *Ladies' Garland and Family Wreath*, December 1838.
4. Hoban, Jr., "Character of Woman," 129.

5. Hoban, Jr., "Character of Woman," 129.
6. Hoban, Jr., "Character of Woman," 129.
7. Baym, *Woman's Fiction*, 53.
8. Karcher, "Sedgwick in Literary History," 6.
9. Shapiro, "Providence of Class," 200. See, respectively, Fichtelberg, *Critical Fictions*; Templin, *Panic Fiction*; and Shapiro.
10. Okker, *Our Sister Editors*, 159.
11. Hartigan-O'Connor, "Political Economy," 339.
12. Templin, *Panic Fiction*, 12.
13. Smith, *Riches Without Wings*, 12, 13.
14. Block, *Nation of Agents*, 445. See also Sandage, *Born Losers*, 48.
15. Mihm, *Nation of Counterfeiters*, 3.
16. Block, *Nation of Agents*, 446. He cites here, among other novels, Sedgwick's *The Linwoods* (1835).
17. Gamer, "Maria Edgeworth," 235.
18. Gamer explains that texts in the genre "claim to occupy both poles [the probable and the improbable] simultaneously, promising to delight readers while delivering the pedagogical heft of an empirically verified 'real'" ("Maria Edgeworth," 238).
19. In her analysis of didactic panic fiction, Sánchez links this genre to the commercial crisis of 1837, and she cites texts that oppose "romance" (unreality) and "real life" (reality) in financial terms. Such fiction thus prescribes "learning to properly read, to distinguish between 'romance' and 'life'" (*Reforming the World*, 73).
20. Sánchez, *Reforming the World*, 73.
21. Sedgwick, "Romance in Real Life," 237. All subsequent references, cited parenthetically in the text, are to this edition and abbreviated "RRL."
22. "Miss Sedgwick's Sketches," *Southern Literary Messenger*, January 1836. Tales in the genre commonly turned on such vicissitudes, as revealed, for instance, by one piece from the era's magazines titled "Remarkable Reverse of Fortune" (*New-York Mirror*, October 1834).
23. Sánchez, *Reforming the World*, 32.
24. Dewey, *Catharine M. Sedgwick*, 250.
25. Put otherwise, here Sedgwick confronts what we might be tempted to call the *financial sublime*. In analyzing contemporary literature, Shonkwiler uses this term to refer "to the full range of mystifications of capital . . . that make it difficult or impossible to distinguish the actuality of money from the increasing unreality of global capitalism" ("Financial Sublime," 249). For me, Sedgwick's sense of this catastrophe is more in tune with a romantic sensibility of the sublime—awe and terror. And the end result is the exposure of the reality of commercial exchange, rather than the unreality of it—the exposure of a reality, that is, from which Americans had strayed, but to which they can return.
26. Dewey, *Catharine M. Sedgwick*, 250.
27. Dewey, *Catharine M. Sedgwick*, 250.
28. Marx, "Crisis Theory," 450.
29. Dewey, *Catharine M. Sedgwick*, 250.
30. Dewey, *Catharine M. Sedgwick*, 250–51.

31. Ware to Sedgwick, January 31, 1835, in Dewey, *Catharine M. Sedgwick*, 239. See also Ware, *Memoir*, 2:129–30.

32. And for good reason. As Homestead has cogently argued in the context of the "shape of Sedgwick's career," her "authorial scope and ambition appear much broader if we give equal weight to her fictions across subgenres" ("Shape of Sedgwick's Career," 187); Homestead here riffs on Baym's classic study of Hawthorne, *The Shape of Hawthorne's Career*, a revisionist project that she (Homestead) has continued recently in "Augusta Jane Evans"). I would add to Homestead that attending to works—private and public, nonfictional and fictional—across Sedgwick's career reinforces the "scope and ambition" of her economic critique within the antebellum era as well.

33. Robbins, "Periodizing Authorship," 3–4; Dewey, *Catharine M. Sedgwick*, 239.

34. Robbins, "Periodizing Authorship," 1.

35. Shapiro, "Providence of Class," 200.

36. Shapiro, "Providence of Class," 203. Shapiro's work complicates prior critics' dismissal of this novella as didactic and ideological. Lewis, for instance, has sharply addressed its "unnuanced treatment of the benefits of poverty and the disadvantages of wealth" ("Little Charity," 263). See also Gates, "American Poor."

37. Shapiro, "Providence of Class," 200.

38. Dewey, *Catharine M. Sedgwick*, 239.

39. Mihm, *Nation of Counterfeiters*, 180.

40. Sobel, *Panic on Wall Street*, 39.

41. Hammond, *Banks and Politics*, 453. For a contemporary account of the "wild and visionary speculations" that would eventually result in the Panic of 1837, see Hildreth, *History of Banks*.

42. Andrew Jackson, "July 10, 1832: Bank Veto," https://millercenter.org/the-presidency/presidential-speeches/july-10-1832-bank-veto.

43. Unlike Melville's *The Confidence-Man* (see chapter 4), which, as Mihm notes, offers a sophisticated critique of the era's banking system, in which the line separating "real" banks and counterfeiters was often imperceptible, Sedgwick's novella does not engage with the reputability of paper money (*Nation of Counterfeits*, 4). For Sedgwick, perhaps, counterfeit money was like a romance hopelessly adrift from the "real"—a genre that could not be moderated and, therefore, one that was beyond the pale of her (and her characters') interests.

44. Germana, "Counterfeiters," 300.

45. Block, *Nation of Agents*, 544.

46. Block, *Nation of Agents*, 544.

47. Balleisen, *Navigating Failure*, 34.

48. Balleisen, *Navigating Failure*, 94.

49. Anthony, *Paper Money Men*, 107.

50. Robbins, "Periodizing Authorship," 17.

51. Shapiro, "Providence of Class," 209. As I discuss earlier, my work adds to Shapiro's depiction of Sedgwick's political economy by demonstrating the extent to which her classed worldview relies, fundamentally, on a generic understanding of capitalism as a "romance in real life" that ought to temper go-aheadism.

52. Balleisen, *Navigating Failure*, 159.

53. Larson, *Market Revolution*, 92.

54. Miss Sedgwick to Miss K. M. (Katherine Maria) Sedgwick, April 24, 1837, in Dewey, *Catharine M. Sedgwick*, 265.

55. Sedgwick to Sedgwick, April 24, 1837, in Dewey, *Catharine M. Sedgwick*, 265.

56. "Convention of Business Men," *Niles' Weekly Register*, August 12, 1837.

57. Sedgwick to Sedgwick, April 24, 1837, in Dewey, *Catharine M. Sedgwick*, 265.

58. Sedgwick to Sedgwick, April 24, 1837, in Dewey, *Catharine M. Sedgwick*, 265.

59. Sedgwick to Sedgwick, April 24, 1837, in Dewey, *Catharine M. Sedgwick*, 265.

60. Sedgwick to Sedgwick, April 24, 1837, in Dewey, *Catharine M. Sedgwick*, 265.

61. Sedgwick to Sedgwick, April 24, 1837, in Dewey, *Catharine M. Sedgwick*, 264.

62. Sedgwick to Sedgwick, April 24, 1837, in Dewey, *Catharine M. Sedgwick*, 264.

63. Sedgwick to Sedgwick, April 24, 1837, in Dewey, *Catharine M. Sedgwick*, 264–65.

64. Miss Sedgwick to Mr. Charles Sedgwick, May 24, 1837, in Dewey, *Catharine M. Sedgwick*, 267.

65. Catharine M. Sedgwick, "Who, and What, Has Not Failed," *New-Yorker*, June 17, 1837.

66. Sedgwick, "Who, and What."

67. Sedgwick, "Who, and What."

68. Sedgwick, "Who, and What."

69. Charles Sedgwick, *Public and Private Economy*, 133.

70. Sedgwick, "Who, and What."

71. Sedgwick, "Who, and What."

72. Sedgwick, "Who, and What."

73. Sedgwick, "Who, and What."

74. Sedgwick, "Who, and What."

75. In 1836, Sedgwick published a different short story called "New Year's Day" (no hyphen) in Samuel G. Goodrich's annual, *The Token and Atlantic Souvenir*.

76. Sedgwick, "New-Year's Day," *Columbian Lady's and Gentleman's Magazine*, February 1846.

77. Sedgwick, "New-Year's Day."

78. Sedgwick, "New-Year's Day."

79. Sedgwick, "New-Year's Day."

80. Sedgwick, "New-Year's Day." In moving Mercer's mercantile activity to East Asia, Sedgwick's tale partakes of a long cultural history detailed by Weyler, "Speculating Spirit."

81. Sedgwick, "New-Year's Day." Thoreau makes a joke of this midcentury practice. He writes in *Walden* that "bankruptcy and repudiation are the springboards from which much of our civilization vaults and turns its somersets," pointing to a social reality of life under capitalism that Sedgwick's fiction would like to alter (*Walden*, 22).

Chapter Three

1. "Editor's Table: Cheerfulness," *Harper's New Monthly Magazine* 16 (December 1857): 122.

2. "Cheerfulness," 122.

3. "Cheerfulness," 122.

4. "Success," in Emerson, *Collected Works*, 7:143. Subsequent references to this edition of Emerson's writing, abbreviated *CW*, will be cited in the text parenthetically by volume and page number.

5. Kern, "Emerson and Economics," 678.

6. For the former, see Newfield, *Emerson Effect*, where he strenuously critiques Emerson's idealist fidelity to moral laws as licensing the material excess of the nineteenth-century United States.

7. Sandage, *Born Losers*; Levy, *Freaks of Fortune*, 84; Sklansky, *Soul's Economy*, 33–72.

8. Sklansky, *Soul's Economy*, 6.

9. Sklansky, *Soul's Economy*, 6.

10. Bromell, *Sweat of the Brow*, 2.

11. I quote here from the lecture, "Man the Reformer" (1841), but this sentiment abides in the essay "Wealth" (1870). See *CW*, 6:60.

12. Newfield's analysis blames Emerson for the rise of the corporate ethos in the United States—mine would indict him for something like that corporation's expectation for a full-time employee to participate in strategic planning while on vacation.

13. Emerson, *Journals and Miscellaneous Notebooks*, 5:327. References to this edition of Emerson's journals, abbreviated *JMN*, will be cited parenthetically in the text.

14. Frothingham, *Hard Times*, 4.

15. Emerson's friend and former colleague, Frothingham, finds that the "commercial world," indeed, "is governed by rules that are peculiar," and the "vexed questions concerning credit and capital," "the laws of currency," and the "fluctuations of trade" are "too complicated" for the pulpit (*Hard Times*, 4).

16. An important exception here is Brownson's May 1837 sermon, *The Spirit of Gain*, a scathing diatribe that, with its dialectical framework, anticipates his later argument in "The Laboring Classes" (1840). For an economic critique of Brownson, see Pickford, "Fungible Scrip."

17. Lears, *Something for Nothing*, 3.

18. See, for example, "Money Market," *Daily National Intelligencer*, April 11, 1837.

19. Bosco and Myerson, *Emerson Brothers*, 316.

20. Emerson, *Letters*, 1:232. References to this edition, abbreviated *L*, will be cited parenthetically in the text.

21. Bosco and Myerson, *Emerson Brothers*, 578.

22. Grusin, "'God in Your Debt,'" 43n3.

23. Packer, *Emerson's Fall*, 99.

24. Bell, "Hard Currency," 735.

25. Bell, "Hard Currency," 735.

26. Block, *Nation of Agents*, 333.

27. Block, *Nation of Agents*, 460. There is (in my view, at least) a pronounced compatibility between Block's integrative thesis, derived from his social history of US capitalist selfhood, and Newfield's, which stems from his political-ethical take on Emerson. The latter finds in Emerson a body of writing that makes the transformation of the self into a capitalist agent (in Block's idiom) "*feel OK*" (*Emerson Effect*, 4; emphasis original).

28. "Address on Education," in Emerson, *Early Lectures*, 2:197. References to this edition, abbreviated *EL*, will be cited parenthetically in the text.
29. Block, *Nation of Agents*, 26.
30. See also Rezneck, "Social History," 664.
31. Pfister, *Surveyors of Customs*, 15.
32. Frothingham, *Hard Times*, 8.
33. Frothingham, *Hard Times*, 12.
34. Emerson would consistently valorize this commitment to "a work of my own," even while he acknowledged that it was (for him) always enmeshed in the structure of financial capitalism. In his journal entry about declining an invitation to the experiment at Brook Farm, he writes, "I have a work of my own which I know I can do with some success. . . . My Genius loudly calls me to stay where I am, even with the degradation of owning bank-stock and seeing poor men suffer whilst the Universal Genius apprises me of this disgrace" (*JMN*, 9:62). He realizes that financial returns permit such practice, and this brings ambivalence, no doubt. But he remains steadfast in using these returns for his own ends.
35. This opposition is a foundational insight of classical political economy. See Smith, *Wealth of Nations*, 314–15. And Emerson here co-opts "mechanical metaphors," which his friend and correspondent Thomas Carlyle worries will "imprison us" (Bronk, *Romantic Economist*, 24).
36. "The Downfall of Speculation," *New-Yorker*, October 12, 1839.
37. "Convention of Business Men," *Niles' Weekly Register*, August 12, 1837.
38. Martineau, *Society in America*, 238. Emerson commented of this volume in his *Journals*: "I have read Miss Martineau's first volume with great pleasure" (*JMN*, 5:354).
39. Newfield, *Emerson Effect*.
40. Dewey, *Moral Views*, 81.
41. Buell, *Emerson*, 244.
42. Smith, "Disciplines of Attention," 889.
43. Smith, "Disciplines of Attention," 909.
44. Smith, "Disciplines of Attention," 909.
45. Block, *Nation of Agents*, 460.
46. Sellers, *Market Revolution*, 261. See also Sandage, *Born Losers*, 7, and Balleisen, *Navigating Failure*, 80.
47. See also an article in Greeley's *New-Yorker*, which even cited failure in business as one of the "various modern causes of suicide." The piece refers the reader to the case of "a merchant, aged 32, who had lost his fortune, and was left without resources," and thus determined to commit suicide ("Remarkable Suicides," *New-Yorker*, December 7, 1839, 180).
48. Maibor, joining Bromell, Gilmore, and Pfister, uses Emerson's early lecture series to emphasize his thinking about labor. She extensively reads the early lecture series, *The Philosophy of History* (December 1836–March 1837) and *Human Culture* (December 1837–February 1838), in addition to his occasional addresses from the 1840s, as evidence of Emerson's idealization of the division of labor: "The division of labor, occurring naturally by everyone heeding his individual calling, would strengthen humanity; occurring falsely through societal pressures and limitations, it weakens and

stunts us all" (Maibor, *Labor Pains*, 5). For a related critique of Emerson's liberalism, see Dolan, *Emerson's Liberalism*, which demonstrates Emerson's affinities with classical political economy. I aim to clarify that Emerson's thinking engages, more particularly, the era's financial instability and the categories of self this unrest necessitated.

49. "Getting Along Slowly," *Hunt's Merchants' Magazine* 35, 1856, 393. For an overview of the cultural work of the genre of conduct literature and a detailed bibliography, see Newton, *Learning to Behave*.

50. Horwitz, *Law of Nature*.

51. Block, *Nation of Agents*, 473.

52. For more on this process of renaturalizing forms of attention, see Smith, "Disciplines of Attention."

53. "Getting Along Slowly," 394.

54. The passage "our safety is in our speed" slightly emends an October 19, 1837 passage from the *Journals* (*JMN*, 5:402), and it appears in the essay "Prudence" (*CW*, 2:138). In a revaluation of "Prudence," Hanlon remarks, "Prudence is for Emerson in 1841 the genius of managing outward reality with an eye to its betterment, and doing so requires us to give social, economic, and political circumstance its due" (*Emerson's Memory Loss*, 82).

55. Block, *Nation of Agents*, 473–74.

56. "Perpetual Forces," in Emerson, *Later Lectures*, 2:300.

57. Insko analyzes this same tendency in the essay "Circles," but sees it as expressing Emerson's immediatist abolitionism, rather than his response to business enterprise's influence on the self. See Insko, *History*, 121.

58. Lee, *Uncertain Chances*, 148.

59. Knight, *Reading the Market*.

60. US Congress, *Financial Crisis*, 11.

61. US Congress, *Financial Crisis*, 12.

62. US Congress, *Financial Crisis*, 13.

63. Greenspan, *Age of Turbulence*, 520.

64. US Congress, *Financial Crisis*, 13.

65. Greenspan, *Age of Turbulence*, 515.

66. US Congress, *Financial Crisis*, 13.

67. Berlant first articulates this idea in *Queen of America*, 222; they elaborate on it in "Cruel Optimism," 23. In the latter work, they link "technologies of patience" to "the violence of normativity," a fair description, in my estimation, of Emerson's account of the self, and its long game, in the context of economic crisis ("Cruel Optimism," 23).

68. Here we can see Greenspan's faith in what Balakrishnan critiques as "capitalism's distinctive capacity for creative destruction, for periodic renewal through downturns that liquidate inefficient conditions of production and life forms, opening up frontiers for the next round of expansion" ("Speculations," 6). Balakrishnan's Schumpterian frame ("creative destruction") implies, further, how capitalist apologetics, including Emerson's, diminish the significance of a local event through a long temporal frame, an idealist angle of vision that leads to material consequences in the "next round of expansion."

Chapter Four

1. Following Levine's recommendation in citing "Hawthorne and His Mosses," this chapter refers to the consecutive issues of Literary World, rather than the reprint included in Parker's Norton edition of Moby-Dick. See Levine, "Teaching and Writing."
2. Melville, "Hawthorne and His Mosses," Literary World, August 17, 1850, 125.
3. Melville, "Hawthorne," 125.
4. Melville, "Hawthorne," 125.
5. Weinauer, "Plagiarism," 701.
6. Weinauer, "Plagiarism," 701.
7. Weinauer, "Plagiarism," 710.
8. Pfister, Surveyors of Customs, 33. What I am calling a "sustained interest" here has also been termed "ambivalence," the latter being a keyword of studies of "American Romanticism" and the market. In this context, see Gilmore, American Romanticism. For me, this phenomenon is interesting because it leads us to consider the individual psychological affordances of "the market" in Hawthorne's and Melville's views, rather than only focusing on the fact that they needed the market to earn a living by selling their writing.
9. Pfister, Surveyors of Custom, 32. For a sense of how the word "soft" continued to circulate around Hawthorne's author effect, see James, Hawthorne, in which the realist novelist lingers with Hawthorne's "soft philosophy" (53).
10. Temple, "Fluid Identity," 464.
11. In emphasizing here the unmaking of the self, I bring an economic approach to bear on an ongoing conversation about how writers like Hawthorne and Melville critique the ideology of the Romantic self. Inspired by Sharon Cameron (Impersonality), formalist and deconstructive critics like Larson have generated subtle readings of Hawthorne and Melville's unsettling of the notion of a coherent self.
12. The Letters, 1813–1843, from Hawthorne, Centenary Edition, 15:138–39.
13. Block, Nation of Agents, 341.
14. Twice-Told Tales, from Hawthorne, Centenary Edition, 9:3. Subsequent references to Twice-Told Tales, abbreviated TT and cited parenthetically, are to this edition.
15. McGill, Culture of Reprinting, 222.
16. McGill, Culture of Reprinting, 222.
17. McGill, Culture of Reprinting, 222.
18. McGill, Culture of Reprinting, 226.
19. McGill, Culture of Reprinting, 226.
20. Although remote from my concerns here, in an analysis of a similarly patient affect in transcendentalist discourse, Insko reads what he calls this "romantic presentism" as related to the era's immediatist abolitionism, rather than a critical response to its go-aheadism. See Insko, History, 96.
21. James, Hawthorne, 53.
22. Hawthorne develops this non-anxious but critical relation to go-aheadism elsewhere, as he recasts his years of "obscurity" as a kind of training for a more turbulent—and "hard[er]"—social life. In 1840, he recounts his days before the publication of Twice-Told Tales "imprisoned . . . in this lonely chamber" as "happy" ones. The experience of living life "as if I were already in the grave" actually prepared him for the

"world." For "if I had sooner made my escape . . . I should have grown hard and rough, and been covered with earthly dust, and my heart might have become callous by rude encounters with the multitude" (Hawthorne, *American Note-Books*, 223).

23. Hawthorne, "Custom-House," 17.
24. "Hints to Young Ambition," *New-England Magazine*, June 1832.
25. "The Workingmen," *New-England Magazine*, August 1831.
26. "Workingmen."
27. Phillips, *Political Economy*, 255.
28. As Urakova observes, "much work [on Hawthorne's tales] has been recently done in recontextualizing Hawthorne and reading him against the periodical culture of his day" ("Hawthorne's Gifts," 588). I read these neglected stories not against the "periodical culture of his day," but instead alongside the dominant go-ahead ethos of the mid-1800s.
29. See Cohen, "Peddling Authorship."
30. Cohen, "Peddling Authorship," 370.
31. Melville, "Bartleby," 14.
32. Melville, "Bartleby," 14.
33. Melville, "Bartleby," 14.
34. Melville, "Happy Failure," 255.
35. Melville, "Happy Failure," 255.
36. Melville, "Happy Failure," 258.
37. Melville, "Happy Failure," 258.
38. Melville, "Happy Failure," 260. Whereas I am reading "The Happy Failure" as a critique of the pace of antebellum capitalism, Stauffer finds evidence in this story of Melville's preference for a gradual—rather than immediate—abolition of enslavement (Stauffer, "American Dilemma").
39. Melville, "Happy Failure," 255.
40. Melville, "Happy Failure," 255.
41. Melville, "Happy Failure," 260.
42. Melville, "Happy Failure," 260.
43. Melville, "Happy Failure," 260.
44. On Melville's personal financial situation, see Parker, *Herman Melville*.
45. Sobel, *Panic on Wall Street*, 80.
46. Gibbons, *Banks of New-York*, 344.
47. *Hunt's Merchants' Magazine* 38, January 1858, 100, quoted in Rezneck, *Business Depressions*, 104.
48. Gibbons, *Banks of New-York*, 346. The language of the "avalanche" also suggests how the public increasingly feared that financial pressures were indiscriminate. See Lepler, "Pictures of Panic."
49. Edward W. Clark to Jay Cooke, September 29, 1857, quoted in Huston, *Panic of 1857*, 18.
50. Temple, "Fluid Identity," 453.
51. Seybold reads this critique of the novel's forward-looking logic differently: as an elaborate prank, which uses the structure of the April Fool's Day joke, on the reader in Melville's era and in ours. See Seybold, "Original Failure."

52. Sklansky, *Soul's Economy*, 38. The phrase I quote is embedded in Sklansky's critique of Emerson's thought and its "legitimating conception of market society" (38). My point is that Hawthorne and Melville critique this psychological structure that "became the unquestioned organizing principle of American society and culture" (Luskey, *On the Make*, 20). To my mind, there is an obvious overlap here, in the emphasis on the illusory hope for liberation from the market culture, with Block's psychological history of US capitalism as well.

53. Melville, *Confidence-Man*, 31. Subsequent references to *Confidence-Man*, abbreviated *CM* and cited parenthetically in the text, are to this edition.

54. Jackson, *Week in Wall Street*, 130.

55. Jackson, *Week in Wall Street*, 130.

56. Jackson, *Week in Wall Street*, 131.

57. Temple, "Fluid Identity," 452. Here, Temple follows a tradition initiated by Van Vechten, who coins the novel a "great satire of Transcendentalism" (Van Vechten, "Later Work," 19).

58. Perhaps the distinction would not have been lost on the few people who purchased Melville's novel. In a February 1858 financial column, a writer for *The Bankers' Magazine and Statistical Register* shows that what separates a speculation from an investment is the degree of risk assumed in the transaction. Differentiating railway bonds (debt) from railway stocks (equity)—some of the very instruments at the center of the Panic of 1857—the anonymous writer explains, "these securities [bonds] being generally held for investment and not for speculation, there is less fluctuation observable in them than in railroad shares [stocks]" ("Notes on the Money Market: New York, February 28, 1858," *Bankers' Magazine and Statistical Register*, March 1858). *The Bankers' Magazine* thus anticipates by 100 years Benjamin Graham's classic investing guide *The Intelligent Investor*, which distinguishes between investment and speculation in similar terms: "Here the term [investor] will be used in contradistinction to 'speculator.' In our textbook *Security Analysis* we attempted a precise formulation of the difference between the two as follows: 'An investment operation is one in which, upon thorough analysis, promises safety of principal and a satisfactory return. Operations not meeting these requirements are speculative" (Graham, *Intelligent Investor*, 3). Graham later defines the "defensive investor" as "one interested chiefly in safety plus freedom from bother" (9).

59. Previous scholars have emphasized the "commodification" of the individual as central to the novel's critique; in addition to Gale, see also Dimock, *Empire for Liberty*, and Cole, "Limits of Identity."

60. Thompson, "Early Books on Investing," 88.

61. Armstrong, *Stocks and Stock-Jobbing in Wall Street*; Crosthwaite, Knight, and Marsh, "Economic Humanities," 669.

62. Crosthwaite, Knight, and Marsh, "Economic Humanities," 669.

63. In making this claim, I have in mind a temporal insight from Bloom, in which he describes the paradox of "capitalist subjectivity" as "the attachment of psychological wholeness to fantasies of soon to be achieved economic success" ("Capitalist Future," 165).

64. Picking up on the detail of the spermaceti candles, Parker advances a compelling psychobiographical reading of this dream and relates it to Melville's financial trouble after the commercial failure of *Moby-Dick*. See *CM*, 340–43.

65. Balleisen, *Navigating Failure*, 196.

66. Balleisen, *Navigating Failure*, 197.

67. In the context of analyzing twenty-first century "crisis narratives," Bloom describes this phenomenon as "a fantasy promoting the need to 'go back to the capitalist future'" ("Capitalist Future," 167).

68. Matthiessen, *American Renaissance*, 493.

69. Davis and Gilman, *Letters of Herman Melville*, 188n9.

70. Davis and Gilman, *Letters of Herman Melville*, 188n9.

71. Davis and Gilman, *Letters of Herman Melville*, 188n9.

72. Herman Melville to George William Curtis, in Davis and Gilman, *Letters of Herman Melville*, 188.

73. Herman Melville to George William Curtis, in Davis and Gilman, *Letters of Herman Melville*, 188.

74. Hawthorne to William D. Ticknor, January 19, 1855, in Hawthorne, *Letters*, 1:75.

75. Hawthorne to William D. Ticknor, January 19, 1855, in Hawthorne, *Letters*, 1:75.

76. Hawthorne to William D. Ticknor, February 2, 1855, in Hawthorne, *Letters*, 1:78.

77. Hawthorne to William D. Ticknor, February 2, 1855, in Hawthorne, *Letters*, 1:78.

78. Cohen, "Making Hero Strong," 98.

79. Wood, "Scribbling Women."

80. Fern, *Ruth Hall*, 64. Subsequent references to *Ruth Hall*, abbreviated as *RH* and cited parenthetically in the text, are to this edition.

81. Although beyond the purview of this Coda, the subject of Fern's—and other popular women writers denounced by Hawthorne—use of probability would complement Lee's emphasis on canonical writers' relation to these discourses; see *Uncertain Chances*.

82. Classic readings here include Berlant, "Female Woman," and Brown, *Domestic Individualism*. For two readings against the grain of Hall as performing middle-class proprieties, see Sánchez, "Re-Possessing Individualism," and Weyler, "Literary Labors."

83. Kelley, *Private Woman*.

84. Sánchez, "Re-Possessing Individualism," 26. Sánchez reads this scene much differently than I do, positing that Hall's relation to her class position "is never reducible" to her wealth and evinces an "anti-market individualism," whereby Hall's identity pursues the "elusive quality" of "class," rather than an achieved self (Sánchez, "Re-Possessing Individualism," 26).

Chapter Five

1. Spires, *Practice of Citizenship*, 3.

2. Spires, *Practice of Citizenship*, 30. Spires sees in Black print culture evidence that indirectly supports Block's overarching thesis of (in Spires's phrasing) the "United States as tending toward economic citizenship, a structure in which the market dis-

places civil society as the privileged space of citizenship practices and civic identity" (30). Although Spires does not engage Block, he does cite Sklansky, thereby implying at least a loose affiliation with the new history of capitalism. The present chapter further considers the possibility of this line of inquiry.

3. Marable, *Capitalism*, 60.

4. Marable, *Capitalism*, 61; emphasis original. See also Spires, *Practice of Citizenship*, 124, and Peterson, "Capitalism."

5. Coates, "Case for Reparations."

6. Coates, "Case for Reparations."

7. Equiano, *Interesting Narrative*, 95–96.

8. Spires, *Practice of Citizenship*, 125.

9. Harris, *Shadow of Slavery*, 228.

10. Abraham Lincoln, quoted in Sandage, *Born Losers*, 220.

11. Abraham Lincoln, quoted in Sandage, *Born Losers*, 220.

12. Webb, *Garies and Their Friends*, 280. Subsequent references, abbreviated *GaTF*, are to this edition and are cited parenthetically within the text.

13. Beckert, "Clear Connection."

14. Beckert, "Clear Connection."

15. "Introduction: Slavery's Capitalism," in Beckert and Rockman, *Slavery's Capitalism*, 2; see also Huston, *Panic of 1857*, 61.

16. "Lessons of the Panic," *Liberator*, October 1857.

17. "Our Slave System," *National Era*, August 6, 1857.

18. "Our Slave System," 126.

19. "The Panic and Abolitionism," *Liberator*, October 23, 1857.

20. "Panic and Abolitionism," 43.

21. "Panic and Abolitionism," 43.

22. "Panic and Abolitionism," 43.

23. This elision is obvious in Clay's lithograph, *The Times*, which does not represent a single person of color. This elision, further, is stark given the financial value of enslaved Black people in the midcentury United States. According to the historian Blight: "Slaves by 1860 were worth approximately $3.5 billion. That was the largest single asset in the entire US economy. That was worth more than all railroads, more than all manufacturing, all other assets combined" (Blight, "Historian Says '12 Years,'" quoted in Coates, "Case for Reparations").

24. "Our Slave System," 126.

25. "Our Slave System," 126.

26. "Our Slave System," 126.

27. "'The Times Are Out of Joint': The Financial Crisis," *DeBow's Review*, December 1857.

28. "'Out of Joint,'" 655.

29. "'Out of Joint,'" 655.

30. Hewitt goes further and suggests that the *DeBow's Review* imagined slavery perversely to enable a superior literary culture ("Romances of Real Life," 21n37).

31. George Fitzhugh, "Trade and Panics," *DeBow's Review*, August 1859.

32. Fitzhugh, "Trade and Panics," 160.

33. Fitzhugh, "Trade and Panics," 160.
34. Fitzhugh, "Trade and Panics," 160.
35. Fitzhugh, "Trade and Panics," 162.
36. Fitzhugh, "Trade and Panics," 161. Fitzhugh's critique can seem to resonate with republican-based criticisms of free market capitalism, even among abolitionists, that decry the immiseration of the wage laborer. As Du Bois points out, though, it is essential to remember that "there was in 1863 a real meaning to slavery different from that we may apply to the [wage] laborer today. It was in part psychological. . . . It was the helplessness" (*Black Reconstruction*, 9).
37. Fitzhugh, "Trade and Panics," 161–62.
38. Fitzhugh, "Trade and Panics," 162.
39. Fitzhugh, "Trade and Panics," 161–62. See the dovetailing of terms with Emerson's late essay, "Success," in which the Sage of Concord ironizes Viking "restless[ness]" (*CW*, 7:145).
40. Spires, *Practice of Citizenship*, 137.
41. In his study of early Black newspapers, Fagan finds that "the newspaper was designed not only to connect readers to a community but also to inspire members of that community to act in a certain way" (*Black Newspaper*, 7). I am emphasizing the financial elements of this conduct literature as a response to business turbulence.
42. Samuel Cornish and John Brown Russwurm, *Freedom's Journal*, March 23, 1827, quoted in Fagan, *Black Newspaper*, 28. See also Peterson, *Black Gotham*.
43. "Facts for Colored Americans," *Colored American*, May 6, 1837, 2.
44. Delany, *Condition*, 191.
45. Ball, *Antislavery Life*, 22.
46. Easton, *Treatise*, 45.
47. Ball, *Antislavery Life*, 22.
48. "Colored Population," *Colored American*, March 4, 1837.
49. *Colored American*, April 22, 1837.
50. Ball, *Antislavery Life*, 21.
51. "Purchase of Real Estate," *Colored American*, August 5, 1837; "Spirit of the Age," *Colored American*, May 6, 1837.
52. "Spirit of the Age."
53. "Spirit of the Age."
54. "The Cause of the Hard Times," *Colored American*, June 17, 1837.
55. "Our Banking System," *Colored American*, July 1, 1837.
56. "Our Banking System."
57. "Purchases of Real Estate."
58. Baker, *Afro-American Literature*, 48.
59. Hammond, *Banks and Politics*, 572.
60. Kirkland, *New Home*, 192. According to Bodenhorn, "free banking created a sort of gold-rush mentality in 1837 Michigan. . . . Massive entry was followed by widespread failure" (*State Banking*, 9).
61. Mihm, *Nation of Counterfeiters*, 8.
62. Hammond, *Banks and Politics*, 601.
63. "Narrative of the Life," preface to Brown, *Clotel*, 26.

64. "Narrative of the Life," 27.

65. "Narrative of the Life," 28.

66. In research that was published after I completed my own, the historian Edwards shows the inverse relationship between an enslaver's immersion in financial capitalism and the enslaved person's autonomy. Brown's writing thus links the supposed freedom of "free banking" and the loss of autonomy for the striving subject. See Edwards, *Unfree Markets*.

67. "Narrative of the Life," 9.

68. Germana, *Standards of Value*, 11.

69. "Memoir of the Author," preface to Brown, *Black Man*, 18–19.

70. "Memoir of the Author," 20.

71. "Memoir of the Author," 20.

72. "Memoir of the Author," 22.

73. Jacobs, *Incidents*, 193. Jacobs's text has long been a site of interest for an economic critique of midcentury African American literature. See Lovell, "Labor and Economy"; Cope, "Free Woman"; and Stanley, *Bondage to Contract*. A recent line of inquiry frames these issues, especially Jacobs's subjectivity, as routed through financial "modalities," through the lens of Foucault's critique of neoliberalism—see Diran, "Scenes of Speculation," 698. On the enslaved body as a financial asset in the antebellum economy, see Baptist, *Never Been Told*.

74. Walker, *History of Black Business*, 1:62.

75. I insert this qualification to acknowledge Mitchell's recent thesis regarding the durability, and independence, of Black success (*From Slave Cabins*).

76. Gardner, "Gentleman," 297.

77. For a recent appraisal of Mary E. Webb's performances and abolitionist eloquence, see Mielke, *Provocative Eloquence*.

78. Webb, *Biographical Sketch*.

79. Webb, *Biographical Sketch*.

80. Webb, *Biographical Sketch*.

81. Webb, *Biographical Sketch*.

82. Webb, *Biographical Sketch*.

83. *Oxford English Dictionary*, "appal (v.), sense I.1," March 2025, https://doi.org/10.1093/OED/9875689834.

84. Webb, *Biographical Sketch*.

85. Webb, *Biographical Sketch*.

86. Webb, *Biographical Sketch*.

87. Webb, *Biographical Sketch*.

88. Webb, *Biographical Sketch*.

89. Peterson, "Capitalism," 560; see especially 577–79.

90. Augst, *Clerk's Tale*, 11.

91. Purvis, *Appeal*, 9.

92. Clymer, *Family Money*, 163n24.

93. Kinney, *Amalgamation*, 93.

94. Clymer, *Family Money*, 27. See also Spires, *Practice of Citizenship*, and Luskey, *On the Make*, 68–69. Luskey briefly cites Webb's novel as cultural evidence of the challenges

that would-be-clerks face even within supposedly friendly—because putatively abolitionist—businesses (69).

95. See Stockton, "Property of Blackness," 484.

96. See Stockton, "Property of Blackness," 483.

97. Runcie, "'Hunting.'" As another historian reports, a citizens committee investigating the cause of an August 1834 riot known as "Flying Horses" blamed "the frequent hiring of Negroes during periods of depression" for "white unemployment" (Litwack, *North of Slavery*, 101).

98. For Sandage, Douglass "encounter[s] . . . success and failure as the definitive categories of human worth in postemancipation America" (Sandage, *Born Losers*, 225). Du Bois saw the "American Assumption"—the name he gives to the ideology that "wealth is mainly the result of its owner's effort and that any average worker can by thrift become a capitalist"—as a failed promise for African Americans that ended with the Panic of 1873 (*Black Reconstruction*, 183).

99. Blight, *Frederick Douglass*, 470. See also Douglass, *Life and Times*, 374, 376.

100. Douglass, "Self-Made Men," 556. At the beginning of this speech, Douglass directly refers to Emerson, particularly his essay, "Uses of Great Men" (548).

101. Douglass, "Self-Made Men," 557.

102. Douglass, "Self-Made Men," 557.

103. Douglass, "Self-Made Men," 557.

104. Douglass, "Self-Made Men," 557.

105. Douglass, "Black Man Wants," 164.

106. Douglass, "Black Man Wants," 164.

107. Buccola, *Political Thought*, 165.

108. Buccola, *Political Thought*, 165.

109. Buccola, *Political Thought*, 165.

110. Buccola, *Political Thought*, 165. Here, Buccola also analyzes the Supreme Court Justice Clarence Thomas's use of this same passage in Douglass.

Epilogue

1. Sandage, *Born Losers*, 225.

2. Sandage, *Born Losers*, 225. This expansion also entailed a transformation of individualism, in Sandage's account. I follow Block here, however, in seeing continuity between the ante- and postbellum eras in an account of agency subjectivity.

3. Luskey, *On the Make*, 19.

4. Luskey, *On the Make*, 19.

5. Hager and Marrs, "Against 1865," 266.

6. Renker, "Melville," 486. See also Renker, *Realist Poetics*.

7. Sandage, *Born Losers*, 225.

8. Hager and Marrs, "Against 1865." For a fuller articulation of the concept of the "transbellum," see also Marrs, *Long Civil War*.

9. Downs, *After Appomattox*, 92.

10. Wilson, *Business of Civil War*, 36.

11. Wilson, *Business of Civil War*, 36.

12. Downs, *After Appomattox*, 92.

13. Downs, *After Appomattox*, 92.

14. Downs, *After Appomattox*, 92.

15. Samuel Wilkeson to Jay Cooke, April 11, 1865, quoted in Downs, *After Appomattox*, 93.

16. McCulloch, *Men and Measures*, 217–18.

17. McCulloch, *Men and Measures*, 182. McCulloch states further that "if I were asked to designate the man whose services, next to Mr. Lincoln's, were of the greatest value to the country, from March, 1861, to July, 1864, I should unhesitatingly name Salmon P. Chase" (182). Chase had a distinguished, and unusually wide-ranging, political career and served as Lincoln's Treasury Secretary from 1861 to 1864. McCulloch would succeed Chase's successor, William Fessenden, as Treasury Secretary.

18. Luskey, *On the Make*, 227.

19. Melville, *Battle-Pieces*, 173.

20. Levine, "Infrastructuralism," para. 53.

21. Melville, *Battle-Pieces*, 43.

22. Melville, *Battle-Pieces*, 173.

23. Melville, *Battle-Pieces*, 44–45.

24. Melville, *Battle-Pieces*.

25. Melville, *Battle-Pieces*, 108.

26. Melville, *Battle-Pieces*, 177.

27. Anthony, *Paper Money Men*, 185.

28. Berlant, "Cruel Optimism," 23.

29. Melville, "Bartleby," 15.

30. Melville, "Bartleby," 18.

31. Melville, "Bartleby," 18.

32. Anthony, *Paper Money Men*, 184.

33. Melville, "Bartleby," 19.

Bibliography

Newspapers and Magazines

Atlantic Monthly
Bankers' Magazine and Statistical Register
Colored American
Columbian Lady's and Gentleman's
  Magazine
Daily National Intelligencer
DeBow's Review
Freedom's Journal
Harper's New Monthly Magazine
Hunt's Merchants' Magazine
Ladies' Garland and Family Wreath
Liberator
Literary World
National Era
New-England Magazine
New-Yorker
New-York Mirror
New York Times
Niles' Weekly Register
North American Review
North-American Review and Miscellaneous
  Journal
Panoplist, and Missionary Herald
Philadelphia Register and National
  Recorder
Southern Literary Messenger
Virginia Evangelical and Literary
  Magazine

Books, Articles, Speeches, and Published Documents

'37 and '57: A Brief Popular Account of All the Financial Panics and Commercial Revulsions in the United States from 1690 to 1857. New York: J. C. Haney, 1857.

Agnew, Jean-Christophe. *Worlds Apart: The Market and the Theater in Anglo-American Thought, 1550–1750*. Cambridge: Cambridge University Press, 1986.

Alger, Horatio. *Ragged Dick and Struggling Upward*. New York: Penguin, 1986.

Anthony, David. *Paper Money Men: Commerce, Manhood, and the Sensational Public Sphere in Antebellum America*. Columbus: Ohio State University Press, 2009.

Armstrong, William A. *Stocks and Stock-Jobbing in Wall-Street*. New York: New-York Publishing Company, 1848.

Arthur, T. S. (Timothy Shay). *Making Haste to Be Rich; or The Temptation and Fall*. New York: J. M. Fairchild, 1855.

Augst, Thomas. *The Clerk's Tale: Young Men and Moral Life in Nineteenth-Century America*. Chicago: University of Chicago Press, 2003.

Baker, Houston, Jr. *Blues, Ideology, and Afro-American Literature: A Vernacular Theory*. Chicago: University of Chicago Press, 1984.

Baker, Jennifer J. *Securing the Commonwealth: Debt, Speculation, and Writing in the Making of Early America*. Baltimore, MD: Johns Hopkins University Press, 2005.

Balakrishnan, Gopal. "Speculations on the Stationary State." *New Left Review* 59 (2009): 5–26.

Ball, Erica L. *To Live an Antislavery Life: Personal Politics and the Antebellum Black Middle Class*. Athens: University of Georgia Press, 2012.

Balleisen, Edward J. *Navigating Failure: Bankruptcy and Commercial Society in Antebellum America*. Chapel Hill: University of North Carolina Press, 2001.

Baptist, Edward E. *The Half Has Never Been Told: Slavery and the Making of American Capitalism*. New York: Basic Books, 2014.

———. "Toxic Debt, Liar Loans, and Securitized Human Beings: The Panic of 1837 and the Fate of Slavery." *Commonplace: The Journal of Early American Life* 10, no. 3 (April 2010).

Bartlett, John Russell. *Dictionary of Americanisms*. New York: Bartlett and Welford, 1848.

Baucom, Ian. *Specters of the Atlantic: Finance Capital, Slavery, and the Philosophy of History*. Durham, NC: Duke University Press, 2005.

Bauman, Zygmunt. *Liquid Times: Living in an Age of Uncertainty*. Cambridge, MA: Polity Press, 2007.

Baym, Nina. *Woman's Fiction: A Guide to Novels by and About Women in America 1820–1870*. Ithaca, NY: Cornell University Press, 1978.

Beckert, Sven. "The Clear Connection Between Slavery and American Capitalism." Interview by Dina Gerdeman. *HBS Working Knowledge*, Forbes, May 3, 2017. www.forbes.com/sites/hbsworkingknowledge/2017/05/03/the-clear-connection-between-slavery-and-american-capitalism/?sh=295444607bd3.

———. "History of American Capitalism." In *American History Now*, edited by Eric Foner and Lisa McGirr, 314–35. Philadelphia: Temple University Press, 2011.

Beckert, Sven, and Seth Rockman, eds. *Slavery's Capitalism: A New History of American Economic Development*. Philadelphia: University of Pennsylvania Press, 2016.

Beckert, Sven, Augus Burgin, Peter James Hudson, Louis Hyman, Naomi Lamoreaux, Scott Marler, Stephen Mihm, Julia Ott, Philip Scranton, and Elizabeth Tandy Shermer. "Interchange: The History of Capitalism." *Journal of American History* 101, no. 2 (September 2014): 503–36.

Bell, Ian F. A. "The Hard Currency of Words: Emerson's Fiscal Metaphor in Nature." *ELH* 52, no. 3 (1985): 733–53.

Bell, Michael Davitt. *The Development of American Romance: The Sacrifice of Relation*. Chicago: University of Chicago Press, 1980.

Benjamin, Walter. *The Arcades Project*, edited by Rolf Tiedemann and translated by Howard Eiland and Kevin McLaughlin. Cambridge, MA: Harvard University Press, 1999.

Berlant, Lauren. "Cruel Optimism." *differences: A Journal of Feminist Cultural Studies* 17, no. 3 (2006): 20–36.

———. "The Female Woman: Fanny Fern and the Form of Sentiment." *American Literary History* 3, no. 3 (Autumn 1991): 429–54.

———. *The Queen of America Goes to Washington City: Essays on Sex and Citizenship*. Durham, NC: Duke University Press, 1997.

Blight, David W. *Frederick Douglass: Prophet of Freedom*. New York: Simon & Schuster, 2018.

———. "Historian Says '12 Years' Is a Story the Nation Must Remember." Interview by Terry Gross. *Fresh Air*, NPR, October 24, 2013. www.npr.org/2013/10/24/240491318/historian-says-12-years-is-a-story-the-nation-must-remember.

Block, James E. *A Nation of Agents: The American Path to a Modern Self and Society*. Cambridge, MA: Harvard University Press, 2002.

Bloom, Peter. "Back to the Capitalist Future: Fantasy and the Paradox of Crisis." *Culture and Organization* 22, no. 2 (2016): 158–77.

Bodenhorn, Howard. *State Banking in Early America: A New Economic History*. New York: Oxford University Press, 2003.

Bosco, Ronald A., and Joel Myerson. *The Emerson Brothers: A Fraternal Biography in Letters*. New York: Oxford University Press, 2006.

Brantlinger, Patrick. *Fictions of State: Culture and Credit in Britain, 1694–1994*. Ithaca, NY: Cornell University Press, 1996.

Brevoort, Henry, Jr. "Review of *The Sketch Book*, No. 1." In *Critical Essays on Washington Irving*, edited by Ralph M. Aderman, 46–47. Boston: G. K. Hall, 1990.

Briggs, Charles F. *The Adventures of Harry Franco: A Tale of the Great Panic*. 2 vols. New York: Saunders, 1839.

———. *Bankrupt Stories*, edited by Harry Franco. New York: John Allen, 1843.

Bromell, Nicholas K. *By the Sweat of the Brow: Literature in Antebellum America*. Chicago: University of Chicago Press, 1993.

Bronk, Richard. *The Romantic Economist: Imagination in Economics*. Cambridge: Cambridge University Press, 2009.

Brown, Gillian. *Domestic Individualism: Imagining Self in Nineteenth-Century America*. Berkeley: University of California Press, 1992.

Brown, Wendy. *Undoing the Demos: Neoliberalism's Stealth Revolution*. Brooklyn, NY: Zone Books, 2015.

Brown, William Wells. *The Black Man: His Antecedents, His Genius, and His Achievements*. 2nd ed. New York: Thomas Hamilton, 1863.

———. *Clotel; or, The President's Daughter*, edited by M. Giula Fabi. New York: Penguin, 2004.

Buccola, Nicholas. *The Political Thought of Frederick Douglass: In Pursuit of American Liberty*. New York: New York University Press, 2012.

Buell, Lawrence. *Emerson*. Cambridge, MA: Belknap Press of Harvard University Press, 2004.

Burstein, Andrew. *The Original Knickerbocker: The Life of Washington Irving*. New York: Basic Books, 2007.

Cameron, Sharon. *Impersonality: Seven Essays*. Chicago: University of Chicago Press, 2007.

Channing, Walter. "Reflections on the Literary Delinquency of America." *North-American Review and Miscellaneous Journal* 2, no. 4 (1815): 33–43.

Charvat, William. *The Profession of Authorship in America, 1800–1870*. Columbus: Ohio State University Press, 1968.

Clegg, John. "Capitalism and Slavery." *Critical Historical Studies* 2, no. 2 (2015): 281–304.

Clymer, Jeffory A. *Family Money: Property, Race, and Literature in the Nineteenth Century*. New York: Oxford University Press, 2012.

Coates, Ta-Nehisi. "The Case for Reparations." *Atlantic,* June 2014.
Cohen, Daniel A. "Making Hero Strong: Teenage Ambition, Story-Paper Fiction, and the Generational Recasting of American Women's Authorship." *Journal of the Early Republic* 30, no. 1 (Spring 2010): 85–136.
Cohen, Michael C. "Peddling Authorship in the Age of Jackson." *ELH* 79, no. 2 (Summer 2012): 369–88.
Cole, Rachel. "At the Limits of Identity: Realism and American Personhood in Melville's *Confidence-Man.*" *NOVEL* 39, no. 3 (2006): 384–401.
Collman, Charles Albert. *Mysterious Panics, 1830–1930.* 1931. Reprint, New York: Greenwood, 1968.
Conkin, Paul Keith. *Prophets of Prosperity: America's First Political Economists.* Bloomington: Indiana University Press, 1980.
Cooper, James Fenimore. *Early Critical Essays (1820–1822) by James Fenimore Cooper,* edited by James F. Beard. Gainesville, FL: Scholars' Facsimiles and Reprints, 1955.
———. *The Spy: A Tale of the Neutral Ground.* 1822. Reprint, New York: AMS Press, 2002.
Cope, Virginia. "'I Verily Believed Myself to Be a Free Woman': Harriet Jacobs's Journey into Capitalism." *African American Review* 38, no. 1 (2004): 5–20.
Crosthwaite, Paul, Peter Knight, and Nicky Marsh. "The Economic Humanities and the History of Financial Advice." *American Literary History* 31, no. 4 (Winter 2019): 661–86.
Davis, Gerald F., and Suntae Kim. "Financialization of the Economy." *Annual Review of Sociology* 41 (2015): 203–21.
Delany, Martin R. "*The Condition, Elevation, Emigration, and Destiny of the Colored People of the United States.*" In *Martin R. Delany: A Documentary Reader,* edited by Robert S. Levine, 189–216. 1852. Reprint, Chapel Hill: University of North Carolina Press, 2003.
Dewey, Mary E., ed. *The Life and Letters of Catharine M. Sedgwick.* New York: Harper Bros., 1872.
Dewey, Orville. *Moral Views of Commerce, Society, and Politics.* 2nd ed. New York: Felt, 1838.
Dimock, Wai Chee. *Empire for Liberty: Melville and the Poetics of Individualism.* Princeton, NJ: Princeton University Press, 1989.
Diran, Ingrid. "Scenes of Speculation: Harriet Jacobs and the Biopolitics of Human Capital." *American Quarterly* 71, no. 3 (2019): 697–718.
Ditz, Toby. "Shipwrecked; or, Masculinity Imperiled: Mercantile Representations of Failure and the Gendered Self in Eighteenth-Century Philadelphia." *Journal of American History* 81, no. 1 (1994): 51–80.
Doherty, Robert W. *Society and Power: Five New England Towns, 1800–1860.* Amherst: University of Massachusetts Press, 1977.
Dolan, Neal. *Emerson's Liberalism.* Madison: University of Wisconsin Press, 2009.
Douglass, Frederick. *Life and Times of Frederick Douglass.* New York: Macmillan, 1962.
———. "Self-Made Men." In *The Frederick Douglass Papers,* Series One: Speeches, Debates, and Interviews, vol. 5, edited by John W. Blassingame and John R. McKivigan, 545–74. New Haven, CT: Yale University Press, 1992.

———. "What the Black Man Wants." In *The Life and Writings of Frederick Douglass*, vol. 4, edited by Philip S. Foner, 157–65. New York: International Publishers, 1955.

Downs, Gregory P. *After Appomattox: Military Occupation and the Ends of War*. Cambridge, MA: Harvard University Press, 2015.

Du Bois, W. E. B. *Black Reconstruction in America*. 1935. Reprint, New York: Russell & Russell, 1963.

Easton, Hosea. *A Treatise on the Intellectual Character, and Civic and Political Condition of the Colored People of the United States*. Boston, 1837.

Edwards, Justene Hill. *Unfree Markets: The Slaves' Economy and the Rise of Capitalism in South Carolina*. New York: Columbia University Press, 2021.

Emerson, Ralph Waldo. *The Collected Works of Ralph Waldo Emerson*, edited by Robert E. Spiller, Alfred R. Ferguson, Joseph Slater, Jean Ferguson Carr, Wallace E. Williams, Douglas Emory Wilson, Philip Nicoloff, et al. 10 vols. Cambridge, MA: Harvard University Press, 1971–2013.

———. *The Early Lectures of Ralph Waldo Emerson*, edited by Stephen E. Whicher, Robert E. Spiller, and Wallace E. Williams. 3 vols. Cambridge, MA: Harvard University Press, 1959–72.

———. *Journals and Miscellaneous Notebooks of Ralph Waldo Emerson*, edited by William H. Gilman, Alfred R. Ferguson, George P. Clark, Merrell R. Davis, Merton M. Sealts, Jr., Ralph H. Orth, A. W. Plumstead, et al. 16 vols. Cambridge, MA: Belknap Press of Harvard University Press, 1960–82.

———. *The Later Lectures of Ralph Waldo Emerson*, edited by Ronald A. Bosco and Joel Myerson. 2 vols. Athens: University of Georgia Press, 2010.

———. *The Letters of Ralph Waldo Emerson*, edited by Ralph L. Rusk and Eleanor Tilton. 10 vols. New York: Columbia University Press, 1939–96.

Epstein, Gerald A. *Financialization and the World Economy*. Cheltenham, UK: Edward Elgar, 2005.

Equiano, Olaudah. *The Interesting Narrative of the Life of Olaudah Equiano, or Gustavus Vassa, the African, Written by Himself*, edited by Werner Sollors. 1789. Reprint, New York: Norton, 2001.

Fabian, Ann. "Speculation on Distress: The Popular Discourse of the Panics of 1837 and 1857." *Yale Journal of Criticism* 3, no. 1 (Fall 1989): 127–42.

Fagan, Benjamin. *The Black Newspaper and the Chosen Nation*. Athens: University of Georgia Press, 2016.

Fern, Fanny. *Ruth Hall*. 1855. Reprint, New York: Penguin, 1997.

Fichtelberg, Joseph. *Critical Fictions: Sentiment and the American Market, 1780–1870*. Athens: University of Georgia Press, 2003.

Fitzhugh, George. *Cannibals All! Or, Slaves Without Masters*. Richmond, VA: A. Morris, 1857.

———. *Sociology for the South, or, The Failure of Free Society*. Richmond, VA: A. Morris, 1854.

Foucault, Michel. *The Birth of Biopolitics. Lectures at the Collège de France, 1978–1979*. New York: Picador, 2008.

Franklin, Wayne. *James Fenimore Cooper: The Early Years*. New Haven, CT: Yale University Press, 2007.

Frothingham, N. L. (Nathaniel Langdon). *Duties of Hard Times: A Sermon Preached on to the First Church, on Sunday Morning, April 23, 1837*. Boston: Munroe & Francis, 1837.

Galbraith, John K. *Money: Whence It Came, Where It Went*. Princeton, NJ: Princeton University Press, 2017.

Gallagher, Catherine. *The Body Economic: Life, Death, and Sensation in Political Economy and the Victorian Novel*. Princeton, NJ: Princeton University Press, 2006.

Gamer, Michael. "Maria Edgeworth and the Romance of Real Life." *NOVEL* 24, no. 2 (Spring 2001): 232–66.

Gardner, Eric. "'A Gentleman of Superior Cultivation and Refinement': Recovering the Biography of Frank J. Webb." *African American Review* 35, no. 2 (2001): 297–308.

Gates, Sondra Smith. "Sedgwick's American Poor." In *Catharine Maria Sedgwick: Critical Perspectives*, edited by Lucinda Damon-Bach and Victoria Clements, 192–208. Boston: Northeastern University Press, 2003.

Germana, Michael. "Counterfeiters and Con Artists: Money, Literature, and Subjectivity." *American Literary History* 21, no. 2 (Summer 2009): 296–305.

———. *Standards of Value: Money, Race, and Literature in America*. Iowa City: University of Iowa Press, 2009.

Gibbons, J. S. [James Sloan]. *The Banks of New-York, Their Dealers, the Clearing House, and the Panic of 1857*. New York: Appleton, 1859.

Gilmore, Michael T. *American Romanticism and the Marketplace*. Chicago: University of Chicago Press, 1985.

Graham, Benjamin. *The Intelligent Investor*. New York: Harper, 1959.

Greene, Asa. *The Perils of Pearl Street, Including a Taste of the Dangers of Wall Street, by a Late Merchant*. New York: Betts & Anstice, and Peter Hill, 1834.

Greenspan, Alan. *The Age of Turbulence: Adventures in a New World*. New York: Penguin, 2008.

Grusin, Richard. "'Put God in Your Debt': Emerson's Economy of Expenditure." *PMLA* 103, no. 1 (January 1988): 35–44.

Hager, Christopher, and Cody Marrs. "Against 1865: Reperiodizing the Nineteenth Century." *J19: The Journal of Nineteenth-Century Americanists* 1, no. 2 (Fall 2013): 259–84.

Hammond, Bray. *Banks and Politics in America from the Revolution to the Civil War*. Princeton, NJ: Princeton University Press, 1957.

Hanlon, Christopher. *Emerson's Memory Loss: Originality, Communality, and the Late Style*. New York: Oxford University Press, 2018.

Harris, Leslie M. *In the Shadow of Slavery: African Americans in New York City, 1626–1863*. Chicago: University of Chicago Press, 2003.

Hartigan-O'Connor. "The Personal Is Political Economy." *Journal of the Early Republic* 36, no. 2 (Summer 2016): 335–41.

Hawthorne, Nathaniel. *The Centenary Edition of the Works of Nathaniel Hawthorne*, edited by William Charvat, Roy Harvey Pearce, and Claude M. Simpson. 23 vols. Columbus: Ohio State University Press, 1962–94.

———. "The Custom-House." In *The Scarlet Letter and Other Writings*, 2nd ed., edited by Leland S. Person, 7–33. New York: Norton, 2017.

———. *The House of the Seven Gables*. Vol. 2 of *The Centenary Edition of the Works of Nathaniel Hawthorne*, edited by William Charvat, Roy Harvey Pearce, Claude M. Simpson, Fredson Bowers, Matthew J. Bruccoli, and L. Neal Smith. Columbus: Ohio State University Press, 1971.

———. *Letters of Hawthorne to William D. Ticknor, 1851–1864*. 2 vols. Newark, NJ: Cartaret Book Club, 1910.

———. *Passages of the American Note-Books of Nathaniel Hawthorne*. Vol. 9 of *The Complete Works of Nathaniel Hawthorne*, edited by George Parsons Lathrop. Boston: Houghton Mifflin, 1914.

Hedges, William L. *Washington Irving: An American Study, 1802–1832*. Baltimore, MD: Johns Hopkins University Press, 1965.

Henderson, Andrea K. *Romantic Identities: Varieties of Subjectivity, 1774–1830*. Cambridge: Cambridge University Press, 1996.

Hewitt, Elizabeth. "Romances of Real Life; or, the Nineteenth-Century American Business Magazine." *American Periodicals* 20, no. 1 (2010): 1–22.

———. *Speculative Fictions: Explaining the Economy in the Early United States*. New York: Oxford University Press, 2020.

Higham, John. *From Boundlessness to Consolidation: The Transformation of American Culture, 1848–1860*. Ann Arbor: University of Michigan Press, 1969.

Hildreth, Richard. *The History of Banks*. Boston: Hilliard, Gray, 1837.

Homestead, Melissa J. *American Women Authors and Literary Property, 1822–1869*. Cambridge: Cambridge University Press, 2005.

———. "Augusta Jane Evans." In *American Literature in Transition: The Long Nineteenth Century, 1851–1877*, edited by Cody Marrs, 42–57. Cambridge: Cambridge University Press, 2022.

———. "The Shape of Sedgwick's Career." In *The Cambridge History of American Women's Literature*, edited by Dale M. Bauer, 185–203. Cambridge: Cambridge University Press, 2012.

Horwitz, Howard. *By the Law of Nature: Form and Value in Nineteenth-Century America*. New York: Oxford University Press, 1991.

———. "Rip Van Winkle and Legendary National Memory." *Western Humanities Review* 58, no. 2 (2004): 34–47.

Huehls, Mitchum. *After Critique: Twenty-First Century Fiction in a Neoliberal Age*. New York: Oxford University Press, 2019.

Huston, John L. "Economic Landscapes Yet to Be Discovered: The Early American Republic and Historians' Unsubtle Adoption of Political Economy." *Journal of the Early Republic* 24, no. 2 (July 2004): 219–31.

———. *The Panic of 1857 and the Coming of the Civil War*. Baton Rouge: Louisiana State University Press, 1987.

Insko, Jeffrey. *History, Abolition, and the Ever-Present Now in Antebellum American Writing*. New York: Oxford University Press, 2018.

Irving, Pierre M., ed. *The Life and Letters of Washington Irving*. 3 vols. New York: Putnam, 1863.

Irving, Washington. *The Complete Works of Washington Irving*, edited by Henry A. Pochmann, Herbert L. Kleinfeld, and Richard D. Rust. 30 vols. Boston: Twayne, 1969–89.

———. *The Sketch Book of Geoffrey Crayon, Gent.* Vol. 8 of *The Complete Works of Washington Irving*, edited by Haskell Springer. Boston: Twayne, 1978.

Jackson, Frederick. *A Week in Wall Street by One Who Knows*. New York, 1841.

Jackson, Leon. *The Business of Letters: Authorial Economies in Antebellum America*. Redwood City, CA: Stanford University Press, 2008.

Jacobs, Harriet A. *Incidents in the Life of a Slave Girl*, edited by Jean Fagan Yellin. Enlarged ed. Cambridge, MA: Harvard University Press, 2002.

James, Henry. *Hawthorne*. New York: Harper & Bros., 1880.

Jones, Gavin. *Failure and the American Writer: A Literary History*. New York: Cambridge University Press, 2014.

Karcher, Carolyn. "Catharine Maria Sedgwick in Literary History." In *Catharine Maria Sedgwick: Critical Perspectives*, edited by Lucinda L. Damon-Bach and Victoria Clements, 5–15. Boston: Northeastern University Press, 2003.

Kelley, Mary. *Private Woman, Public Stage: Literary Domesticity in Nineteenth-Century America*. Chapel Hill: University of North Carolina Press, 1984.

Kern, Alexander. "Emerson and Economics." *The New England Quarterly* 13, no. 4 (1940): 678–96.

Kinney, James. *Amalgamation! Race, Sex, and Rhetoric in the Nineteenth-Century American Novel*. Westport, CT: Greenwood, 1985.

Kirkland, Caroline [Mrs. Mary Clavers, pseud.]. *A New Home—Who'll Follow?; or, Glimpses of Western Life*. 4th ed. New York: 1850.

Knight, Peter. *Reading the Market: Genres of Financial Capitalism in Gilded Age America*. Baltimore, MD: Johns Hopkins University Press, 2016.

Kopec, Andrew. "Fiction, Finance, and Eliza Wharton's 'Awful Futurity' in Early America." *ELH* 84, no. 4 (Winter 2017): 919–42.

Kornblugh, Anna. *Realizing Capital: Financial and Psychic Economies in Victorian Form*. New York: Fordham University Press, 2014.

Krippner, Greta R. *Capitalizing on Crisis: The Political Origins of the Rise of Finance*. Cambridge, CT: Harvard University Press, 2011.

La Berge, Leigh Claire. *Scandals and Abstraction: Financial Fiction of the Long 1980s*. New York: Oxford University Press, 2014.

Larson, John Lauritz. *The Market Revolution in America: Liberty, Ambition, and the Eclipse of the Common Good*. New York: Cambridge University Press, 2010.

Lears, Jackson. *Something for Nothing: Luck in America*. New York: Viking, 2003.

Lee, Maurice S. *Uncertain Chances: Science, Skepticism, and Belief in Nineteenth-Century American Literature*. New York: Oxford University Press, 2013.

Lepler, Jessica M. *The Many Panics of 1837: People, Politics, and the Creation of a Transatlantic Crisis*. Cambridge: Cambridge University Press, 2013.

———. "Pictures of Panic: Constructing Hard Times in Words and Images." *Common-Place* 10, no. 3 (April 2010). https://commonplace.online/article/pictures-panic/.

Leverenz, David. *Manhood and the American Renaissance*. Ithaca, NY: Cornell University Press, 1989.

Levine, Caroline. "Infrastructuralism, or the Tempo of Institutions." In *On Periodization: Selected Essays from the English Institute*, edited by Virginia Jackson, paras. 43-123. Cambridge, MA: English Institute collaboration with the American Council of Learned Societies, 2010. http://hdl.handle.net/2027/heb.90047.0001.001.

Levine, Robert S. "Why We Should Be Teaching and Writing About *The Literary World*'s 1850 'Hawthorne and His Mosses.'" *J19: The Journal of Nineteenth-Century Americanists* 5, no. 1 (Spring 2017): 179-89.

Levy, Jonathan. "Capital as Process and the History of Capitalism." *Business History Review* 91, no. 3 (Autumn 2017): 483-510.

———. *Freaks of Fortune: The Emerging World of Capitalism and Risk in America*. Cambridge, MA: Harvard University Press, 2014.

Lewis, Paul. "'Lectures or a Little Charity': Poor Visits in Antebellum Literature and Culture." *New England Quarterly* 73, no. 2 (June 2000): 246-73.

Litwack, Leon. *North of Slavery: The Negro in the Free States, 1790-1860*. Chicago: University of Chicago Press, 1961.

Lovell, Thomas B. "By Dint of Labor and Economy: Harriet Jacobs, Harriet Wilson, and the Salutary View of Wage Labor." *Arizona Quarterly* 52, no. 3 (1996): 1-32.

Luck, Chad. *The Body of Property: Antebellum American Fiction and the Phenomenology of Possession*. New York: Fordham University Press, 2014.

Lukács, Georg. *The Historical Novel*. London: Merlin Press, 1989.

Luskey, Brian P. *On the Make: Clerks and the Quest for Capital in Nineteenth-Century America*. New York: New York University Press, 2010.

Lynch, Deidre Shauna. *The Economy of Character: Novels, Market Culture, and the Business of Inner Meaning*. Chicago: University of Chicago Press, 1998.

Mackay, Charles. *Memoirs of Extraordinary Popular Delusions*. 2 vols. London: Bentley, 1841.

Maibor, Carolyn R. *Labor Pains: Emerson, Thoreau, and Alcott on Work, Women, and the Development of the Self*. New York: Routledge, 2003.

Marable, Manning. *How Capitalism Underdeveloped Black America: Problems in Race, Political Economy, and Society*. Chicago: Haymarket, 2015.

Marrs, Cody. *Nineteenth-Century Literature and the Long Civil War*. Cambridge: Cambridge University Press, 2015.

Martineau, Harriet. *Society in America*. 1837. Reprint, New York: Anchor, 1962.

Marx, Karl. *Capital, Volume One*. In *The Marx-Engels Reader*, 2nd ed., edited by Robert C. Tucker, 294-438. New York: Norton, 1978.

———. "Crisis Theory." In *The Marx-Engels Reader*, 2nd ed., edited by Robert C. Tucker, 443-65. New York: Norton, 1978.

Marx, Karl, and Friedrich Engels. *Manifesto of the Communist Party*. In *The Marx-Engels Reader*, 2nd ed., edited by Robert C. Tucker, 469-99. New York: Norton, 1978.

Matson, Cathy. "Introduction: The Ambiguities of Risk in the Early Republic" (Introduction to Special Forum: Reputation and Uncertainty in Early America). *Business History Review* 78, no. 4 (2004): 595-606.

Matthiessen, F. O. *The American Renaissance*. Oxford: Oxford University Press, 1941.

McClanahan, Annie. *Dead Pledges: Debt, Crisis, and Twenty-First Century Culture*. Redwood City, CA: Stanford University Press, 2017.

McCulloch, Hugh. *Men and Measures of Half a Century: Sketches and Comments*. New York: Charles Scribner's Sons, 1888.

McGill, Meredith L. *American Literature and the Culture of Reprinting, 1834–1853*. Philadelphia: University of Pennsylvania Press, 2003.

McTiernan, Dave. "The Novel as 'Neutral Ground': Genre and Ideology in Cooper's *The Spy*." *Studies in American Fiction* 25, no. 1 (1997): 3–20.

Melville, Herman. "Bartleby, the Scrivener: A Story of Wall-Street." In *The Piazza Tales and Other Prose Pieces, 1839–1860*, 13–45.

———. *Battle-Pieces*. Vol. 10 of *The Works of Herman Melville*. New York: Russell & Russell, 1963.

———. *The Confidence-Man: His Masquerade*, 2nd ed., edited by Hershel Parker and Mark Niemeyer. New York: Norton, 2006.

———. "The Happy Failure: A Story of the River Hudson." In *The Piazza Tales and Other Prose Pieces, 1839–1860*, 254–61.

———. "Hawthorne and His Mosses." *Literary World* (August 17 and August 24, 1850).

———. *The Letters of Herman Melville*, edited by Merrell R. Davis and William H. Gilman. New Haven, CT: Yale University Press, 1960.

———. *Moby-Dick*, 3rd ed., edited by Hershel Parker. New York: Norton, 2018.

———. *The Piazza Tales and Other Prose Pieces 1839–1860*, edited by Harrison Hayford, Alma A. MacDougall, and G. Thomas Tanselle. Evanston, IL: Northwestern University Press and Newberry Library, 1987.

Michaels, Walter Benn. *The Gold Standard and the Logic of Naturalism: American Literature at the Turn of the Century*. Berkeley: University of California Press, 1987.

Mielke, Laura L. *Provocative Eloquence: Theater, Violence, and Antislavery Speech in the Antebellum United States*. Ann Arbor: University of Michigan Press, 2019.

Mihm, Stephen. *A Nation of Counterfeiters: Capitalists, Con Men, and the Making of the United States*. Cambridge, MA: Harvard University Press, 2007.

Miller, Harry E. *Banking Theories in the United States Before 1860*. 1927. Reprint, Clifton, NJ: Augustus M. Kelley, 1972.

Mitchell, Koritha. *From Slave Cabins to the White House: Homemade Citizenship in African American Culture*. Urbana: University of Illinois Press, 2020.

Murison, Justine S. *The Politics of Anxiety in Nineteenth-Century American Literature*. Cambridge: Cambridge University Press, 2011.

Newfield, Christopher. *The Emerson Effect: Individualism and Submission in America*. Chicago: University of Chicago Press, 1996.

Newton, Sarah E. *Learning to Behave: A Guide to American Conduct Books*. New York: Greenwood Press, 1994.

Nguyen, Duy Lap. "Capitalism and Primal History in Walter Benjamin's *Arcades Projects*." *differences: A Journal of Feminist Cultural Studies* 25, no. 3 (2015): 123–43.

O'Brien, John. *Literature Incorporated: The Cultural Unconscious of the Business Corporation, 1650–1850*. Chicago: University of Chicago Press, 2016.

Okker, Patricia. *Our Sister Editors: Sarah J. Hale and the Tradition of Nineteenth-Century American Women Editors*. Athens: University of Georgia Press, 1995.

Packer, B. L. *Emerson's Fall*. New York: Continuum, 1982.
Parker, Hershel. *Herman Melville: A Biography*. 2 vols. Baltimore, MD: Johns Hopkins University Press, 2002.
Parrington, Vernon Louis. *Main Currents of American Thought*. 3 vols. New York: Harcourt, 1958.
Peterson, Carla L. *Black Gotham: A Family History of African Americans in Nineteenth-Century New York City*. New Haven, CT: Yale University Press, 2012.
———. "Capitalism, Black (Under)Development, and the Production of the African American Novel in the 1850s." *American Literary History* 4, no. 4 (1992): 559–83.
Pfister, Joel. *Surveyors of Customs: American Literature as Cultural Analysis*. New York: Oxford University Press, 2016.
Phillips, Willard. *A Manual of Political Economy, with Particular Reference to the Institutions, Resources, and Condition of the United States*. Boston: Hilliard, Gray, Little, and Wilkins, 1828.
Pickford, Benjamin. "Toward a Fungible Scrip: Orestes Brownson's *Boston Quarterly Review* and the Valuation of American Literature." *Open Library of Humanities* 2, no. 1 (2016). https://olh.openlibhums.org/articles/10.16995/olh.48/.
Pocock, J. G. A. *The Machiavellian Moment: Florentine Political Thought and the Atlantic Republican Tradition*. Princeton, NJ: Princeton University Press, 1975.
Poovey, Mary. *Genres of the Credit Economy: Mediating Value in Eighteenth- and Nineteenth-Century Britain*. Chicago: University of Chicago Press, 2008.
Pratt, Lloyd. *Archives of American Time: Literature and Modernity in the Nineteenth Century*. Philadelphia: University of Pennsylvania Press, 2009.
Purvis, Robert. *Appeal of Forty Thousand Citizens, Threatened with Disenfranchisement, to the People of Pennsylvania*. Pennsylvania: Merrihew and Gunn, 1838.
Raymond, Daniel. *Thoughts on Political Economy*. Baltimore, MD: Fielding Lucas, 1820.
Renker, Elizabeth. "Melville the Realist Poet." In *A Companion to Herman Melville*, edited by Wyn Kelly, 482–96. Malden, MA: Blackwell, 2006.
———. *Realist Poetics in American Culture, 1866–1900*. New York: Oxford University Press, 2018.
Rezneck, Samuel. *Business Depressions and Financial Panics*. New York: Greenwood, 1968.
———. "The Social History of an American Depression, 1837–1843." *American Historical Review* 40, no. 4 (1935): 662–87.
Rifkin, Mark. *Settler Common Sense: Queerness and Everyday Colonialism in the American Renaissance*. Minneapolis: University of Minnesota Press, 2014.
Robbins, Sarah. "Periodizing Authorship, Characterizing Genre: Catharine Maria Sedgwick's Benevolent Literacy Narratives." *American Literature* 76, no. 1 (2004): 1–29.
Rockman, Seth. "What Makes the History of Capitalism Newsworthy?" *Journal of the Early Republic* 34, no. 3 (Fall 2014): 439–66.
Rotundo, E. Anthony. *American Manhood: Transformations in Masculinity from the Revolution to the Modern Era*. New York: Basic Books, 1993.
Rubin-Dorsky, Jeffrey. *Adrift in the Old World: The Psychological Pilgrimage of Washington Irving*. Chicago: University of Chicago Press, 1988.

Runcie, John. "'Hunting the Nigs' in Philadelphia: The Race Riot of August 1834." *Pennsylvania History: A Journal of the Mid-Atlantic Studies* 39, no. 2 (1972): 187–218.

Ryan, Susan M. *The Moral Economies of American Authorship: Reputation, Scandal, and the Nineteenth-Century Literary Marketplace*. New York: Oxford University Press, 2016.

Sánchez, María Carla. *Reforming the World: Social Activism and the Problem of Fiction in Nineteenth-Century America*. Iowa City: University of Iowa Press, 2008.

———. "Re-Possessing Individualism in Fanny Fern's *Ruth Hall*." *Arizona Quarterly* 56, no. 4 (Winter 2000): 25–56.

Sandage, Scott. *Born Losers: A History of Failure in America*. Cambridge, MA: Harvard University Press, 2006.

Sawaya, Francesca. *The Difficult Art of Giving: Patronage, Philanthropy, and the American Literary Market*. Philadelphia: University of Pennsylvania Press, 2014.

Sedgwick, Catharine Maria. *The Poor Rich Man and the Rich Poor Man*. New York: Harper Bros., 1836.

———. "Romance in Real Life." In *Tales and Sketches*, 237–78. Philadelphia, PA: Carey, Lea, and Blanchard, 1835.

Sedgwick, Theodore. *Public and Private Economy*. New York: Harper Bros., 1836.

Sellers, Charles. *The Market Revolution: Jacksonian American, 1815-1846*. New York: Oxford University Press, 1991.

Seybold, Matt. "Quite an Original Failure: Melville's Imagined Reader in *The Confidence-Man*." *reception* 8 (2016): 73–92.

Seybold, Matt, and Michelle Chiara, eds. *The Routledge Companion to Literature and Economics*. London and New York: Routledge, 2019.

Shapiro, Joe. "The Providence of Class: Catharine Maria Sedgwick, Political Economy, and Sentimental Fiction in the 1830s." *American Literary History* 27, no. 2 (Summer 2015): 199–225.

Shapiro, Stephen. *The Culture and Commerce of the Early American Novel: Reading the Atlantic World-System*. University Park: Pennsylvania State University Press, 2008.

Shonkwiler, Alison. "Don DeLillo's Financial Sublime." *Contemporary Literature* 51, no. 2 (2010): 246–82.

———. *The Financial Imaginary: Economic Mystification and the Limits of Realist Fiction*. Minneapolis: University of Minnesota Press, 2017.

Sklansky, Jeffrey. "The Elusive Sovereign: New Intellectual and Social Histories of Capitalism." *Modern Intellectual History* 9, no. 1 (2012): 233–48.

———. *The Soul's Economy: Market Society and Selfhood in American Thought, 1820-1920*. Chapel Hill: University of North Carolina Press, 2002.

Smith, Adam. *Wealth of Nations*. New York: Modern Library, 1937.

Smith, Caleb. "Disciplines of Attention in a Secular Age." *Critical Inquiry* 45, no. 4 (2019): 884–909.

Smith, Elizabeth Oakes [Mrs. Seba Smith, pseud.]. *Riches Without Wings, or The Cleveland Family*. Boston: George W. Light, 1839.

Smith, Rachel Greenwald. *Affect and American Literature in the Age of Neoliberalism*. Cambridge: Cambridge University Press, 2015.

Sobel, Robert. *Panic on Wall Street: A History of America's Financial Disasters*. New York: Macmillan, 1968.

Spiller, Robert E. *Fenimore Cooper: Critic of His Times*. New York: Russell & Russell, 1963.
Spires, Derrick R. *The Practice of Citizenship: Black Politics and Print Culture in the Early United States*. Philadelphia: University of Pennsylvania Press, 2019.
Stanley, Amy Dru. *From Bondage to Contract: Wage Labor, Marriage, and the Market in the Age of Slave Emancipation*. Cambridge: Cambridge University Press, 1998.
Stauffer, John. "Melville, Slavery, and the American Dilemma." In *A Companion to Herman Melville*, edited by Wyn Kelly, 214–30. Malden, MA: Blackwell, 2006.
Stockton, Elizabeth. "The Property of Blackness: The Legal Fiction of Frank J. Webb's *The Garies and Their Friends*." *African American Review* 42, no. 2–3 (Summer/Fall 2009): 473–86.
Stowe, Harriet Beecher. *Uncle Tom's Cabin*, 3rd ed., edited by Elizabeth Ammons. New York: Norton, 2018.
Strong, George Templeton. *The Diary of George Templeton Strong*, 4 vols., edited by Allan Nevins and Milton H. Thomas. New York: Macmillan, 1952.
Temple, Gale. "Fluid Identity in *Israel Potter* and *The Confidence-Man*." In *A Companion to Herman Melville*, edited by Wyn Kelly, 451–66. Malden, MA: Blackwell, 2006.
Templin, Mary. *Panic Fiction: Women and Antebellum Economic Crisis*. Tuscaloosa: University of Alabama Press, 2014.
Thompson, James. *Models of Value: Eighteenth-Century Political Economy and the Novel*. Durham, NC: Duke University Press, 1996.
Thompson, Joel E. "Early Books on Investing at the Dawn of Modern Business in America." *Accounting Historians Journal* 35, no. 1 (2008): 83–110.
Thoreau, Henry David. *Walden*. In *Walden and Resistance to Civil Government*, 2nd ed., edited by William Rossi, 1–233. New York: Norton, 1992.
Urakova, Alexandra. "Hawthorne's Gifts: Re-Reading 'Alice Doane's Appeal' and 'The Great Carbuncle' in *The Token*." *New England Quarterly* 89, no. 4 (2016): 587–613.
US Congress. House of Representatives. Committee on Oversight and Government Reform. *The Financial Crisis and the Role of Federal Regulators: Hearing Before the Committee on Oversight and Government Reform*. 110th Cong., 2nd sess., October 23, 2008.
Van Vechten, Carl. "The Later Work of Herman Melville." *The Double Dealer: A National Magazine from the South* 3 (January 1922): 9–20.
Walker, Juliet E. K. *The History of Black Business in America: Capitalism, Race, Entrepreneurship*. 2 vols. 2nd ed. Chapel Hill: University of North Carolina Press, 2009.
Ware, John. *Memoir of the Life of Henry Ware Jr., by His Brother, John Ware, M.D.* 2 vols. Boston: Munroe, 1846.
Webb, Frank J. *Biographical Sketch*. London: Sampson, 1856. http://utc.iath.virginia.edu/uncletom/xianslav/xsesfjwat.html.
———. *The Garies and Their Friends*, edited by William Hunting Howell and Megan Walsh. 1857. Reprint, Peterborough, ON: Broadview, 2016.
Weinauer, Ellen. "Plagiarism and the Proprietary Self: Policing the Boundaries of Authorship in Herman Melville's 'Hawthorne and His Mosses.'" *American Literature* 69, no. 4 (December 1997): 697–717.

Welter, Barbara. "The Cult of True Womanhood." *American Quarterly* 18, no. 2 (1966): 151–74.

Wertheimer, Eric. *Underwriting: The Poetics of Insurance in America, 1722–1872*. Redwood City, CA: Stanford University Press, 2006.

Weyler, Karen A. *Intricate Relations: Economic Desire in American Fiction, 1789–1814*. Iowa City: University of Iowa Press, 2004.

———. "Literary Labors and Intellectual Prostitution: Fanny Fern's Defense of Working Women." *South Atlantic Review* 70, no. 2 (Spring 2005): 96–131.

———. "'A Speculating Spirit': Trade, Speculation, and Gambling in Early American Fiction." *Early American Literature* 31, no. 3 (1996): 207–42.

Whale, John C. "The Making of a City of Culture: William Roscoe's Liverpool." *Eighteenth Century Life* 29, no. 2 (2005): 91–107.

Whitman, Walt. *Democratic Vistas*, edited by John Valente. 1871. Reprint, New York: Liberal Arts Press, 1949.

———. Preface. In *Leaves of Grass and Other Writings*, edited by Michael Moon, 616–36. New York: Norton, 2002.

———. "Song of Myself." In *Leaves of Grass and Other Writings*, edited by Michael Moon, 26–78. New York: Norton, 2002.

———. "To Those Who've Fail'd." In *Leaves of Grass and Other Writings*, edited by Michael Moon, 426. New York: Norton, 2002.

Wilentz, Sean. *The Rise of American Democracy*. New York: Norton, 2005.

Williams, Stanley T. *The Life of Washington Irving*. 2 vols. 1935. Reprint, New York: Octagon, 1971.

Wilson, Mark R. *The Business of the Civil War: Military Mobilization and the State*. Baltimore, MD: Johns Hopkins University Press, 2006.

Winthrop, John. "A Model of Christian Charity." In *Beginnings to 1820*, vol. A of *The Norton Anthology of American Literature*, 8th ed., edited by Nina Baym, Robert S. Levine, Wayne Franklin, Philip F. Gura, and Arnold Krupat. New York: Norton, 2012.

Wood, Ann Douglas. "The 'Scribbling Women' and Fanny Fern: Why Women Wrote." *American Quarterly* 23, no. 1 (Spring 1971): 3–24.

Wood, Gordon. *The Creation of the American Republic, 1776–1789*. Chapel Hill: University of North Carolina Press, 1998.

Zakim, Michael, and Gary J. Kornblith, eds. *Capitalism Takes Command: The Social Transformation of Nineteenth-Century America*. Chicago: University of Chicago Press, 2012.

Zimmerman, David A. "Commentary." *American Literary History* 23, no. 1 (2010): 56–68.

———. *Panic! Market, Crises, and Crowds in American Fiction*. Chapel Hill: University of North Carolina Press, 2006.

Index

Note: Italic page numbers refer to illustrations.

abolitionism: abolitionist press, 107–9, 115; money and finances of, 123
"Address on Education" (Emerson), 69–70, 76
The Adventures of Harry Franco (Briggs), 7
African Americans: Black literature as normative for racial uplift, 111–12; Black newspapers, 160n41; economic agency of, 122–26; emancipation of, 106; market capitalism, 109–10, 116; racist barriers, 117–24; real estate investment and property ownership of, 112–13, 127–28; and suffrage, 120. *See also* enslavement
African American writers, 18, 105–7, 128–30; abolitionist literature and business fluctuations, 107–16; on enslavement, 20; narratives of formerly enslaved writers, 105–7. *See also The Garies and Their Friends* (Webb)
"agency civilization," 54, 56, 113
The Age of Turbulence (Greenspan), 80–81
Agnew, Jean-Christophe, 6, 7
Alger, Horatio, 2, 7
ambition: cultural context of, 131–32; in *Twice-told Tales* (Hawthorne), 84–86, 88; lack of, 31, 93; prevalence of, 63, 70–71, 106. *See also* go-aheadism
"The Ambitious Guest" (Hawthorne), 20, 83, 87–89, 93
American exceptionalism, 1–2
American Literary History (journal), 17
"The American Scholar" (Emerson), 19, 65, 70–75
Analectic Magazine, 31, 36

Anthony, David: on "Bartleby, the Scrivener" (Melville), 136; on "capitalist selfhood," 9, 10; on financial success and failure, 55; on *The House of the Seven Gables* (Hawthorne), 11; on Washington Irving, 3, 23; *Paper Money Men*, 143n65, 143n67; "paper money men," 7, 30
antislavery newspapers, 107–9, 115. *See also* abolitionism
anxiety: of African Americans, 117; in "Mr. Higginbotham's Catastrophe" (Hawthorne), 89–90; over economic uncertainty, 5, 9–10, 142–43n56; Washington Irving's financial anxieties, 30–31, 32–35
Appeal of Forty Thousand Citizens (Purvis), 120
Armstrong, William, 97
assimilationism, 39–40
Augst, Thomas, 8, 119

Baker, Houston A., 113
Baker, Jennifer J., 9, 39
Balakrishnan, Gopal, 154n68
Baldwin, Henry, 24–25
Ball, Charles, 113
Ball, Erica L., 111
Balleisen, Edward J., 25, 34, 57, 99, 140n17
banking: Bank of the United States, 42, 43, 52; free-banking systems, 113; in *Narrative* (Brown), 114–15; after Panic of 1837, 111–12; Wells Fargo, 105–6; wildcat banks, 113–14, 123

179

bankruptcy: as adaptability, 57; and anxiety, 33; and credit markets, 54–55; opportunity following, 55–56, 99; P. & E. Irving, 29–32; after Panic of 1819, 22; romanticization of, 37. *See also* debt
Bankrupt Stories (Briggs), 7, 9–10
"Bartleby, the Scrivener" (Melville), 21, 91–93, 121, 135–37
Bartlett, John Russell, 8
Battle-Pieces (Melville), 21, 134–36
Baucom, Ian, 35
Bauman, Zygmunt, 16
Baym, Nina, 44
Bell, Ian F. A., 67
Bell, Michael Davitt, 23, 34
Benjamin, Walter, 139n9
Benton, Thomas Hart, 22
Berlant, Lauren, 81, 136, 154n67
Bewick's History of Birds (Bewick), 53
Bibb, Henry, 113
Black Americans. *See* African Americans
Black American writers. *See* African American writers
The Black Man (Brown), 115
"Black plunder," 105, 107, 113, 114, 126
Black Reconstruction (Du Bois), 106
Block, James E.: on "agency civilization," 54, 56, 113, 136–37; and modernity, 14, 39–40; *A Nation of Agents*, 28, 152n27; on "renunciation of boundaries," 83; and secular movement, 46, 93; on "universal striving," 67–68, 74, 76
Bradstreet, Anne, 50
Brevoort, Henry, Jr., 31–32, 34, 147n74; review of *The Sketch-Book*, 38
Bridgen, Thomas, 24
Briggs, Charles Frederick, 7, 16
Bromell, Nicholas K., 64
Brown, Gillian, 11, 15
Brown, Wendy, 18
Brown, William Wells, 20, 105, 113–15, 123
Brownson, Orestes, 152n16

Buccola, Nicholas, 129–30
Buell, Lawrence, 72
business culture: business cycle vs. business fluctuations, 140n19; business failure, 6–7; entrepreneurial individualism, 131–32; habits and character, 90; and identity formation, 40; laws of profit accumulation, 72; nineteenth-century shift to financialization, 2; speed in, 76. *See also* capitalism; market economy; panics

Calyo, Nicolino, 48, 49
Cannibals All! (Fitzhugh), 109
Capital (Marx), 141–42n46
capitalism: and American identity, 30–31; in antebellum United States, 8–11; Black striving in marketplace, 109–10, 116; escapism from, 12; "expectant," 116; failure and success paradigm, 45, 52; gradual development of, 75–76; and identity formation, 68–69, 95, 97–99, 123; and innovation, 63–64; market capitalism and slavery, 105–6; and natural disaster, 50–51; soft, 83
"The Case for Reparations" (Coates), 105
Channing, Walter, 22, 23
Charvat, William, 18, 22–23, 29; materialist model of, 145n13
Chase, Salmon P., 163n17
Chesnutt, Charles W., 127, 131
Chevalier, Michele, 14
Christian principles and themes, 8, 38, 51
The Christian Slave (Stowe), 116–17
"Circles" (Emerson), 78
citizenship, economic, 105, 106–7, 111–12, 158–59n2
Civil War, 131–37
class stratification: binary of rich vs. poor, 51–52; and class oppression, 92, 141n36; "educated" vs. "industrial" class, 70; and gender roles, 147–48n88; and income inequality, 92; and real estate investment, 112; and working-class population, 10. *See also* wealth

Clay, Edward Williams, 3, *3*, 55, *58*, 70
Clymer, Jeffory A., 122
Coates, Ta-Nehisi, 105
Cohen, Michael C., 89
Colored American (Cornish), 110, 111–13, 118, 126
Columbian Lady's and Gentleman's Magazine, 61
commodification of individuals, 1, 8, 64, 76, 157n59
Communist Manifesto (Marx and Engels), 5
"The Condition, Elevation, Emigration, and Destiny of the Colored People of the U.S." (Delany), 111
The Conduct of Life (Emerson), 65, 79
The Confidence-Man (Melville), 20, 83, 94–101, 109, 114, 126–27
Cooke, Jay, 132
Cooper, James Fenimore, 2; on economic policy-tract review, 24–26, 28; on free trade vs. protectionism, 28; *The Last of the Mohicans*, 29; on literature as capital, 26; *Precaution*, 24; *The Spy*, 19, 23, 26–28
Cooper, Susan F., 27–28
Cooper, William, 24
Cornish, Samuel, 110, 111–12
corporate culture. *See* business culture
counterfeit currency, 46, 150n43
Crayon, Geoffrey, 30, 36–38. *See also* Irving, Washington
Cummins, Maria Susanna, 102
currency: counterfeit, 46, 150n43; mercantilism and shift to paper money, 30; security of, 114; symbolism of, 79
Curtis, George William, 101
"The Custom-House" (Hawthorne), 17, 86

De Bow, James, 109
DeBow's Review (magazine), 108–9
debt: Melville's, 94, 99; and Panic of 1819, 22; reliance on, 16; repudiation process, 62. *See also* bankruptcy
Delany, Martin R., 110
Democratic Review (magazine), 59

Democratic Vistas (Whitman), 1, 139n4
Denning, Michael, 10
Dewey, Orville, 72
Dictionary of Americanisms (Bartlett), 8
"discipline of attention," 73
"Doctrine of the Hands" (Emerson), 75–76
domesticity, 19, 37. *See also* women's roles
Douglass, Frederick, 2, 20, 105, 106, 110, 113, 128–30
Downs, Gregory P., 132
Du Bois, W. E. B., 106, 152n98

Easton, Hosea, 111
Economic Humanities (project), 10, 16–17, 97
economy: economic citizenship, 105, 111–12; economic swings, 79–81; enslavement and US financial history, 107–8; mercantilism and shift to paper money, 30; and unrest and volatility, 5–7
Edenic frameworks, 15
Edgeworth, Maria, 46
Embargo Act, 29
Emerson, Ellen Tucker, 19, 66
Emerson, Ralph Waldo, 2, 19–20, 51, 63–81; "Address on Education," 69–70, 76; "The American Scholar," 19, 65, 70–75; business education of, 69–70; "Circles," 78; commitment of to writing, 153n34; *The Conduct of Life*, 65, 79; "Doctrine of the Hands," 75–76; *English Traits*, 77; as "family banker," 66; financial ideals of after Panic of 1837, 75–79; "General Views," 77; and geology, 66–67; idealism of, 68; *Journals*, 19; "Language," 68; "Man, the Reformer," 76–77; *Nature*, 68; and Panic of 1837, 65–70; "Perpetual Forces," 78; "The Poet," 19, 71; "Self-Reliance," 77–79; *Society and Solitude*, 63; "Success," 63–64; on transcendentalism and market economy, 64–65; "Wealth," 77, 79, 80

Index 181

Emerson, William, 66
English Traits (Emerson), 77
enslavement, 20; enslavers as investors, 115; slave markets, 114; slave narratives, 105; and US financial history, 107–8
Equiano, Olaudah, 105, 106
exceptionalism, American, 1–2
Extraordinary Popular Delusions (Mackay), 41

failure: in capitalism, 59; reactions to, 117; and success, 1–2, 65. *See also* success
Fern, Fanny, 2, 101–4
The Fighting Temeraire (Turner), 134
financialization, 139n9
financial sublime, 149n25
Fitzhugh, George, 106, 109–10, 113, 160n36
Foucault, Michel, 18
Franklin, Wayne, 25–26
Freedom's Journal (newspaper), 110
free trade: and protectionism, 28; and tariffs, 24–25. *See also* market economy
Frothingham, Nathaniel Langdon, 70–71, 74, 152n15
Fugitive Slave Law, 117
Fuller, Hiram, 69

Gamer, Michael, 46
Gardiner, W. H., 26–27
Gardner, Eric, 116
The Garies and Their Friends (Webb), 20, 106–7, 116, 118–28; and Black achievement, 127–28; and Black economic agency, 124–26; capitalism in, 122–23; racial capitalism in, 127–28
Garrison, William Lloyd, 107
The Gem of the Season (annual), 61
gender roles, 19; and class stratification, 147–48n88; letter writing and male identity, 34. *See also* women's roles

"General Views" (Emerson), 77
geology, 66–67
Germana, Michael, 52, 114–15
Gibbons, J. S., 94
Gilded Age, 137
Gilmore, Michael T., 11, 64
globalization, 92
go-aheadism, 8, 19–21, 52, 56, 78; in "Bartleby, the Scrivener" (Melville), 136–37; challenges to, 63; Emerson's approach to, 65; "go ahead" age, 45; Hawthorne's response to, 87; lack of in South, 109–10; Melville's critique of, 92; and women's roles, 102–4; and work ethic, 129. *See also* ambition
Great Fire of New York (1835), 48–50, 49, 95
Greeley, Horace, 71
Greene, Asa, 7
Greene Street School (Providence, RI), 69–70
Greenspan, Alan, 79–81, 105, 154n68

Hager, Christopher, 131
Hall, Ruth, 121
Hammond, Bray, 52
"The Happy Failure" (Melville), 20, 83, 92–94
Harper's New Monthly Magazine, 63, 92
Hawthorne, Nathaniel, 2, 78; "The Ambitious Guest," 20, 83, 87–89, 93; "The Custom-House," 17, 86; "Hints to Young Ambition," 86; *The House of the Seven Gables*, 11–16, 78, 83–84, 88; *Mosses from an Old Manse*, 82; "Mr. Higginbotham's Catastrophe," 20, 83, 87, 89–91, 93; *New-England Magazine* tales, 20; *The Scarlet Letter*, 86; and Ticknor, 101–2; *Twice-Told Tales*, 84–91, 101
"Hawthorne and His Mosses" (Melville), 82–83, 93, 97
Hedges, William, 36
"Hints to Young Ambition," 86

The History of Black Business in America (Walker), 116
History of New York (Irving), 31
Hoban, James, Jr., 44, 46
Homestead, Melissa J., 150n32
Hone, Philip, 48
Hopkinson, Joseph, 15
Horwitz, Howard, 39, 75
The House of the Seven Gables (Hawthorne), 11–16, 78, 83–84, 88
Howells, William Dean, 131
Hunt, Freeman, 44, 75
Hunt's Merchants' Magazine, 75, 94

identity formation: and achieved identity, 51–52; and Black Americans, 106–7, 126; and business culture, 40; and capitalism, for white workers, 123; capitalist identity, 68–69, 97–99; capitalist identity in Hawthorne, 11–16, 83–84; competitive self-making, 8–9; "feeling like a capitalist" (Alger), 7; and go-aheadism, 8; and male correspondence, 34; and risk-taking, 116, 121; schools and character formation, 53–54; selfhood and hopefulness, 94–95; selfhood and market identity, 7–8; of women, 103–4. See also selfhood
Incidents in the Life of a Slave Girl (Jacobs), 115, 161n73
indemnity, 47, 99, 124
individualism, 64, 129–30, 158n84; entrepreneurial, 131–32; individualist ethos, 55–56; literary, 82–83; success vs. failure, 100
industrialization, 63–64, 92; language of, 72
insurance industry: indemnity, 47, 99, 124; and natural disaster, 50–51; and risk, 47
investment strategies, 38, 53–54, 56, 97, 112; real estate, 111
Irving, Ebenezer, 29, 35
Irving, Peter, 29, 31–32

Irving, Washington, 2; and capitalization of writing, 35; family bankruptcy, 5; financial anxiety of, 30–31, 32–35; financial reversals (1930s) of, 40–41; *History of New York*, 31; on Mississippi Bubble (1720), 41; and P. & E. Irving (family business), 29–32; "romance of trade," 3; on success vs. failure paradox, 18; "The Wife," 37–39, 44. See also *The Sketch-Book* (Irving)
Irving, William, 29, 34–35

Jackson, Andrew, 3, 22, 42, 43, 52
Jackson, Frederick, 95
Jackson, Leon, 18; *The Business of Letters*, 145n13
Jacobs, Harriet, 20, 105, 113, 115, 161n73
James, Henry, 131
Jay, John, 27
Jefferson, Thomas, 29
Journals (Emerson), 19

Kinney, James, 122
Kirkland, Caroline, 113
The Knickerbocker (magazine), 41
Knight, Peter, 41, 79

Ladies' Garland and Family Wreath (magazine), 44
Lamplighter (Cummins), 102
"Language" (Emerson), 68
Larson, John Lauritz, 27
The Last of the Mohicans (Cooper), 29
Law, John, 41–43
Leaves of Grass (Whitman), 1
"Lecture on Commercial Integrity" (Hopkinson), 15
Lee, Maurice S., 78–79
The Legendary (annual), 46
Letters from an American Farmer (St. John de Crèvecœur), 47
Leverenz, David, 9
Levy, Jonathan, 13, 27, 35, 64
Liberator (newspaper), 107–8

Lincoln, Abraham, 106; fiscal policy of, 132–34, *133*
literary marketplace, 85; Melville's work in, 100–101; and women, 103–4
"literary ownership" model, 82–83
literature as capital, 26, 35, 142n47
Longfellow, Henry Wadsworth, 86–87
Luskey, Brian P., 8, 134

Mackay, Charles, 41
Madison, James, 29
male identity: letter writing, 34; and manhood, 9–10
"Man, the Reformer" (Emerson), 76–77
Marable, Manning, 105, 119
market economy: culture, 9; and Emersonian transcendentalism, 64–65; and literature, 142n47; psychology of, 20; and self-identity, 9–10
marketplaces: and Black identity, 106–7; literary, 85, 100–101, 103–4; and market voluntarism, 28; after Panic of 1837, 3; and race-based barriers, 126
marriage: as partnership, 60; and women's identity, 39
The Marrow of Tradition (Chesnutt), 127
Marrs, Cody, 131
Martineau, Harriet, 6, 14, 72
Marx, Karl, 50, 141–42n46; *Capital*, 141–42n46; *Communist Manifesto*, 5
Matthiessen, F. O., 100
McClanahan, Annie, 16
McCulloch, Hugh, 132–33, 137, 163n17
McGill, Meredith, 11, 84–85
Melville, Herman, 2; "Bartleby, the Scrivener," 21, 91–93, 121, 135–37; *Battle-Pieces*, 21, 134–36; and Civil War, 131–32; *The Confidence-Man*, 20, 83, 94–101, 109, 114, 126–27; "The Happy Failure," 20, 83, 92–94; "Hawthorne and His Mosses," 82–83,

93, 97; in literary marketplace, 100–101; on market culture, 20; "The Paradise of Bachelors and the Tartarus of Maids," 92; *Pierre*, 92; "Poor Man's Pudding and Rich Man's Crumbs," 92
Men and Measures of a Half Century (McCulloch), 132–33
mercantilism, 30
The Merchants' Magazine and Commercial Review, 44
meritocracy myth, 54, 118, 119–20, 122
Michaels, Walter Benn, 11–12
Mihm, Stephen, 46
Mississippi Bubble (1720), 41–43
"A Model of Christian Charity" (Winthrop), 8–9
money. *See* currency
Mosses from an Old Manse (Hawthorne), 82
"Mr. Higginbotham's Catastrophe" (Hawthorne), 20, 83, 87, 89–91, 93

Narrative (Equiano), 106
"narrative of reversal" (Block), 14
Narrative of the Life and Escape of William Wells Brown (Brown), 113–15
National Bank. *See* banking
National Convention of Colored Freemen (1848), 106
National Era (newspaper), 107–8
A Nation of Agents (Block), 14, 28
Nature (Emerson), 68
New Economic Criticism (project), 9
New-England Magazine, 86, 87, 89
A New-England Tale (Sedgwick), 46
Newfield, Christopher, 72
A New Home (Kirkland), 113
New Military Tract, (New York), 24
"New-Year's Day" (Sedgwick), 61–62
New York Evangelist (newspaper), 107–8
Niles' Weekly Register (newspaper), 6; on Panic of 1837, 71–72; on speculation, 35–36

184 *Index*

Ohio Life Insurance & Trust Company, 94
Okker, Patricia, 12, 45
optimism, romantic, 1-2
O'Sullivan, John, 59

Packer, B. L., 67
P. & E. Irving, 29-32; and Washington Irving, 31, 32-34
Panic of 1819, 22
Panic of 1837, 3, 16, 19, 57-60, 58, 110; in *Colored American* (Cornish), 113; Emerson on, 65-70
Panic of 1857, 63, 94, 106; in antebellum South, 107-9
Panic of 1865, 135
panics: economic, 5-7; panic fiction, 38-39, 149n19; psychological aspects of, 95-96
Paper Money Men (Anthony), 7, 30, 143n65, 143n67
"The Paradise of Bachelors and the Tartarus of Maids" (Melville), 92
The Perils of Pearl Street (Greene), 7
"Perpetual Forces" (Emerson), 78
Peterson, Carla L., 119
Pfister, Joel, 70, 83
Phillips, Willard, 87
Pierre (Melville), 92
Pocock, J. G. A., 23, 30
"The Poet" (Emerson), 19, 71
"Poor Man's Pudding and Rich Man's Crumbs" (Melville), 92
The Poor Rich Man and the Rich Poor Man (Sedgwick), 19, 51-57
Poovey, Mary, 139n9
Precaution (Cooper), 24
profit accumulation laws, 72
promissory notes, 114
property ownership, 112-13, 125. *See also* real estate investment
"The Providence of Class'" (Shapiro), 150n36, 150n51
Public and Private Economy (Sedgwick), 60
Purvis, Robert, 120

race riots (Philadelphia), 127
racism: business barriers for Black Americans, 117-22, 123-24, 126; in federal policy, 124
Ragged Dick (Alger), 7
railroad companies, 63-64
Raymond, Daniel, 6, 41, 81
real estate investment, 112-13, 126, 127-28. *See also* property ownership
"Reflections on the Literary Delinquency of America" (Channing), 22
Renker, Elizabeth, 131
repudiation of debt, 62
Revolutionary War, 23-24
Rezneck, Samuel, 6, 140n21
Riches Without Wings (Smith), 45
Rifkin, Mark, 11, 13; *Settler Common Sense*, 143n65, 143n67
risk-taking: consequences of, 19; in *The Garies and Their Friends*, 120-21; and identity formation, 116; imprudent, 25; and insurance industry, 47; in nineteenth-century women's fiction, 48; in real estate market, 56-57; rejection of, 110; in *The Spy* (Cooper), 27; women's roles, 103. *See also* speculation
Robbins, Sarah, 51, 56
Rockman, Seth, 141n36
romance genre, 46-47
"Romance in Real Life" (Sedgwick), 46-48, 50-51, 99
"romance of trade" (Irving), 3
Roscoe, William, 36-37
Rubin-Dorsky, Jeffrey, 23, 30
ruin (theme), 31, 32-34, 36, 44, 49-50, 57, 77, 99-100, 102-3, 123
Russwurm, John Brown, 110
Ruth Hall (Fern), 83, 101-4
Ryan, Susan M., 29

Sánchez, María Carla, 47
Sandage, Scott A., 8, 64, 131, 162n98
The Scarlet Letter (Hawthorne), 86
Securing the Commonwealth (Baker), 9

Sedgwick, Catharine Maria, 2, 16, 19, 44–62; on Great Fire of New York (1835), 48–50, 95; "New-Year's Day," 61–62; and Panic of 1837, 57–60; *The Poor Rich Man and the Rich Poor Man*, 51–57; on romance vs. self-discipline, 46–51; on success vs. failure paradox, 18, 19; on women's economic agency, 45–46; and women's fiction, 44–45
Sedgwick, Charles, 59
Sedgwick, Katherine "Kate" Maria, 57–58, 59
Sedgwick, Theodore, 60
selfhood: in economic institutions, 16–17; fluid frameworks of, 105; identity and bank panics, 6; and market identity, 4, 7–8; and personal striving, 8. *See also* identity formation
"Self-Made Men" (Douglass), 129
self-reliance, 129–30
"Self-Reliance" (Emerson), 77–79
Shapiro, Joe, 51
Sherman, William Tecumseh, 132
"Shinplasters," 114
Shonkwiler, Alison, 17–18
"sink or swim," (phrase), 2
The Sketch-Book (Irving), 5, 19, 23, 34–40; ruin as theme in, 36
Sklansky, Jeffrey, 64, 95, 157n52
Smith, Caleb, 73
Smith, Elizabeth Oakes, 45
Society and Solitude (Emerson), 63
Society in America (Martineau), 6
Sociology of the South (Fitzhugh), 109
"Song of Myself" (Whitman), 2
Southern Literary Messenger (magazine), 47
speculation: on currency, 114; Emerson on, 71–72; and inflation, 35–36; and investment, 157n58; Mississippi Bubble (1720), 41–43; in "New-Year's Day" (Sedgwick), 61–62; in railroad stock, 63; and stock manipulation, 126–27. *See also* risk-taking

Spiller, Robert E., 24
Spires, Derrick R., 105, 106, 110, 158–59n2
The Spy (Cooper), 19, 23, 26–28
St. John de Crèvecœur, J. Hector, 46–47
stock manipulation, 126–27
Stocks and Stock-Jobbing in Wall Street (Armstrong), 97
Stockton, Elizabeth, 125
Stowe, Harriet Beecher, 107, 116; *The Christian Slave*, 116–17; *Uncle Tom's Cabin*, 107, 116, 124
striving, 20–21
success: critique of, 97; and failure, 85–86, 88–89, 92–93; and individualism, 100; post-bankruptcy, 99; psychology of, 10. *See also* failure
suffrage, Black, 120
suicide, 74, 153n47

Tales and Sketches (Sedgwick), 46–48
tariffs, 24–25
Temple, Gale, 94–95
Templin, Mary, 38–39
temporal concerns: and boundaries, 8, 15; and gradual development of business frameworks, 66, 72, 75–76, 154n68
Thoreau, Henry David, 73, 151n81
Thoughts on Political Economy (Raymond), 6
Ticknor, William, 101–2
The Times (lithograph), 3, 3–4, 4, 55, 70, 159n23
Tocqueville, Alexis de, 14, 106
"To Those Who've Fail'd" (Whitman), 1
transcendentalism, 75–76, 96
transferable skills, 97
"true womanhood," 37. *See also* women's roles
Turner, J. M. W., 134
Twain, Mark, 131
Twice-Told Tales (Hawthorne), 84–91, 101

186 *Index*

Uncle Tom's Cabin (Stowe), 107, 116, 124
United States: Civil War, 131–37; and literary professionalism, 22–23; optimism of, 1; Southern states, 109–10; War for Independence, 23–24; War of 1812, 25

Van Buren, Martin, 58

Walker, James, 114–15
Walker, Juliet E. K., 116
Wall Street, 28, 95, 135–36. *See also* "Bartleby, the Scrivener" (Melville)
Ware, Henry, Jr., 51
War for Independence, 23–24
War of 1812, 25
wealth: endurance of, 12–13; pursuit of, 38; and restraint of rich, 53, 57; and toxic assets, 80; unearned, 128. *See also* class stratification
"Wealth" (Emerson), 77, 79, 80
Webb, Frank J., 2, 20, 106, 116–18
Webb, Mary E., 116–18
A Week in Wall Street, by One Who Knows (Jackson), 95
Weinauer, Ellen, 82
Wells Fargo (bank), 105–6. *See also* banking
Welter, Barbara, 37

Wharton, Edith, 131
"What the Black Man Wants" (Douglass), 129–30
Whitman, Walt, 37; *Democratic Vistas*, 1, 139n4; *Leaves of Grass*, 1; "Song of Myself," 2
"The Wife" (Irving), 37–39, 44
wildcat banks, 113–14, 123. *See also* banking
Williams, Stanley, 23, 31
Wilson, Mark R., 132
Winthrop, John, 8–9
women's fiction, 44–45; panic fiction, 38–39; *Ruth Hall* (Fern), 101–4
women's roles: and domesticity, 19, 37; and domestic partnership as capital, 60; and go-aheadism, 102–4; "The Wife" (Irving), 37–39, 44; women's dependent status, 37–39
work ethic, 129; work vs. idleness, 86. *See also* go-aheadism
writing: as financially viable occupation, 29–30; and literary marketplace, 34, 85; and "literary ownership" model, 82–83; and professional authorship as vocation, 30–31; as "property" and "stock," 35

Zimmerman, David, 17, 144n96

www.ingramcontent.com/pod-product-compliance
Lightning Source LLC
Chambersburg PA
CBHW021857230426
43671CB00006B/426